Democratic Religion from Locke to Obama

AMERICAN POLITICAL THOUGHT

Wilson Carey McWilliams and Lance Banning
Founding Editors

Democratic Religion from Locke to Obama

Faith and the Civic Life of Democracy

GIORGI ARESHIDZE

UNIVERSITY PRESS OF KANSAS

Published by the University Press of Kansas (Lawrence, Kansas 66045), which was organized by the Kansas Board of Regents and is operated and funded by Emporia State University, Fort Hays State University, Kansas State University, Pittsburg State University, the University of Kansas, and Wichita State University

© 2016 by the University Press of Kansas

Library of Congress Cataloging-in-Publication Data

Names: Areshidze, Giorgi, 1983– author.
Title: Democratic religion from Locke to Obama : faith and the civic life of democracy / Giorgi Areshidze.
Description: Lawrence, Kansas : University Press of Kansas, [2016] | Series: American political thought | Includes bibliographical references and index.
Identifiers: LCCN 2016004955 |
ISBN 9780700622672 (cloth : acid free) |
ISBN 9780700622689 (ebook)
Subjects: LCSH: Democracy—Religious aspects. | Liberalism—Religious aspects. | Religion and politics. | Religious tolerance. | Religious pluralism—Political aspects.
Classification: LCC BL65.P7 A74 2016 |
DDC 201/.72—dc23
LC record available at https://lccn.loc.gov/2016004955.

British Library Cataloguing-in-Publication Data is available.

Printed in the United States of America
10 9 8 7 6 5 4 3 2 1

The paper used in this publication is recycled and contains 30 percent postconsumer waste. It is acid free and meets the minimum requirements of the American National Standard for Permanence of Paper for Printed Library Materials Z39.48–1992.

For my teachers

CONTENTS

ACKNOWLEDGMENTS

I owe a debt of gratitude to many individuals who helped me with this book.

Most of the manuscript was written while I was a postdoctoral fellow at the Jefferson Center at the University of Texas at Austin. I am grateful to Tom and Lorraine Pangle for extending to me the opportunity to spend a year at UT to work on this manuscript. I would also like to thank Jeff Tulis and Devin Stauffer for their advice, support, and crucial intellectual guidance and prodding during the writing process as well as throughout my graduate years. This book would not have been possible without Lorraine Pangle, whose encouragement, advice, and friendly criticism helped push the project to completion. Lorraine read and commented on every chapter of this manuscript, and the argument of the book is stronger thanks to her keen and insightful eye.

I am grateful to the Dean's Office at Claremont McKenna College and my colleagues at the Government Department for helping arrange the leave of absence that was instrumental for the completion of this project.

Mark Blitz and the Salvatori Center provided special assistance and accommodation in the process of my transition between Claremont and UT Austin prior to the start of my postdoctoral appointment.

I am indebted to Chuck Myers, my editor at the University Press of Kansas, for his excellent stewardship of this manuscript and the two anonymous reviewers whose criticisms and suggestions improved it significantly. Larisa Martin handled the production process with diligence and care, and I am grateful for her patience and attention to details that I would have otherwise missed.

Ariel Helfer and Marco Paoli deserve particular recognition for their selfless and extensive contributions to this book. Through countless conversations and workshops (both in person and sometimes over the phone), Marco and Ariel helped me develop this project from a germinating idea into the book that it became, improved my grasp of its core questions and dilemmas, and provided friendly support that helped encourage me throughout the process.

Finally, I would like to thank my brother, Irakly George Arison; my parents, Gia and Nana Areshidze; and my host-parents, Tom and Suzi Modisett. All of these individuals have selflessly invested in my education and my life in America, and they have made it possible for me to pursue my dreams in this country.

CHAPTER ONE

RELIGION AND THE POST-ENLIGHTENMENT LIBERALISM OF JOHN RAWLS

Liberalism and Religious Transformation

In *Bad Religion*, his popular but highly controversial treatment of the fate of American religiosity, *New York Times* columnist Ross Douthat argues that in the last five decades America has become a "nation of heretics" because of its increasing propensity to transform Christianity into newer and newer (and less orthodox) versions of itself.[1] Writing from the perspective of a Catholic conservative, Douthat laments the watering-down of American theology in the second half of the twentieth century and finds the evangelical accommodation with capitalism and the rise of "therapeutic spiritualism" among mainline Protestants deeply troubling from the perspective of traditional religion. In its place, he seeks to remind his readers of the heyday of American religiosity, when religion was both more orthodox and more institutionally robust, and when its cultural role in public life was more universally respected: "A chart of the American religious past would look like a vast delta, with tributaries, streams, and channels winding in and out, diverging and reconverging—but all of them fed, ultimately, by a central stream, an original current, a place where the waters start. This river is Christian orthodoxy."[2] The erstwhile dominance of Christian orthodoxy, according to Douthat, fulfilled important civic purposes in our national life: "Both doubters and believers have benefited from the role that institutional Christianity has traditionally played in our national life," Douthat writes. He cites traditional Christianity's "communal role, as a driver of assimilation and a guarantor of social peace, and its prophetic role, as a curb against our national excesses and a constant reminder of our national ideals."[3] Like others, Douthat traces the transformation of American Christianity to the cultural revolutions that began in the 1960s, which he presents as a kind of historical aberration in an otherwise harmonious theological-political tradition that has animated American history.[4] While he chooses to settle for a call for a Christian renewal that can re-evangelize America, Douthat's study leaves it an open question whether such a revival is at all foreseeable in our day and age.

The leading school of contemporary liberal theory is singularly ill-equipped to assess the civic costs of the transformation of religion that Douthat pinpoints. John Rawls's influential work, which takes its bearings from the fact of moral and religious pluralism, emphasizes the need for a liberalism that secures a limited consensus by maintaining "impartiality" between controversial comprehensive doctrines, including especially religious ones.[5] Rawlsian neutrality has both metaphysical and political consequences: it is not only often thought to imply that liberalism can be theoretically justified independently from metaphysical foundations, but also that it requires a culture of public reasoning that eschews divisive religious appeals in support of coercive laws—a concept popularized by Rawls as the "public reason" requirement of liberalism.[6] Thus, in large part because of the influence of Rawls's approach, debates in political theory in America have often focused more on the narrow question of the rules that should govern the interjection of religious views in public deliberation, and less on the question of whether liberalism presupposes a theological transformation. To be sure, Rawls's paradigm has had its detractors, with critics often asserting that it risks excluding the contribution of religious arguments to democracy's civic life,[7] and in recent years an "inclusivist"[8] alternative that allows for religious argumentation in deliberation has gained prominence.[9] But while these "inclusivists" are friendlier to the contribution of religion than the "exclusivist" Rawlsians, they still retain the original spirit of Rawls's consensus-oriented approach: they claim that liberal neutrality helps bring about a "convergence" between competing viewpoints and traditions of reasoning (both religious and nonreligious) in support of shared political conclusions, even if they do not expect the justificatory foundations of those political conclusions to be mutually acceptable across the various traditions under consideration.[10] Thus, according to this view, religious and nonreligious citizens may come to share liberal political principles without agreeing on the reasons why those principles are fundamentally sound or desirable.

What both the defenders and (to a lesser extent) the critics of public reason may fail to bring into sharper focus, however, is that the contemporary debates about the requirements that should govern public speech take place within the context of a broader transformation of religion in modern democracy. Accordingly, a different group of scholars has emphasized that democratic pluralism itself alters the essential experience of religious faith.[11] These commentators have shown that the cultural pressures that modern democracy generates liberate individual rationality and nurture an attitude that questions the inerrancy (and the authority) of revelation as a source of moral and political guidance. This is a development with consequences for theology that we are still trying to comprehend, although most scholars agree that overall its results include increasing interreligious tolerance and decreasing salience of theological controversy between faith groups.[12] In *American Grace*, their celebrated study of American religiosity, Robert Putnam and David Campbell show that theological flexibility and "religious fluidity" allows Americans to combine exceptional religious devotion with religious diversity while maintaining relatively high levels of toleration.[13] While they claim that religious identities are still distinct and meaningfully intact in spite of this fluidity, their findings simultaneously point to a theological ambiguity underlying America's religious pluralism: Americans appear to have become indifferent to theology—so much so that they believe in an "equal opportunity heaven."[14] Although they neglect to highlight this underlying homogeneity of America's religious landscape, their findings confirm Alan Wolfe's famous conclusion that "Americans impose their individualism on their religious beliefs rather than the other way around."[15]

This book advances the debate by bringing these disparate scholarly foci into critical dialogue with each other. I attempt to evaluate and trace the intellectual sources of this theological development and to assess its implications for the civic life of American democracy. I grapple with the following foundational questions: Can liberalism maintain a posture of neutrality toward religion, as John Rawls famously argued it should in his *Political Liberalism*, or does a liberal regime presuppose (and even bring about) a certain transformation of religious beliefs? Furthermore, has the apparent democratization of religion transpired the way early Enlightenment thinkers, such as Locke, or recent liberal thinkers, such as Rawls, expected it would, and how has this transformation affected religion's capacity to contribute to the moral and civic life of a liberal society? Finally, is there something crucial in religion that is "lost in translation," and should that be a concern for those who care about the health of democracy today? I explore these questions through an investigation of the political and religious thought of John Locke, Alexis de Tocqueville, Abraham Lincoln, Martin Luther King, Jr., Barack Obama, and Jürgen Habermas. In chapters that focus on their political and theological legacies, I place these figures in dialogue with each other as well as with contemporary debates, illustrating in each case how they struggle to navigate the foundational tensions between religion and liberalism.

By stressing the ambiguous effects of the liberal transformation of religion on the civic health of democracy, I offer a new framework for thinking about the role of religion in contemporary democratic life that goes beyond both the Rawlsian and Lockean paradigms of liberalism. Unlike Douthat, most scholars have at least implicitly followed Lockean liberalism in celebrating democracy's relative success at transforming religion and at rendering it in important respects more tolerant and more liberal. Putnam and Campbell are again instructive in this regard, since they are troubled by the "deeply moralistic" and "less tolerant" denominations of American Christianity, and they favor what they call "a faith without fanaticism" insofar as it contributes to America's interreligious tolerance.[16] Not surprisingly, they find the decline in "religious chauvinism," or the percentage of "true believers" that identify their faith as the only path to heaven, to be beneficial for American politics, although it is less than clear that this redounds to the benefit of religion.[17] America would be better off, according to their account, if religious groups emulated the ecumenism of mainline Protestantism. But studies of America's civic culture, among them Putnam's own *Bowling Alone* (published a decade before his *American Grace*), have simultaneously pointed to alarming trends that should leave us less than sanguine about the civic effects of this transformation: democratic culture is increasingly individualized and atomistic, resulting in the erosion of traditional institutions (including especially religious ones) that historically sustained what Putnam refers to as democracy's "social capital," the network of communal and social ties that are necessary for a vibrant civic life.[18]

Following Alexis de Tocqueville, who I show anticipated these troubling developments in democracy, this study highlights a foundational ambiguity in liberalism's posture toward religion: I point to an abiding tension between the civic benefits that religion can provide and the tendency of democracy to make religion increasingly liberal, tolerant, and accordingly theologically easygoing, suggesting that paradoxically a faith that maintains some form of rootedness in tradition and revelation may be more effective at counteracting democratic pathologies than are the liberalized faiths that we frequently encounter today. I ask whether this tension can ever truly be surmounted by liberalism and whether an essentially liberal civic faith is either theoretically coherent or practically feasible. The book suggests that this dissonance between how tolerant we want religion to be and what we expect it to accomplish in our civic life is a consequence of the liberal transformation of religion and may explain some of the deepest spiritual and civic anxieties that continue to beset American democracy.

Rawls's "Public Reason" Liberalism and the Muddle of Contemporary Neutrality

*Post-Enlightenment Liberalism and John Rawls's
Anti-Foundationalism*

Contemporary liberal theory often operates under a blind spot with respect to these theological trade-offs and thus misses the tension between the requirements of liberal tolerance and the fate of religion in democracy. By aspiring to move beyond both rationalism and religion to a liberalism of "neutrality," present-day political theory neglects the ambiguous civic and theological effects of the liberal transformation of religion. A prominent illustration of this approach is John Rawls's *Political Liberalism*, a work that continues to define not just the methodological parameters but also the foundational questions that inform liberal theory today.[19] Taking his bearings from the enduring fact of "reasonable pluralism"[20] of comprehensive doctrines in modern societies, Rawls proposes a teaching of liberalism that would be "political not metaphysical."[21] For Rawls, the "political not metaphysical" formula means that liberalism can achieve political neutrality between competing worldviews by embracing a theoretical abstinence with regard to metaphysical, theological, and moral foundations: political liberalism refrains from passing judgment on the truth of any comprehensive doctrine, even including its own, and thus it need not take an official stand on foundational questions. This strategy, according to Rawls, will enable liberalism to secure an "overlapping consensus," allowing individuals to embrace liberal political principles without at the same time abandoning or altering their privately held comprehensive outlooks. Is this approach theoretically and practically coherent? Can liberalism as a way of life remain neutral with respect to religion and with respect to its own theological (or anti-theological) foundations?

It is important to note that Rawls distinguishes his version of political liberalism from its Enlightenment predecessor, on which his political teaching aims to improve in crucial respects. In Rawls's telling, the Enlightenment "project" was developed in response to the historical problem created by the Reformation, which, he writes, "introduce[d] into people's conceptions of the good a transcendent element not admitting of compromise," thereby transforming politics into an arena of "mortal conflict" and precipitating the European Wars of Religion.[22] The liberal thinkers of the Enlightenment responded to their historical predicament by proposing to replace the reigning religious claims with a morality derived exclusively from secular philosophy, from which derive the principles of separation of church and state and limited constitutional government rooted in individual natural rights (xvii). But Rawls emphasizes that "political liberalism has no such aims": "emphatically, it does not aim to replace comprehensive doctrines, religious or nonreligious, but intends to be equally distinct from both and, it hopes, acceptable to both" (xxxviii). Accordingly, "the intention is not to replace those comprehensive views, nor to give them a true foundation."[23] Indeed, doing so would be "delusional," since Rawls believes no such true foundations can ever be expected to be found.[24] Political liberalism will therefore present a conception of justice that will be essentially "freestanding," i.e., not dependent on any exclusive (and therefore controversial) conception of the good life (10). A great deal hinges on Rawls's ambitious promise that political liberalism can achieve neutrality, since it is such neutrality that will ensure its greater tolerance and inclusiveness, even (apparently) of illiberal theological views: the strategy of neutrality means that "both religious and nonreligious, liberal and nonliberal" comprehensive views "may freely endorse, and so freely live by and come to understand [the] virtues" of political liberalism (xxxviii).

While Rawls presents political liberalism as a practical improvement on Enlightenment liberalism, he also indicates that it does not entail a mere rejection, but rather a revision or an extension, of the Enlightenment's foundational theoretical posture. Indeed, he presents political liberalism's break with the Enlightenment as the ultimate consequence of the Enlightenment's own principle of toleration: "political liberalism applies the principle of toleration to philosophy itself," thus setting aside the whole question of moral and philosophical truth as such from political consideration (10). Political liberalism thus aims to generalize and universalize the Enlightenment's apparent religious strategy: just as Enlightenment thinkers, in Rawls's reading, took "the truths of religion off the political agenda" when they constructed the liberal secular state, "by avoiding comprehensive doctrines" altogether Rawlsian liberalism will in turn seek "to bypass religion and philosophy's profoundest controversies" (152). As Rawls elaborates this point further, we see more fully the far-reaching import that he imputes to his attempt to construct a freestanding liberalism:

> Were justice as fairness to make an overlapping consensus possible it would complete and extend the movement of thought that began three centuries ago with the gradual acceptance of the principle of toleration and led to the nonconfessional state and equal liberty of conscience.

The extension is required for an agreement on a political conception of justice given the political and social circumstances of a democratic society. To apply the principle of toleration to philosophy itself is to leave citizens themselves to settle the questions of religion, philosophy, and morals in accordance with views they freely affirm (154).

In an essay responding to an earlier iteration of Rawls's project, Richard Rorty brings out the anti-foundationalist implications of Rawls's approach. Rorty argues that "Rawls . . . shows us how liberal democracy can get along without philosophical presuppositions," and that this is the ultimate implication of "Rawls's effort to, in his own words, 'stay on the surface, philosophically speaking.'"[25] Accordingly, Rorty can claim that his own pragmatist and postmodern liberalism is in agreement with the "political, not metaphysical" position that Rawls first started sketching in the 1980s and that culminated in his *Political Liberalism*: "We can think of Rawls as saying that just as the principle of religious toleration and the social thought of the Enlightenment proposed to bracket many standard theological topics when deliberating about public policy and constructing political institutions, so we need to bracket many standard topics of philosophical inquiry" (ibid., 180). Rawls's strategy, in Rorty's reading, would then involve taking "Jefferson's avoidance of theology one step further" by extending it to all comprehensive views (182).

In the same essay, Rorty goes on to argue that by bracketing foundational disputes, liberalism allows us "to put aside such questions as an ahistorical human nature, the nature of selfhood, the motive of moral behavior, and the meaning of human life" (180). These topics, once considered the focal point of philosophical and theological dispute—and frequently the spark behind political contestation—become "as irrelevant to politics as Jefferson thought questions about the Trinity and about transubstantiation" should be irrelevant to liberal democracy (180). But for Rorty, the strategy of bracketing truth claims is not merely an expression of neutrality about which comprehensive doctrines are preferable from the perspective of liberalism. Instead, it is intended to advance a specific moral outlook: Rorty makes clear that by so bracketing truth claims in the political arena, liberalism encourages people to become morally indifferent to the contest over truth. As he explains, "truth . . . is simply not relevant to democratic politics; . . . when the two conflict, democracy takes precedence over philosophy" (191–192). Society as a whole would be better off, according to Rorty, if the moral and spiritual "disenchantment of the world" that is already being brought about by science and liberal political principles were to accelerate. Indeed, the diffusion of such disenchantment is the "moral purpose" behind Rorty's philosophical project, as it should be the purpose of Rawls's *Political Liberalism* when its goals are rightly understood: "the encouragement of light-mindedness about traditional philosophical topics serves the same purpose as does the encouragement of light-mindedness about traditional theological disputes," namely, "it helps make the world's inhabitants more pragmatic, more tolerant, more liberal, more receptive to the appeal of instrumental reason."[26]

As we are starting to see, Rorty is willing to draw from this evaluation of Rawls's strategy of neutrality an extremely unsettling conclusion about the price of toleration for the spiritual and moral life of democracy: "the typical character types of liberal democracies are bland, calculating, petty, and unheroic." For Rorty, the promotion of such a truncated human type (a veritable "Last Man" that Nietzsche had identified in harrowing detail) "may be a reasonable price to pay for political freedom," even if this ultimately entails accepting a this-worldly materialistic culture that culminates in an easy-going "narcissism." Moreover, from Rorty's perspective, the more that serious moral and religious commitments (and their consequent controversies) decline, the stronger democracy will become. Although Rorty's reading of Rawls's early work has received some criticism, his intuition that Rawls's anti-foundationalism culminates in theological indifference and religious apathy would clearly render the liberal promise of neutrality illogical. Now contrary to Rorty's painfully frank prediction, Rawls had claimed that (his mature) liberalism would have a practical consequence exactly the opposite of that envisioned by Rorty. As we have already seen, Rawls repeatedly stresses that political liberalism will be distinguished from its Enlightenment predecessor by its "impartiality": political liberalism "does not attack or criticize any reasonable view," nor "does it criticize, much less reject, any particular theory of the truth of moral judgments" (xix–xx). Short of presupposing or promoting philosophical light-mindedness about the deepest questions, Rawls insists that political liberalism will nurture a thriving pluralism of competing comprehensive views, which will nevertheless converge around an overlapping consensus on constitutional essentials: "it would be fatal to the idea of a political conception . . . of justice if it were . . . skeptical about, or indifferent to, truth, much less . . . in conflict with it" (150); instead, Rawls expects that each citizen will endorse political liberalism "from the standpoint of their own comprehensive view, whatever it may be" (ibid.).

How then are we to resolve this ambiguity in political liberalism? How can Rawls and Rorty begin from such similar premises (from the need to move liberalism beyond the Enlightenment's truth claims), and yet reach such different conclusions about the fate of comprehensive doctrines in liberal society? The answer can be gleaned from the fact that while both Rawls and Rorty are committed to articulating liberalism without references to metaphysical foundations, Rawls did not think that such foundations could be dispensed with altogether. As we will see below, in spite of its famous strategy of "neutrality," *Political Liberalism* demonstrates a latent dependence on historically inherited metaphysical and theological foundations that support liberal politics, even though Rawls chooses (for the sake of political expediency and practicality) neither to defend nor to articulate such foundations explicitly. In short, Rawls cannot escape foundationalism, since political liberalism requires those comprehensive views that do not already endorse liberal principles to be either transformed or marginalized; on the other hand, sufficiently "reasonable" and liberalized comprehensive views are necessary for the stability of a liberal political order. This underlying foundationalism of Rawlsian liberalism points to its underappreciated dependence on the Enlightenment's historical legacy, thus highlighting the inherent limits of the type of pluralism that liberalism's (of whichever variety) can ultimately secure.

Rawlsian "Reasonableness" as the Enlightenment's Historical Legacy

We may better grasp the force of Rorty's critique by taking up Rawls's doctrine of "public reason," which is to provide the solution to the political problem presented by incompatible comprehensive doctrines. According to Rawls, public reason is the form of reason that should govern citizens of a liberal democracy in their deliberations when "constitutional essentials and matters of basic justice are at stake" (215), which he also designates as the "special subject of public reason" (214). While citizens in a democracy will continue to hold divergent metaphysical, moral, and religious commitments in their private lives, the ideal that Rawls constructs would require them to draw only upon "widely shared" public principles when engaging in political deliberation about constitutional essentials (224–225). In Rawls's words, when justifying the use of political power, we are to "appeal to those *presently accepted* general beliefs and forms of reasoning found in common sense, and the methods and conclusions of science when these are not controversial" (224, emphasis added). In practice, this will mean that citizens should abstain from justifying public policies and the use of political power on the basis of their exclusively privately held (and therefore controversial and nonshareable) comprehensive doctrines, drawing instead on principles that are already part of "the public political culture."

Rawls hopes that by adopting his prescription, citizens in a constitutional regime will be able to reach an "overlapping consensus" on political questions while preserving their commitment to a diversity of viewpoints. As I have already mentioned, scholars have focused on the formal restrictions that Rawls places on public reason, with critics rightly pointing out that Rawls's framework risks excluding some of the most important moral and theological contributions to democracy's civic life. Accordingly, Chapters 4 and 5 of this book will evaluate whether Rawls's framework can accommodate the type of moral and theological argumentation that informed the public reasoning of some of America's leading reformers, by focusing on the statesmanship of Abraham Lincoln and Martin Luther King, Jr. But for now, and before turning to the specific implications of public reason for contemporary liberalism, it is worth pointing out that not enough attention has been paid to the historical conundrum to which Rawls's innovative idea points: how did public reason develop, and how did the historical consensus around liberal political principles on which public reason depends emerge in the first place? After all, as Rawls acknowledges at the outset of his work, "religious toleration is now accepted, and arguments for persecution are no longer openly professed; similarly, slavery, which caused our Civil War, is rejected as inherently unjust" (8; 151, 156). Political liberalism, therefore, would seem to take its bearings by the supposition that liberal principles are universally (or near universally) assented to in modern democratic societies, and accordingly Rawls can limit political philosophy to the modest task of "collecting our settled convictions" rather than reshaping or reconstructing them the way Enlightenment thinkers had originally tried to do (8).

This historically contingent dimension of political liberalism is revealed by Rawls's account of the emergence of freedom of conscience in post-Reformation European history. As Rawls acknowledges, "Catholics and Protestants in the sixteenth century" did not subscribe to an "overlapping consensus on the principle of toleration" (148). Indeed, "both faiths held that it was the duty of the ruler to uphold the true religion and to repress the spread of heresy and false doctrine" (148). Toleration initially emerged after the Reformation only as a "modus vivendi," i.e., as a grudgingly accepted temporary cease-fire between the hostile parties, because it provided the "only workable alternative to endless and destructive civil strife" (148, 156). But a mere modus vivendi, according to Rawls, falls short of the requirements of legitimacy that are necessary for political liberalism, since the stability of the former "depend[s] on happenstance and a balance of relative forces" that could very easily unravel (148). Accordingly, as Rawls eventually acknowledges, this cease-fire or "reluctant" modus vivendi had to be transformed into a genuinely cohesive moral agreement uniting the rival parties in a commitment to a tolerant and "reasonable" Christianity, in order to make the intolerant views of sixteenth-century Catholics and Protestants a decided "minority" in our society (147–148). Only after such a historically socialized reformation has succeeded, i.e., only after Catholics and Protestants have been acculturated into theological liberalism and have affirmed tolerance on "moral grounds" (147), can their "judgments converge sufficiently so that political cooperation on the basis of mutual respect can be maintained" (156; see also 458–462).[27]

In the same discussion, Rawls refers to Locke's *A Letter Concerning Toleration* as "a model case" that can illustrate how a "religious doctrine," which is both "general and comprehensive," could be made to support the political conclusions of Rawlsian liberalism. Rawls appeals to Locke's *Letter* because he sees it as a paradigmatic example of a tolerant version of Christianity—that is to say, he see it as a Christian religious argument for the principle of toleration: the *Letter*'s "*religious doctrine* and *account of free faith* lead to a principle of toleration and underwrite the fundamental liberties of a constitutional regime" (145, emphasis added). Later in the same chapter, Rawls acknowledges that to be considered "reasonable" in modern society, a religion must endorse the same Lockean account of free faith, i.e., it must embrace (on religious grounds) a doctrine that upholds the spiritual autonomy and thus the religious freedom of an individual (170–172). In a footnote, Rawls also refers to seven arguments in Locke's *Letter*, which together establish the theological preconditions of a tolerant faith, by subordinating the church to the state while establishing the supremacy of individual conscience in theological matters:

> This idea is illustrated by various of Locke's statements in *A Letter Concerning Toleration* (1690). He says such things as: 1) God has given no man authority over another; 2) no man can abandon the care of his own salvation to the care of another; 3) the understanding cannot be compelled by force to belief; 4) the care of men's souls is not given to the magistrate as that would determine faith by where we were born; 5) a church is a voluntary society, and no man is bound to any particular church and he may leave it as freely as he entered; 6) excommunication

does not affect civil relationships; 7) only faith and inward sincerity gain our salvation and acceptance with God (145, internal citations omitted).

How did these principles win out in Christianity? How and on what basis were they justified to persecuting faiths, so that both Catholics and Protestants today share a consensus around Locke's teaching of toleration? In Chapter 3 of this book, we explore Locke's arguments for toleration in the *Letter* and related works in detail, as well as their contemporary reception among his Anglican critics. Contrary to Rawls's account, Locke had to argue that the principle of toleration was not simply "reasonable," but also true, both from the perspective of human reason as well as from the perspective of Christian revelation—a proposition that was extremely controversial in his time. This book argues that to advance the cause of toleration, Locke developed a form of political philosophy that was directly engaged with theological disputation and cross-examination of revelation, and that his ultimate aim was to transform Christianity into a tolerant faith. Locke is therefore a leading representative of that strand of the modern Enlightenment that advocated theological reform, and he (along with his most important intellectual allies) wished to reform religion in light of modern rationalism. This massive surface impression is confirmed not only by Locke's *A Letter Concerning Toleration*, but also by his *Reasonableness of Christianity*, as well as by Thomas Hobbes's *Leviathan*,[28] Baruch Spinoza's *The Theological-Political Treatise*, and Immanuel Kant's *Religion within the Limits of Human Reason Alone*. The defining feature of Enlightenment thought from which liberalism and toleration emerged was persistent and intransigent engagement with theological questions and their contested political and moral implications. And in contrast to Rawls's anti-foundationalism, Locke's Enlightenment strategy demanded the application of human reason as the foundational authority in all theological matters: "Reason must be *our last judge* and *guide* in everything."[29]

The present work argues that it is only because Locke's theological project has had relative success in liberalizing American Christianity that Rawls's can aim to develop a political philosophy that disengages from foundational questions and refrains from passing judgment on theological issues. In fact, Rawls implicitly acknowledges the dependence of his political teaching on the historical triumph of the religious project that was set into motion by the Enlightenment. Thus, since he expects that religion has already been made thoroughly "reasonable" and sufficiently tolerant, Rawls can confidently discount the challenge that religious fundamentalism poses to his political project as a merely marginal and unserious phenomenon: "except for certain kinds of fundamentalism, all the main historical religions admit of such an account [of free faith] and thus may be seen as reasonable comprehensive doctrines" (170). As he indicates, on the whole, Catholics and Protestants no longer resemble their intolerant sixteenth-century predecessors, and they have largely adopted the Lockean theological outlook: "In a democratic society," according to Rawls, "the authority of churches over its members" is "freely accepted," and since "apostasy and heresy are no longer legal offenses," individuals are free to join and leave churches at their own discretion, just as they do other "associations," without suffering any civil penalties (221). We see here that Rawls's political system presupposes precisely the sort of individualization of the experience of faith and liberalization (and de-politicization) of church authority that are the hallmarks of the Enlightenment's transformative strategy with respect to religion. As far as these bedrock principles that define a "reasonable faith" are concerned, Rawls's political liberalism will be just as absolutist as the Enlightenment liberalism of Locke from which it seeks to distance itself.

This brings us closer to the nerve of Rawls's argument about the types of religious beliefs that can be accommodated by political liberalism. The linchpin of Rawls's position is that political liberalism is compatible not so much with any kind of normative diversity, but with a specific "reasonable" subsection of the plurality of worldviews. The pluralism that Rawls attributes to democratic societies is not "simple pluralism" (164) or "pluralism as such" (144), but rather "reasonable pluralism"—a pluralism that consists of "reasonable comprehensive doctrines," which, he is quick to note, "do not reject the essentials of a democratic regime" (xvi). It should be stressed that Rawls attempts to distinguish "reasonableness" from rationality (and thus also from truth): reasonableness is a "moral sensibility" or a virtue of "social cooperation," whereas rationality is the agent's capacity to pursue chosen ends through the "most effective means" (50). Rawls comes closest to defining reasonableness when he states that "reasonable persons . . . are not moved by the general good as such but desire for its own sake a social world in which they, as free and equal, can cooperate with others on terms all can accept" (50). Because they subordinate the general good of the community to their sense of fair cooperation, reasonable persons will embrace the classical liberal separation of public and private spheres and therefore practice the liberal virtue of tolerance. Accordingly, the litmus test of reasonableness for Rawls is whether or not an individual supports limited constitutional government: "reasonable persons will think it unreasonable to use political power, should they possess it, to repress comprehensive views that are not unreasonable, though different from their own" (60).

In light of this brief overview, one is tempted to follow Judd Owen in asking whether Rawls means by "reasonable" anything other than a "liberal."[30] As we have now seen, the concept of "reasonableness" takes on massive moral significance for Rawls's liberalism, since it enables Rawls to define the boundaries of what is politically acceptable under his "freestanding" liberal order: it allows him to implicitly exclude nonliberal views without declaring such views as untrue or even irrational. But short of resolving the fundamental theological challenge confronting political liberalism, this feature of Rawls's teaching only confounds the problem even more. Recall that Rawls claimed that he developed political liberalism to show how a political conception of justice could be embraced by, and therefore accommodate, "religious and non-religious, liberal and non-liberal views." Such a conception would not rely on contestable foundations. But in crucial sections of *Political Liberalism*, Rawls cannot avoid having to confront potentially illiberal objections to his teaching, and he is forced (albeit reluctantly) to appeal to his own liberal foundationalism:

> in affirming a political conception of justice we may eventually *have to assert at least certain aspects of our own comprehensive religious or philosophical doctrine* (by no means necessarily fully comprehensive). This will happen whenever someone insists, for example, that certain questions are so fundamental that to insure their being rightly settled justifies civil strife. The religious salvation of those holding a particular religion, or indeed the salvation of a whole people, may be said to depend on it. *At this point we may have no alternative but to deny this, or to imply its denial and hence to maintain the kind of thing we hoped to avoid* (152, emphasis added).[31]

Political liberalism therefore cannot ignore the challenge of illiberal views, but must either expect them to liberalize or deny them legitimacy altogether. But in making this concession, Rawlsian liberalism would effectively have to surrender its aspiration to neutrality and would have to acknowledge its dependence on normative presuppositions that cannot be derived from an already established consensus.

Lost in Translation: "Public Reason" and the Civic Life of
Democracy

Having clarified the theological transformation on which political liberalism depends, let us return to a reconsideration of Rawls's doctrine of
"public reason," the framework that he develops for accommodating pluralism in modern societies. Rawls gives at least three different accounts of
the requirements of public reason vis-à-vis the private religious views of
citizens, with each modification raising fundamental questions about both
the viability and the desirability of shareable norms of public deliberation
presupposed by *Political Liberalism.* The first account appears in the cloth-
bound version of *Political Liberalism* and declares that on "fundamental political matters, reasons given explicitly in terms of comprehensive doctrines
are never to be introduced in public reason" (247). By embracing this perplexing requirement, Rawls opens his theory to a set of thorny challenges:
in addition to the common criticism that it imposes an asymmetric burden
on religious citizens today (expecting them to find nonreligious arguments
for their positions), Rawls's framework comes under tremendous strain in
trying to do justice to the greatest moral conflicts and historical reforms
in American history. In particular, Rawls has difficulty explaining how the
religious rhetoric of Martin Luther King, Jr., the abolitionists before him,
and even possibly Abraham Lincoln in his Second Inaugural Address can be
made compatible with public reason. Lest *Political Liberalism* leave out these
notable contributions to democracy's civic life that precipitated advances in
both liberty and equality, Rawls is led to admit that for much of American
history the restrictive view of public reason has been at most an "ideal" to
be strived for rather than a genuine requirement of responsible public deliberation (249–251). He provisionally settles on an exception that accom-
modates the religiously informed contributions of these historic reformers
("the inclusive view" of public reason), but only because they existed in "a
society [that was] not well ordered" and characterized by "a profound division about constitutional essentials" (249). In such a society, Rawls concedes, "nonpublic reasons" were "required to give sufficient strength" to
reforms that would advance equality (251).[32]

Much to his credit, Rawls would reconsider the fairness of such a restrictive position in his important restatement of the public reason framework—"The Idea of Public Reason Revisited." Here, Rawls offers a more
permissive version of public reason that could guide democratic deliberation
even in our day and age. Rawls refers to this modified framework as "the
wide view of public reason," and its chief new feature is the "translation pro-

viso": Rawls now argues that we are allowed "to introduce into political discussion at any time our comprehensive doctrine, religious or nonreligious, provided that, in due course, we give properly public reasons to support the principles and policies our comprehensive doctrine is said to support" (462). But there are important ambiguities in Rawls's reformulated position, since he nowhere specifies on whom the duty of translation is incumbent and at what point of time its requirement begins to operate. While at first glance this standard appears to be more accommodating of religious speech, as Jeffrey Stout and other critics of Rawls have pointed out, it is only marginally so since it makes the legitimacy of religious appeals contingent on whether or not sufficiently nonreligious reasons are also eventually supplied. According to Stout, the translation requirement amounts to the view that "you have not fulfilled your justificatory obligations until you have" rendered your reasoning in nonreligious language.[33] But as Stout also insists, this is a perplexing requirement, especially when viewed in light of American history: the abolitionists taught the nation about the moral urgency of the antislavery cause, while "the speeches of King and Lincoln represent high accomplishments in our political culture," and they are rightly regarded as "paradigms of discursive excellence."[34] As Stout contends (and as Rawls appears to admit in *Political Liberalism*),[35] it would be a strech to say that these actors abided by the translation proviso since they drew upon controversial comprehensive doctrines in their speeches.[36] It would therefore be "a strong count against" Rawls's position if these speakers would "barely squeak by," if they do so at all, on the basis of Rawls's public reason criteria.[37]

As I show in subsequent chapters, these historical exceptions that challenge the requirements of Rawls's public reason framework are not mere technicalities. Instead they illuminate what is truly at stake in Rawls's position, a fact confirmed by Rawls's discussion in the original cloth-bound *Political Liberalism* of the "ideal" type of deliberation that should characterize democracies in our day and age. The liberal principle of legitimacy that public reason embodies, Rawls argues, imposes on citizens "a duty of civility" that has direct implications for the nature of democratic deliberation: "the ideal of citizenship imposes a moral, not a legal, duty—the duty of civility— to be able to explain to one another on those fundamental questions . . . of constitutional essentials . . . how the principles and policies they advocate and vote for can be supported by the political values of public reason."[38] In this context Rawls clarifies and emphasizes that the public forum in which he expects public reason to operate extends well beyond "official forums" such as courts and legislatures: although he exempts "civil society" and the "background culture" from the norms of public reason (220–222; cf. 443–444), Rawls nevertheless expects its requirements to obtain "when [citizens] engage in political advocacy in the public forum" (215). In particular, public reason extends to the polling booth, and so it applies to citizens when they think about how to cast their ballots; otherwise, Rawls warns, public discourse would "run the risk of being hypocritical: citizens [would] talk to one another one way and vote another" (215). It is true that Rawls eventually reverses his position in "The Idea of Public Reason Revisited" and offers a more narrow definition of the "public forum," which exempts citizens from the requirements of public reason in their capacity as voters and activists. But even here he insists that "the commitment to constitutional democracy is publicly manifested" only when citizens accept "the [translation] proviso and only then come into debate" (463).

As becomes clear in what follows in this manuscript, the original articulation of the Rawlsian paradigm misses not only the scope of the democratic transformation of religion, but also the degree to which democratic deliberation and civic life can be fruitfully enriched by the contribution of religious viewpoints. This is a tremendous civic and moral cost that classical (Enlightenment) liberalism already exerts on modern life, and which the restrictions of public reason liberalism risk aggravating even more in the name of securing an overlapping consensus. Political liberalism shares with Enlightenment liberalism the deep distrust of religiously fueled political instability. But because it refuses to follow its Enlightenment predecessor in declaring religious objections to liberalism as irrational, political liberalism must settle for the less confrontational (but also less coherent and clear-sighted) alternative: it merely seeks to encourage religious viewpoints to converge around basic liberal principles of justice through the framework of public reason. But this emphasis on consensus leads Rawls and his followers to neglect the constructive role of moral and theological debate and intransigent but principled intellectual disagreement and conflict in democratic civic life. As this book will demonstrate, religious traditions can serve as the vehicle for both critique and renewal of liberal democracy, and sometimes they are most effective at fulfilling this task when they have not been entirely reshaped to simply mirror democracy's cultural and political currents. Religious traditions can do so by appealing to principles of justice that go beyond both classical liberal rationalism as well as the historically inherited notions of public reason championed by Rawls, and by drawing on a rich reservoir of thinking grounded in natural theology and in Christian revelation. When religious traditions take on this role, they enrich our cultural and civic life and compel democracy to measure itself against worthwhile normative challenges.

Plan of the Book

Before outlining the project, I would like to avert one possible source of confusion: the book does not proceed chronologically. After the overview of Rawlsian liberalism in the present chapter, Chapter 2 presents a study of Barack Obama's understanding of the role of religion in democracy, illustrating his ambiguous attempt to balance Rawlsian public reason with the tradition of American civil religion. Chapter 3 returns us to the Enlightenment roots of toleration in the philosophy of John Locke in order to highlight the religious transformative ambitions of Locke's project that are often neglected by contemporary theories of liberal neutrality. Chapters 4 and 5 fast-forward to two formative periods of American political development—the Civil War struggle over slavery and the civil rights movement—focusing on the religious statesmanship of Abraham Lincoln and Martin Luther King, Jr. By studying these historical case studies of the role of religion in American political development in light of our readings of Locke and Rawls, we confront them with fresh eyes, paying particular attention to how these statesmen challenge both the Lockean and Rawlsian paradigms while simultaneously advancing liberalizing trends in American Christianity. Chapter 6 returns us to the basic question of the book and evaluates the civic costs and ambiguous results of the liberal transformation of religion through an engagement with Alexis de Tocqueville and Jürgen Habermas.

I begin with an evaluation of Barack Obama's understanding of the role of religion in democracy. Obama presents an illuminating case study of the tension between the two alternative approaches to religion in American democracy that are explored throughout this work: "civil religion" and Rawls's "public reason." More than any other contemporary American politician, Obama has espoused a commitment to pragmatism and to the deliberative ideal of democracy that draws upon the consensus-based approaches to political liberalism that were inspired by John Rawls. At the same time, however, and in contrast to many liberal political theorists today, Obama is deeply appreciative of the contribution of religion to formative reform movements in American political history—most notably, to the abolitionist and civil rights movements. This leads him to call for a political liberalism that is more accommodating of religion in public life and to champion what Michael Sandel has described as a more "faith friendly form of public reason."[39] These competing priorities in Obama's approach reveal an abiding but often underappreciated tension within modern liberal approaches to religion. In short, religion poses a challenge to deliberative democracy, which Obama understands as "requiring a rejection of absolute truths." But at the same time, Obama appears to be much more keenly sensitive to American democracy's need to tap into the moral and civic underpinnings historically provided by Christianity than are contemporary Rawlsian scholars. But because our pluralistic age is characterized by a loss of consensus about theological truth and especially by a division between religious and secular Americans, Obama attempts to transform American civil religion to make it sustainable in a "post-Christian" age. But it is unclear whether this form of liberalized "faith that admits doubt, and uncertainty, and mystery," would share much with the religious and moral fervor of abolitionism and the civil rights movement, and thus whether it would be capable of yielding similar civic benefits. The theological dilemma that is revealed by Obama's leadership is a reflection of a deeper ambiguity within political liberalism, whose aspiration to transcend metaphysical, moral, and theological foundations may turn out to be more a hope than a reality.

In the next chapter, I turn to the early modern Enlightenment thought of John Locke, whose political and philosophic works laid the foundations for both religious disestablishment and toleration. Locke points us to an unresolved question about the liberal project and its effect on religion: does liberalism leave religious beliefs essentially intact, or does a culture of tolerance presuppose the diffusion of philosophical and theological skepticism? There are deeply conflicting answers to this question. The predominant view in scholarship denies that toleration requires skepticism, and a popular interpretation of Locke holds that his political teaching is based on post-Reformation Protestant theology. A persistent but decided minority of scholars, however, interprets Locke as a covert Hobbesian, one whose tolerationist teaching attempted to weaken Christian orthodoxy on the basis of underlying modern rational principles. I attempt to adjudicate between these conflicting views through an investigation of Locke's *Letter Concerning Toleration* and the *Essay Concerning Human Understanding*.

A comparison between these two works demonstrates that Locke presents not one, but rather two accounts of the foundations of toleration, and that these accounts diverge in crucial respects: the *Essay* grounds toleration in the limits of human knowledge, while the *Letter* bases it on a religious argument about the sanctity of the human conscience. I attempt to explicate this divergence by taking account of Locke's debate with Jonas

Proast, an Anglican divine who accused Locke of promoting "skepticism in religion among us," and whose objections prompted Locke to write three subsequent Letters in defense of his original argument. This chapter suggests that Locke intended to leave behind a richer and more complicated legacy than is usually acknowledged by the two dominant interpretations of his work—the "Christian Locke" (the view embraced by Jeremy Waldron and many others) and the "rational" or skeptical Locke (usually favored by some Straussian interpretations). Because Locke's teaching can succeed only at muting the tension between these two sides of his teaching, but not at resolving it altogether, scholars will continue to see in his writings the evidence of both Christian and skeptical foundations. But for his popular audience, Locke hoped that his approach would provide an alternative to the unpalatable choice between orthodoxy and irreligion and encourage in its place a synthesis that would be conducive to both toleration and religious belief.

Next, in Chapters 4 and 5, I turn to two formative periods of American political development, the Civil War struggle over slavery and the civil rights movement. These chapters evaluate whether the Enlightenment's effort to transform and privatize religion can be understood to have been a success when that project is viewed from the perspective of American political history and civic life. In spite of its tremendous influence on Thomas Jefferson and James Madison, Locke's project was highly controversial among his contemporaries in Europe, and it has had only mixed success in American political practice. Not only was it resisted among later political theorists like Alexis de Tocqueville, but its influence among American democracy's greatest reformers, such as Abraham Lincoln and Martin Luther King, Jr., has been deeply ambiguous. These statesmen sought to recruit the theological resources of Christianity for distinctively civic and moral purposes, and they relied on religion to confront the moral challenge that slavery and racial inequality posed to American democracy in a way that Locke may not have imagined to be necessary in a secular society. They judged, moreover, that the moral life of liberal democracy is enriched when it can draw upon the deep wellspring of civic and self-sacrificial conviction that religion provides. For them, neither mere rationalism nor democratic self-interest could overcome the obstacles to American equality, and both viewed theological principles as necessary supplements (and moderating counterweights) to democratic liberty. My book therefore points to the limits of the Lockean project not just in theory, but also in practice.

Lincoln and King provide instructive contrasts to the Lockean and Rawlsian approaches. Even though they are working under the shadow of Enlightenment rationalism and the Lockean imperative to reform Christianity, Lincoln and King show that a democracy cannot be publicly indifferent to theological disputes, especially with respect to God's judgment about the deepest moral questions confronting human beings. At the same time, contrary to the assumptions of "neutralist" approaches to liberalism that are popular today, the success of the antislavery and antisegregation efforts championed by Lincoln and King required them to advance a new liberal theology of equality, which blended the natural rights tradition of America's founding principles with a liberal and egalitarian interpretation of the Bible. As I show in Chapters 4 and 5, the challenge that the theological rhetoric of Lincoln and King poses to his framework of public reason compelled Rawls to reevaluate the restrictive standards of deliberation that he had initially proposed in his *Political Liberalism* and encouraged him to develop a framework that was more accommodating of religious speech. In the end, I argue that because of his overriding emphasis on consensus Rawls failed to do justice to the reconstructive influence of theology in the liberal statesmanship of these two reformers. Instead, I uncover a "Tocquevillian strategy" behind the religious statesmanship of Lincoln and King: while these statesmen employ liberalizing theologies in their public rhetoric, in demonstrating the capacity of religion to act as a moral counterforce reshaping America's moral and public consciousness, they also reveal the limits of Enlightenment rationalism and "public reason" liberalism.

This study closes with a consideration of two very different assessments of the Enlightenment's transformative agenda and theological legacy: Alexis de Tocqueville, the French Catholic aristocrat who authored the two-volume *Democracy in America* after visiting the United States in the early 1800s, and Jürgen Habermas, arguably the most influential living political philosopher in Europe today and the heir to the rationalist project of the European Frankfurt School. Although writing from two very different vantage points, both Tocqueville and Habermas are led to religion by way of a moral and civic critique of liberalism, and both argue that religion provides something unique that secular reason cannot replicate. But where Tocqueville judges it necessary to preserve religion (even and especially in its traditional form) as a unique voice that can moderate democracy's "savage instincts," Habermas concludes that secular reason should seek to appropriate religion (through a "rescuing" or "salvaging translation") as a resource that can supplement liberalism. While Tocqueville will agree with Habermas's recent judgment that "religion is here to stay," from his perspective the resilience of religion is the result not of an incomplete process of secularization (as Habermas somewhat reluctantly suggests), but of the enduring longings and spiritual needs that are inscribed in human nature and that point beyond the moral and cultural horizon of liberalism. The persistence of religion will therefore continue to nourish a dynamic dissonance within liberalism, which explains the spiritual anxieties and civic dissatisfactions that Tocqueville predicted with uncanny accuracy, and which Habermas has started to recognize in our day and age.

CHAPTER TWO

BARACK OBAMA'S CIVIC FAITH:
A POST-CHRISTIAN CIVIL RELIGION
OR RAWLS'S PUBLIC REASON?

Contemporary Liberalism and Obama's Civic Faith

When Barack Obama was sworn in for his second term as president in January 2013, he took the oath of office with his hand placed not on a single but on two Bibles—one used by Abraham Lincoln in his 1861 Inauguration, the other "the traveling Bible" of Martin Luther King, Jr. Throughout both of his presidential campaigns, Obama preached a gospel of social change imbued with the hopeful creed of civil rights Christianity. In his 2011 National Prayer Breakfast remarks, President Obama stressed that it was precisely the religious character of the civil rights movement that inspired him to choose public service as his career: "despite the absence of a formal religious upbringing my earliest inspirations for a life of service ended up being the faith leaders of the civil rights movement."[1] Not only has he been remarkably outspoken about his own spiritual journey to religious faith, but he is also comfortable drawing upon the Bible in his public pronouncements, and one scholar has even described him as "arguably the most theologically serious politician in modern American political history."[2] The *Washington Post* columnist E. J. Dionne suggested that Obama's keynote address delivered in 2006 at Jim Wallis's annual "Call to Renewal" conference offered "the most important pronouncement by a Democrat on faith and politics since John F. Kennedy's Houston speech in 1960 declaring his independence from the Vatican." Even while some of the leading liberal political theorists of the last generation, such as John Rawls and Richard Rorty, have been calling for a liberalism of neutrality or for the "de-divinization" of politics, Obama presents himself as a practitioner of a kind of public theology of liberalism.[3]

To hear Obama speak is to be reminded of the language and the cadences of the African American pulpit. Obama's speeches often effortlessly mine the social justice teaching of the civil rights–era black church, transposing its theological resources into the public oratory of egalitarian liberalism.

This becomes especially vivid during the emotional zenith of Obama's Inaugural Addresses, in which godly references abound as the theological bedrock of American equality. In his First Inaugural, Obama calls on the nation to "reaffirm our enduring spirit" and to renew the promise of the "noble idea" that has been "passed on from generation to generation: the God-given promise that all are equal, all are free, and all deserve a chance to pursue their full measure of happiness."[4] Similarly, in his Second Inaugural, Obama refers to the Declaration's "exceptional" view of the self-evidence of "unalienable rights," which he interprets as the proposition that "while freedom is a gift from God, it must be secured by His people here on Earth." In speaking about the divine sources of equality and of the egalitarian polity as embodying the best of the human spirit, Obama is drawing on a rich strand of religious rhetoric in American political history, a tradition that Robert Bellah described as America's "civil religion."[5]

Many scholars discern in these and similar statements a sign of Obama's rhetorical shrewdness, aimed at reopening the Democratic Party to the language of values and religion, a goal he has been consciously pursuing since his debut in national politics.[6] The keynote address that Obama delivered at the Democratic National Convention in 2004 gave the nation the first taste of Obama's unique blend of post-partisanship, which extends not just to politics but to religion as well: "there's not a liberal America and a conservative America—there's the United States of America. . . . We worship an awesome God in the Blue States, and we don't like federal agents poking around our libraries in the Red States." Stephen Mansfield has argued that Obama's appeal to an "awesome God" in his DNC speech was "a conscious attempt to reclaim the religious voice of the American political left. [Obama intended] to echo the footsteps of nuns and clergymen who marched with Martin Luther King, Jr., or the religiously faithful who protested the Vietnam War or helped build the labor movement."[7] Obama was in effect signaling that bridging what scholars regularly refer to as the "God gap," the Democratic Party's seeming deficit among the so-called "value voters," would require a new conception of pragmatism, one that would not embrace Rorty's view that religion is necessarily a "conversation stopper."[8]

In this chapter, I intervene in this debate about the place of religion in contemporary liberalism, but from an orientation that is distinct from the partisan and electoral concerns that inform the debate about the "God gap." I follow Michael Sandel's invitation to evaluate Obama's attempt to reopen liberal progressivism to religion by developing "a more capacious, faith friendly form of public reason."[9] If Sandel's characterization is correct, Obama presents an intriguing litmus test of contemporary theoretical paradigms of political liberalism and of their capacity to accommodate religious reasoning in the public sphere.[10] I show that Obama's attempt to nudge liberalism in a direction that is less antithetical to religion leads him to a rather paradoxical impasse. On the one hand, Obama presents a more thorough appreciation of the contribution of Christianity to crucial reform movements in American history than any other contemporary politician from the left. He often suggests that a healthy liberal democracy cannot exist without a vibrant civic faith, perhaps one that is even informed by a tradition of Christian activism, that can bind its citizens together in pursuit of shared moral goals. This strand of the president's public philosophy draws on the religiously sensitive critique of democratic individualism offered by Alexis de Tocqueville and points to the neglected link between democracy's spiritual and civic life. On the other hand, Obama's public philosophy embodies a long-standing commitment to deliberative politics, which he shares with contemporary (secular) liberal theorists, and which shapes his view of what a healthy democratic public discourse should look like.[11] The theoretical basis of this vision of liberalism receives its most powerful expression in John Rawls's *Political Liberalism*, and Obama provides an illuminating litmus test of the implications of Rawlsian liberalism for religion.[12] While it is by no means inherently hostile to religious participation in the public sphere, Rawlsian political liberalism leads Obama to embrace an ideal of "public reason" that has the effect of limiting the permissibility of appeals to religious arguments in public deliberation.

For both Rawls and Obama, the challenge confronting contemporary liberalism is the challenge of deep value pluralism, and by this pluralism they mean, above all, the diversity of religious beliefs characteristic of modern free societies. The need "to *reconcile faith* with our modern, *pluralistic democracy*,"[13] Obama argues, is both the preeminent challenge of the contemporary age as well as the source of America's deep political polarization.[14] To accomplish this goal, Obama argues that traditional civil religion needs to be refashioned and updated, to take into account America's increasing pluralism, and this in turn requires us to transcend the Christian foundations of civil religion: "whatever we once were, we are no longer just a Christian nation," because our pluralism today includes not only non-Christian faiths, but also a growing number of "unbelievers." To effect this transformation, Obama puts forward a solution that eschews, as much as possible, public confrontation with theological arguments drawn from revelation, proposing instead "that the religiously motivated translate their concerns into universal, rather than religion-specific, values." Like Rawls, Obama is looking to secure a consensus, and his preferred strategy of translation is meant to facilitate that goal, since one of its primary aims is to make contributions to public discourse (whether religious or nonreligious) less absolutist, and therefore more amenable to compromise and shared consensus-building.[15] Through it, Obama seeks to preserve the religious and moral diversity characteristic of twenty-first century America, while securing an "overlapping consensus" on the core elements of national identity that can sustain our communal aspirations on a non-Christian (and therefore less divisive and more pluralistic) foundation.[16]

What emerges from this "Rawlsian" reimagining of American civil religion is highly paradoxical, since Obama ultimately refuses to sort out what will replace the theological heritage that he himself argues previously sustained democratic social justice and egalitarianism in America. Christianity, after all, was the source of a "higher truth" that Obama believes animated American reform movements during the Civil War and the civil rights movement. The speeches of Martin Luther King, Jr., and Abraham Lincoln are for the president a testament to the power of religion to act as a moral counterforce and an agent of change in democracy, by rendering the moral truths underpinning democratic equality vivid in theological terms. In fact, Obama even goes so far as to suggest that democracy is rooted in Christianity, and that our way of life cannot be conceived independently of the moral foundations that it supplies: "our law is by definition a codification of morality, much of it grounded in the Judeo-Christian tradition."[17] But because Obama's view of democratic deliberation is grounded in a theory of public reason that he believes requires "the rejection of absolute truth,"[18] we are left to wonder whether it can accommodate the type of morally rich and theologically divisive public argumentation that characterized both abolitionism and the civil rights movement—and that continues to define some of the most intractable public debates today. This chapter therefore points to an abiding tension between Obama's appreciation for the historic role of religion as a moral counterforce capable of challenging the status quo, and his view that pluralism requires democratic citizens to frame their contributions to public debate in terms of public reason.

A Civil Religion for a Post-Christian Nation?

Barack Obama's most definitive statement on the role of religion in politics appeared in his 2006 keynote address at the Sojourners Call to

Renewal, a faith-based movement organized by Jim Wallis and dedicated to overcoming poverty in America.[19] Obama chose to include an expanded version of the speech as a chapter on "Faith" in his campaign book, *The Audacity of Hope*, suggesting that it provides a crucial window into the president's understanding of the relationship between religion and politics.[20] The speech is noteworthy for presenting a moderate critique of the secular left, a constituency that Obama chastises for abandoning "the field of religious discourse" to the conservative right out of a misplaced fear of religion. Obama also blames the left for failing to develop a viable alternative to the traditional language of faith through which to communicate about social and civic values in a way that resonates with the American public. Commentators have interpreted the speech as a conscious break with the tradition of strict religious neutrality that the Democratic Party has favored in the twentieth century,[21] and as an implicit rebuke of John F. Kennedy's famous 1960 address to Protestant clergy at the Greater Houston Ministerial Association, in which he declared that he believed in a "president whose religious views are his own private affair." This study suggests that Obama's approach is more puzzling than a simple repudiation of JFK's method of privatization, insofar as he seeks to preserve the civic values that we partially inherit from an erstwhile religious tradition but without any longer explicitly affirming their dependence on either the Bible or on Christianity more broadly.[22] The latter move, Obama hopes, can help transition America's civil religion to an era of post-Christian pluralism, and thereby make its civic contributions shareable among believers and unbelievers alike.

Obama frames the speech from the beginning as an effort to "tackle head-on the mutual suspicion that sometimes exists between religious America and secular America."[23] During a televised debate in the Illinois senatorial campaign in 2004, Alan Keys (his Republican opponent) had charged that "Christ would not vote for Barack Obama," because he "has voted in a way that it is inconceivable for Christ to have behaved."[24] Keys was objecting to Obama's support for abortion rights and gay marriage, alleging, in effect, that "Mr. Obama says he is a Christian . . . and yet he supports a lifestyle that the Bible calls an abomination." Obama was personally offended by Keys's presumption "to speak for my religion, and my God." But instead of questioning the "literalist" approach to the Bible that informed his opponent's views, Obama confesses that he "answered with what has come to be the typically liberal response in such debates—namely, I said that we live in a pluralistic society, that I can't impose my own religious views on another, that I was running to be the U.S. Senator of Illinois and not the Minister of Illinois."[25]

In Obama's telling, the confrontation with Key's provided a microscopic reflection of the "broader debate we've been having in this country for the last thirty years over the role of religion in politics."[26] The biggest "gap" in party affiliation, Obama argues, is "not between men and women, or those who reside in so-called Red States and those who reside in Blue, but between those who attend church regularly and those who don't."[27] The religious gulf between the two parties exacerbates our political culture, and Obama does not hesitate to put some of the blame squarely on Republican doorsteps, since "conservative leaders have been all too happy to exploit this gap." However, Obama is quick to turn his criticism closer to home. "Democrats, for the most part, have taken the bait," Obama argues, for their discomfort with religion has allowed Republicans to monopolize the value debate and the religious vote. The vast majority of secularists "avoid conversation about religious values altogether" out of misguided fear of "offending anyone," insisting that "regardless of our personal beliefs . . . constitutional principles tie our hands." Others, a decided but vocal minority, go even further, "dismissing religion in the public square as inherently irrational and intolerant, insisting on a caricature of religious Americans that paints them as fanatical."[28] Although such "strategies of avoidance" have been politically convenient (and, one could add, as the popularity of Rawlsian neutrality demonstrates, intellectually appealing), Obama stresses that they "fail to acknowledge the power of faith in people's lives," and their long-term consequences disadvantage not just the Democratic Party, but the nation as a whole.

Obama is dealing with a problem that is endemic to liberal political theory: the perception that because liberalism is committed to formal neutrality and individual autonomy, it neglects to care for the civic and social values on which the sustenance of liberalism depends. While a number of prominent attempts have been made to defend a version of "civic liberalism" that would be more effective at nurturing liberal social virtues without recourse to religious values, Obama does not choose to follow this path to stem the erosion of "social capital."[29] Instead, his position is closer to Stephen Carter's eloquent argument in the *Culture of Disbelief* (1994) that liberalism impoverishes itself when it becomes estranged from religion, insofar as this entails ruling out of bounds the most formative commitments of human life.[30] For Obama, the problem is not just that progressivism is rhetorically disadvantaged through its discomfort with and avoidance of religion; his more serious concern is that such discomfort *morally* impoverishes the nation's political character. It is true, Obama acknowledges, that "some of the problem here is rhetorical—if we scrub language of all religious content, we forfeit the imagery and terminology through which millions of Americans understand both their personal morality and social justice."[31] But the progressive "fear of getting 'preachy,'" Obama adds, "may also lead us to discount the role that values and culture play in some of our most urgent social problems." For the vast majority of Americans, Obama stresses, religion "is not something [that can be] set apart from [other] beliefs and values," since for the religiously devout faith continues to be the deepest wellspring of such moral values. To use Michael Sandel's terminology, Obama perceives human beings as "encumbered selves," constituted by prepolitical moral and spiritual commitments that drive their deepest motives and shape their highest priorities.[32] In what could easily be interpreted as a concession to the popular communitarian critiques of liberalism, Obama concludes that the progressive failure to appreciate religion constitutes a failure "to tap into the moral underpinnings of the nation."[33]

This concession has tremendous consequences for Obama's understanding of the role of organized religion in a free society, for it leads him to reject the conventional view, popularized by Rawls's *Political Liberalism* and selectively embraced by the US Supreme Court's religious jurisprudence, that liberalism requires the privatization of faith. While he acknowledges this theoretical expectation built into liberalism about the constricted place of religion in a democratic society, Obama is keenly aware that it does not square with the reality of how faith is actually practiced in religious communities and among believers. As he argues in the *Audacity of Hope*, "religion is rarely practiced in isolation; organized religion, at least, is a very public affair. The faithful may feel compelled by their religion to actively evangelize wherever they can."[34] A living faith will seek to reshape its community in its own image, and it therefore cannot be "neatly confined as a matter of individual conscience" in the private sphere.[35] Religious believers "may feel that a secular state promotes values that directly offend their beliefs," and one cannot simply expect them to submit without resistance, for it is only natural that those who are committed to religion will "want the larger society to validate and reinforce their views."[36] It is precisely because religion seeks to make itself heard in the social arena that it possesses a unique power to nurture a prophetic and transformative perspective on the status quo, which is one of its distinctive contributions to democracy. Insofar as liberalism seeks to discourage such religious activism and attempts to inhibit religion's capacity to publicly engage in moral and social debates, it deprives itself of a valuable contribution that it cannot replace on its own. For Obama, this positive role of religion is especially conspicuous in the tradition of African American religious activism, and it constitutes one of the chief traits that helped Obama gravitate toward the Christian social justice teaching of the black church: "I believed and still believe in the power of the African-American religious tradition to spur social change, a power made real by some of the leaders here today. Because of its past, the black church understands in an intimate way the Biblical call to feed the hungry and clothe the naked and challenge powers and principalities. And in its historical struggles for freedom and the rights of man, I was able to see faith as more than just a comfort to the weary or a hedge against death, but rather as an active, palpable agent in the world. As a source of hope."[37]

Now that we see the prism of social justice through which Obama views the historic contribution of Christianity to democratic equality, we are better prepared to understand why he is so willing to push the envelope and draw a conclusion that is so mystifying to those who view him as a secularist in the conventional liberal mold. Obama's message is nothing less than an eloquent reminder to secularists that they have an obligation to resist the temptation of viewing religion only negatively, as an undesirable but unfortunate problem to be managed, compartmentalized, or bracketed by the modern state. His words seek to elicit an attitude in his audience that encourages them to view faith as a positive good and to recognize it as an abiding wellspring of moral insight instead of intolerance and prejudice. It is unfortunate, Obama observes, that "we discuss religion only in the negative sense of where or how it should not be practiced, rather than in the positive sense of what it tells us about our obligations toward one another."[38] Religion is, after all, special, Obama suggests, not so much because of the special challenges that it poses to a liberal state, but because it is a uniquely powerful (though, as we will see, not the exclusive) source of moral insight, agency, and action. As Obama stresses repeatedly, religion has "sparked some of the most powerful political movements, from abolition to civil rights to the prairie populism of William Jennings Bryan."[39] It is on the basis of this premise that Obama leads his audience to confront an unsettling conclusion, one that demands a reexamination of their instinctive suspicion of the use of religious speech in public discourse: "Secularists are wrong when they ask believers to leave their religion at the door before entering into the public square. Frederick Douglass, Abraham Lincoln, Williams Jennings Bryan, Dorothy Day, Martin Luther King, Jr.—indeed, the majority of great reformers in American history—were not only motivated by faith, but repeatedly used *religious language* to argue for their cause. So to say that men and women should not inject their 'personal morality' into public policy debates is a practical absurdity."[40] This statement, which Obama eventually qualifies and nearly contradicts later in the same speech, puts him in tension with many liberal theorists who believe that religious contributions to democratic deliberation should undergo a process of translation into secular language that is accessible to believers and unbelievers alike.

The resilient power of faith in America is not simply "the result of successful marketing," nor is it the outcome of shrewd packaging of polarizing social issues for religious constituencies, for Obama understands that religion "speaks to a hunger" in the American soul "that goes beyond any particular issue or cause."[41] The root of the vitality of American religiosity, Obama argues, is the spiritual longing that underlies the experience of faith: Americans "want a sense of purpose, a narrative arc to their lives," and they suffer from a "chronic loneliness" that cannot be satiated by mere comfortable self-preservation and the "busyness" of daily lives devoted to family and work.[42] Obama does not explicitly say that religion is rooted in a natural human longing for self-transcendence, but his depiction of its foundations in a psychic or spiritual "hunger" comes very close to the argument that Alexis de Tocqueville presents in *Democracy in America* for the naturalness of religion. Rejecting the early Enlightenment's judgment that religion was rooted in superstitious fear and ignorance, Tocqueville presented an arresting depiction of the natural foundations of religion in the experience of human hope: "Religion is therefore only one particular form of hope, and it is as natural to the human heart as hope itself. Only by a kind of aberration of the intellect and with the aid of a sort of moral violence exercised on their own nature do men stray from religious beliefs; an invincible inclination leads them back to them. Disbelief is an accident; faith alone is the permanent state of humanity."[43] Obama appears to agree with the considered judgment of the French philosopher, for he notes that Americans are attracted to religion because they "need an assurance that somebody out there cares about them, is listening to them—that they are not just destined to travel down that long highway toward nothingness."[44]

But even these words evince the characteristic ambivalence that runs beneath the surface of so many of Obama's statements on faith, for it can be just as easily interpreted not as a Tocquevillian longing for self-transcendence, but rather as a reflection of the human, all too human, desire for this-worldly cultural and social belonging. This is very much the impression that Obama leaves in the *Audacity of Hope* about the place of religion in his own upbringing. Obama notes that he was "not raised in a particularly religious household"—his father was born a Muslim but became an atheist in his adulthood, while his anthropologist mother was raised by "non-practicing Baptists and Methodists . . . but grew up with a healthy skepticism of organized religion itself."[45] He is unequivocal in the book in attributing his childhood explorations of various faiths ("religious samplings" requiring "no introspective exertion or self-flagellation") to his mother's deeply ambivalent but culturally appreciative attitude toward religion: "Religion was an expression of human culture, she would explain, not its wellspring, just one of the many ways—and not necessarily the best way—that man attempted to control the unknowable and understand the deeper truths about our lives."[46] His mother "viewed religion through the eyes of the anthropologist," as "a phenomenon to be treated with a suitable respect, but with a suitable detachment as well. Moreover, as a child I rarely came in contact with those who might offer a substantially different view of faith."[47] But, crucially, Obama stresses that this "anthropological" exposure to religious pluralism did not aim at satisfying a mere cultural curiosity. His mother intended it to be constructive and hoped that it would reinforce in her son (through critical learning, but not through religious conversion) the social values that she believed the great religious traditions shared with her secular ethos, especially "honesty, empathy, delayed gratification, and hard work."[48]

Obama depicts his own religious conversion through a story of the discovery of faith that simultaneously stresses his internal doubts about religious dogma while celebrating the capacity of faith to anchor an individual in a larger community and to elicit in him a moral concern for a cause greater than self-interest. When he found himself working for social improvement and fighting poverty with churches in Chicago shortly after graduating from Occidental College, the fellowship of Christians that took him in saw that Obama knew "their Book and . . . shared their values and sang their songs," but they also recognized that he remained "removed, detached. . . . an observer in their midst."[49] Obama stresses that it was his short-lived effort at church-based community organizing in the south side of Chicago that led him to push up against the limits of his mother's detached perspective on religious faith. He came to realize that "something was missing" from an approach that merely appreciated religion as an element of culture, without at the same time considering it as a source of moral and spiritual guidance and the foundation of communal attachment: "Without a vessel for my beliefs, without a commitment to a particular community of faith, I would always remain apart, alone. . . . I found myself drawn—not just to work with the church, but to be in the church."[50] Obama seems to recognize that the skepticism and detachment that he took away from his mother proved to be partially incomplete, and their deficiencies ultimately lead him to undergo a conversion at the Trinity United Church under the spiritual guidance of Jeremiah Wright.

Even this most direct account of Obama's attraction to faith is replete with ambivalence about whether he views organized religion as a distinctive source of beliefs, or whether he understands it primarily as a "vessel" in which he seeks to deposit the values that he already embraces. As Obama will go on to indicate, his mother's indifference to religion proves deficient not so much for intellectual or theoretical reasons as it does for social and psychological ones, for it reveals itself to be a poor foundation for an active life devoted to social change and justice. Indeed, Obama stresses that he might have remained a thoroughgoing skeptic, "had it not been for the particular attributes of the historically black church, attributes that helped me shed some of my skepticism and embrace the Christian faith."[51] And what the African American church offered Obama was the social and psychological benefits of religious acceptance and commitment without the price of spiritual otherworldliness and theological dogmatism: "It was because of these newfound understandings—that religious commitment did not require me to suspend critical thinking, disengage from the battle for economic and social justice, or otherwise retreat from the world that I knew and loved—that I was finally able to walk down the aisle of Trinity United Church of Christ one day and be baptized."[52] As Stephen Mansfield observes, the way that Obama depicts his religious conversion is similar to how "many of his generation" understand the decision to join a church—"not so much to join a tradition as to find belonging among a people; not so much to accept a body of doctrine as to find welcome for what they already believe; not so much to surrender their lives but to enhance who they already are."[53]

We are now in a better position to assess Obama's ambiguous and puzzling relationship to the tradition of public theological reasoning that is often described as American civil religion. As we have seen, Obama identifies America's increasing religious diversity as the defining fact that informs his approach to the role of religion in democracy. Because it is impossible to achieve agreement over religious truths under conditions of diversity, pluralism renders religious-informed public appeals increasingly divisive, and for Obama this means that "the dangers of sectarianism have never been greater."[54] Instead of desperately clinging to an illusory religious consensus about our national identity that no longer exists, we should openly acknowledge "that our patchwork heritage is a strength,"[55] and that it is flexible enough to accommodate both believers and unbelievers:

> Whatever we once were, we're no longer just a Christian nation; we are also a Jewish nation, a Muslim nation, a Buddhist nation, a Hindu nation, and a nation of non-believers. We should acknowledge this and realize that when we're formulating policies from the statehouse to the Senate floor to the White House, we've got to work to translate our reasoning into values that are accessible to every one of our citizens, not just members of our own faith community.[56]

In what one commentator described as an effort to put "nonbelievers on the same footing as religious Americans,"[57] Obama became the first president in US history to acknowledge in an Inaugural Address that there are Americans who do not believe in God.[58] Obama's repeated references to nonbelievers in his speeches would therefore seem to follow a trend in scholarship that suggests that pluralism has fundamentally altered the nature of the relationship between America's political and constitutional values and the nation's religious heritage.[59] Obama appears to agree with Frederick Gedicks that "pluralism and sectarianization make it unlikely that American civil religion in its current [i.e., Christian] form could function as a source of American identity and national unity."[60] But this emerging consensus remains paradoxical, because while the nation's increasing pluralism is undeniable, neither Obama nor Gedicks wish to simply jettison the social and civic benefits that the now bygone era of religiously informed politics seemed to provide to American civic life.[61] As we have seen, Obama is explicit in stressing the unique contribution that religion (viz., Christianity) made to advances in democratic freedom, and he cherishes the heritage of political equality in which it culminated: "Imagine Lincoln's Second Inaugural Address without references to 'the judgments of the Lord.' Or King's 'I Have a Dream' speech without references to 'all of God's children.' Their summoning of a higher truth helped inspire what had seemed impossible and moved the nation to embrace a common destiny."[62] That America has entered a post-Christian century does not in itself alleviate the need for the civic function that religion fulfilled in the past, but how it can legitimately continue to do so going forward remains an unresolved puzzle for Obama just as much as it does for recent scholarship on civil religion.

Obama's relationship to American civil religion, therefore, is highly paradoxical, both in the way that he understands that tradition and in the way that he employs it. While he aims to continue the politics of civic engagement that he discerns in the abolitionist and the civil rights movements, he seeks to alter and update that tradition's relationship to Christianity, in order to tailor it to what he considers to be the profoundly deeper divisions that confront our society today and to make it sustainable under conditions of religious pluralism in which Christianity no longer commands the type of consensus that it did in the past. As Philip Gorski argues, "Obama's contribution consists in subtly rearranging the pieces" of American civil religion "to yield something both familiar and new. Of particular importance is his attention to religious-cultural pluralism. . . . Obama again and again refers to the religious mosaic of contemporary America and the divide between religious and secular America."[63] On its surface, it may seem paradoxical that a political leader who emphasizes the "divide" between the religious and secular sides of America to the extent that Obama does would simultaneously aspire to preserve the civic benefits that religion supplies to democracy. But as I have tried to show, this is precisely what Obama has been trying to do, by reconceptualizing civil religion so as to render it neutral between religion and irreligion. Obama therefore leaves us with the following question: to what extent is it possible to update American civil religion so as to take into account the nation's increasing pluralism without at the same time diluting religion so much as to render its contribution to democracy practically useless?

Obama's Ambivalent Embrace of Rawls's "Public Reason"

In the remainder of this chapter, I explore the idea of deliberative reasoning that Obama offers as a solution to the political challenges posed by religious pluralism and then attempt to appraise the theoretical coherence of that standard of public deliberation in light of Obama's own demanding moral and theological commitments to social justice. The solution that Obama proposes should be quite familiar to those attentive to debates in liberal political theory over the last few decades, since Obama embraces a standard of public reasonableness that initially appeared in Rawls's *Political Liberalism* (2005) and that has since then gained great influence. Distrustful of biblical certainty and concerned about the polarization of our public discourse, Obama argues that religiously based arguments are not suitable for efforts of political persuasion, both because they are dogmatically uncompromising and because they are inaccessible to those who do not share the faith. In "a pluralistic democracy" we have "no choice" but to demand that public deliberation transpire according to criteria of human reason that are accessible to both believers and unbelievers, and therefore religious reasons should be translated into universal, secular terms.[64] But by insisting on this standard, Obama shows much more clearly than is discernible in Rawls that the theoretical promise of liberal neutrality may be hard to fulfill in practice. While Rawls had insisted that his elegant system of political liberalism is "impartial" between comprehensive views, and that it promotes neither secular nor skeptical views, Obama shows that the standard of public reasonableness requires all claims of revealed religious authority to submit themselves to the tribunal of unassisted human reason.[65]

Obama provides an instructive litmus test of the character of civic life that can be sustained under a version of liberalism that subjects its public discourse to the demands of public reason. The crux of the problem can be stated in the following way: can public reason accommodate the religiously infused reasoning that was the hallmark of the approach that Lincoln and King shared in their quest for racial equality? Obama seems aware of this troubling question, since in some of the more self-critical parts of *The Audacity of Hope* he is compelled to question whether a politics that aims above all at compromise and deliberation can successfully account for historic democratic reform movements such as abolitionism and the civil rights movement. As we will see below, he knows that these historic advancements in equality and democratic decency were the result of the activists' moral urgency, theological certainty, and even absolutism, rather than their pragmatism, humility, and compromise. This disharmony between the moral requirements of civic life and social activism (which often involve bitter disagreement and division) and the expectations of pragmatism (which aims at common ground) will continue to pose a thorny challenge to Obama's Rawlsian solution to democratic pluralism.

Rawls's original view of public reason was rather exclusivist, since it held that on "fundamental political matters, reasons given explicitly in terms of comprehensive doctrines are never to be introduced in public reason."[66] However, Rawls revealingly confesses in a footnote that he was eventually convinced by the friendly criticisms of Amy Gutmann and Lawrence Solum that his "exclusive view" of public reasons "was too restrictive," insofar as it would have excluded the contributions of abolitionists and Martin Luther King, Jr., from the sphere of legitimate public discourse.[67] These objections led Rawls to propose modifications to his conception of public reason on two separate occasions. The first is the "inclusive" view of public reason that he articulates in the cloth-bound version of *Political Liberalism*, which concedes that public reason is an "ideal" that Rawls hopes can obtain in a "well-ordered society" in which principles of justice already obtain and where "profound divisions over constitutional essentials" no longer persist.[68] Under less perfect historical circumstances, however, Rawls grants that it is permissible to appeal to arguments based on comprehensive views when such arguments are judged to be "the best way to bring about a well-ordered and just society in which the ideal of public reason could eventually be honored"—as both the abolitionists and the leaders of the civil rights movement could plausibly argue they did.[69] Rawls offers a different and even more permissive modification on another occasion. In the restatement of his argument that he presents in "The Idea of Public Reason Revisited," Rawls proposes his famous translation "proviso" that would make the use of religious reasons permissible even in a well-ordered society, provided one important qualification: citizens may introduce comprehensive doctrines, including religious ones, "into political discussion at any time, provided that in due course public reasons . . . are presented sufficient to support whatever the comprehensive doctrines are introduced to support."[70] As we have seen, Rawls's theory of public reason has generated a great deal of debate in scholarship, with critics often highlighting the contribution of religious arguments to democracy's civic life that would arguably be left out even under the more inclusive framework that Rawls eventually embraced.[71]

When Obama articulates the "ground rules" that should guide religious believers in public deliberation, he drop Rawls's "proviso" altogether, opting for an absolute translation requirement: "Democracy demands that the religiously motivated translate their concerns into universal, rather than religion-specific, values." As Horwitz points out, "Obama outdoes Rawls himself"[72] on the requirements of public reason, since he urges citizens to provide strictly nonreligious arguments to win a hearing in democracy. From his perspective, anything less than absolute translation of religious views would entail arguments that are not "amenable to reason," and this would impede our ability to engage in deliberative persuasion with each other. To illustrate the limits that this view of deliberation imposes on religiously informed speech, Obama refers to the hot-button example of opposition to abortion: "I may be opposed to abortion for religious reasons, but if I seek to pass a law banning the practice, I cannot simply point to the teachings of my church or evoke God's will. I have to explain why abortion violates some principle that is accessible to people of all faiths, including those with no faith at all." It is doubtless true that in a pluralistic democracy, politically astute citizens will have an incentive to seek arguments that are, to some degree, "accessible to people" of other faiths (including those with no faith at all), since prevailing in democracy ultimately depends on building coalitions that can win majorities. But as Jeffrey Stout points out, to concede this is merely to acknowledge that there may exist "strategic reasons for self-restraint,"[73] and not that there are any moral or constitutional restrictions against the use of religious language in public deliberation. Citizens, after all, "are not *required* to be Rawlsian liberals, even if doing so would help them win political battles," since an important purpose of political debate is to bring into sharp focus the stark alternatives that often endure on intractable moral and policy issues such as abortion. According to Stout, adopting "the policy of restraint" in the case of religious or other private comprehensive views "would cause too much silence at precisely the points where more discussion is most badly needed," because "reasons actually held in common do not get us far enough toward answers to enough of our political questions."[74]

The objections to the translation requirement that Stout and others advance point us to an alternative model of public deliberation that does not share the priority of achieving common ground or an "overlapping consensus" that Obama and Rawls cherish. There is a crucial role for religion in democracy not as a mere supplement to public reason, but instead as its friendly antagonist and sparring partner that can morally challenge the democratic status quo. This is the function of religion that Jeremy Waldron describes as "bearing witness," and that Hugo Heclo refers to as American Christianity's "prophetic stance" toward government and society.[75] We see this role of religion reflected in the Christian reasoning that is at the core of some of the social movements that both Rawls and Obama would endorse and celebrate—not just the abolitionist and the civil rights movements, but also and more recently Evangelical and Catholic teachings opposed to torture and supporting social justice, including especially those that emphasize the need for economic care for the poor.[76] Imposing a strict translation requirement would mean that the breadth, scope, and richness of the moral arguments that can be marshaled in democracy would be diminished and truncated in the process. As Andrew March shows, this would be especially problematic for a democratic society, since religious arguments tend to be extremely effective at "pricking the consciences or enlarging the moral imaginations" of human beings, even and especially for the potentially skeptical recipient of the theological message who may find its social implications appealing.[77] Contrary to Rawls, as March and others have stressed, this role of religion appears to be especially pronounced in times of national crisis or great moral conflict, when public consensus on moral issues and the political status quo are challenged.[78] Accordingly, to insist that religious contributions to public deliberation undergo a rigorous process of translation into public reason may be both unrealistic and undesirable from the perspective of democratic pluralism and justice.

We get a better sense of what Obama's translation requirement would entail for religious views if we consider what he says about faith and reason, and about the meaning and import of biblical revelation in contemporary political life. Where Rawls had insisted that political liberalism would be neutral between comprehensive views, and that the "overlapping consensus" that it would secure would promote neither skepticism nor indifference, Obama explicitly defends a religious outlook that combines faith and doubt.[79] In the Introduction to *The Audacity of Hope*, Obama claims that his attitude about faith grows out of his personal experience as a "Christian and skeptic."[80] Furthermore, in a remarkably candid 2004 interview with Cathleen Falsani in the *Chicago Sun Times*, Obama claimed that he is "very suspicious of religious certainty expressing itself in politics."[81] "I think that religion at its best comes with a big dose of doubt," Obama explained in the same interview. Similarly, in a 2006 *New Yorker* interview with David Remnick, Obama deplored the tendency in this country "to define religion in absolutist, fundamentalist terms."[82] Those who insist on theological dogmatism, Obama explained, are doing the nation a profound disservice, for they encourage the view that "to be a believer is to be a fundamentalist in some fashion." As an alternative to dogmatic theological certainty, Obama proposed his own understanding of faith, which combines religious belief with humility and doubt: "What I was trying to describe is a faith that admits doubt, and uncertainty, and mystery. . . . It's not faith if you're absolutely certain. There's a leap that we all take, and when you admit that doubt publicly, it's a form of testimony."[83] Such a synthesis, Obama stresses, offers indisputably positive political benefits in a pluralistic society: it "allows both the secular and the religious to find some sort of common space" and "is in the best of the United States religious tradition."[84] In short, Obama has in mind a religion that has been moderated by an awareness of the limits of certainty and by pluralism—what Robert Putnam and David Campbell describe as "a faith without fanaticism" in their study of American religiosity.[85]

Doubtless a faith that has been moderated in this way would pose fewer challenges to a pluralistic democracy as well as to liberal theory. But would a religion so transformed have anything solid left to contribute to our political and moral debates? Obama claims that "faith and reason operate in different domains": the domain of political deliberation is the exclusive realm of "reason" and is distinguished from the domain of religion, which Obama claims is the realm of "faith."[86] Both domains make accessible to human beings certain truths, but they do so in crucially different ways. Reason "involves the accumulation of knowledge based on realities we can all comprehend," and in politics this knowledge is tested in "our ability to persuade each other of common aims based on a common reality."[87] Religion, on the other hand, "is based on truths that are not provable through ordinary understanding."[88] The peculiar challenge that religion poses to democracy is that "at some fundamental level, religion does not allow for compromise."[89] Obama here echoes Rawls's formulation in *Political Liberalism* that the "zeal to embody the whole truth in politics is incompatible with an idea of public reason that belongs to democratic citizenship."[90] Sealing this Rawlsian argument, Obama claims that such religious zeal necessarily obstructs the willingness to deliberate and the commitment to compromise that are necessary for nurturing a political process that advances the "overlapping values that both religious and secular people share when it comes to the moral and material direction of our country."[91]

This straightforward dichotomy between faith and reason that Obama and Rawls appear to share is not a peculiar feature of contemporary liberal theory alone. John Locke adopted a similar distinction in his *Letter Concerning Toleration* when he set out to "distinguish exactly the business of civil government from that of religion" and in his *Essay Concerning Human Understanding*, where he urged to make reason (as distinguished from "faith" or mere "probability") our "last judge and guide in everything."[92] There is a long modern philosophical tradition tying together the Enlightenment's effort to "domesticate" religion through privatization with contemporary attempts to develop models of public deliberation that are insulated from divisive religious rhetoric. We have already seen that Obama is aware that this distinction cannot quite do justice to the nature of religious experience in America's civic and political history, and that it would entail the exclusion of the theological contributions of both King and Lincoln from legitimate political debate. But can even a pragmatic liberal like Obama uphold such a standard of rationalism in political practice, or are his moral and theological commitments (including especially his understanding of divine revelation) bound to spill over into his political rhetoric? Can Obama, in short, successfully bracket his theology from politics, as his Rawlsian framework would seem to require, or do his theological views and liberal politics mutually shape and inform each other?

We can begin to uncover an answer to this question by comparing Obama's description of his approach to biblical interpretation with the way he actually employs the Bible in public speeches. On the one hand, Obama's pragmatic rationalism predisposes him to distrust dogmatism in matters of revelation: "When I read the Bible," Obama explains, "I do so with the belief that it is not a static text but the Living Word and that I must be continually open to new revelations—whether they come from a lesbian friend or from a doctor opposed to abortion."[93] Literalist readings of the Bible, Obama writes, are not only untenable in the modern context of pluralism, but unsustainable on the basis of the Bible itself, since many of the stories in the scripture contradict each other. The scripture therefore invites a method of creative interpretation, and while "there are passages of the Bible that make perfect sense to me," Obama writes, many others strain credulity. The Bible's alleged condemnation of homosexuality, for instance, is one example that Obama singles outs as "an obscure line in Romans" that should not be considered "to be more defining of Christianity than the Sermon on the Mount." Obama therefore counsels that believers should make distinctions between such biblical edicts as the Ten Commandments and Christ's divinity that "are central to the Christian faith" and those that "are more culturally specific and may be modified to accommodate modern life." But on what basis are we to distinguish which parts of the Bible are reasonable and which are not, and is there any other standard guiding this interpretative flexibility besides the cultural norms that dominate in our day and age? Obama never explains why religious accommodation with modern life should come at the *expense* of those religious views which do not simply support present-day cultural norms. But by suggesting that liberalism reshapes theology in light of liberal principles, and that therefore the liberal polity is by no means theologically neutral, Obama clarifies a controversial implication of political liberalism that is obscured by the Rawlsian framework of neutrality.

We are left with a final paradox about the implications of Obama's theological skepticism for the social and moral values that he often celebrates and sometimes traces to the Christian tradition. Obama suggests that some of the moral teachings of the Bible can be severed from their biblical foundations, and therefore doubt about religious dogma need not bring into question the social justice teaching that Obama, like many others, believes the Christian tradition supports. Indeed, the latter values of social justice Obama argues are insulated from skepticism, and they constitute unshakable moral truths: "There are some things that I'm *absolutely sure* about—

the Golden Rule, the need to battle cruelty in all its forms, the value of love and charity, humility and grace."[94] Obama does not here explain how one can be absolutely certain about the validity of such principles, although he has at other occasions indicated that he sees the call to service that imbues both his domestic and foreign policy as embodying "the Biblical call to care for the least of these—for the poor; for those at the margins of our society." But whatever may be said about the potential theological foundations of this vision of social justice, surely these are not principles that would meet the demanding test of pragmatism that Obama articulated in his discussion of democracy and its relationship to religion. Pragmatism, or "doing what works" in Obama's formulation, would seem to require the dilution of the certainty and fervor with which one embraces even these moral values, and not merely their theological counterparts. As Obama himself observed in a commencement address at the University of Notre Dame in 2009, while doubt may not ultimately "push us away from our faith," it should certainly "humble us," "temper our passions," and "cause us to be wary of too much self-righteousness."[95]

Conclusion: Religion and the Limits of Deliberative Politics

Obama leaves us with an ambiguity in his understanding of the relation-ship between religion and democracy, an ambiguity that is reflective of a tension within the prevailing view of the foundational neutrality of liberal-ism. Like the anti-foundationalist thinkers such as John Rawls and Richard Rorty, Obama believes that the Constitution commits this nation to delibera-tive democracy, which he understands as requiring the rejection of "absolute truths."[96] Unlike the anti-foundationalists, however, Obama appears to be much more keenly aware of our inescapable need for such "absolute truths" for the civic and moral health of ordinary political life, which is one of the reasons that he seeks to nurture a liberalism that is friendlier to religion. But the awareness of our need for the absolutes that religion provides does not make Obama any less uncomfortable with absolutist politics than was Rawls, which is why Obama insists on the need for translation of our religious com-mitments into public reason. As we have seen, this solution proves less than satisfactory in practice, for while Obama renounces neither public reason nor pragmatism, he demonstrates how easily their requirements can come under strain when confronted with moral conflict and division.

In fact, in the most self-critical parts of the *Audacity of Hope*, Obama voices doubts about whether the gap between public reason and the legacy of antislavery political and social activism can ever successfully be bridged: "I'm reminded that deliberation and the constitutional order may sometimes be the luxury of the powerful, and that it has sometimes been the cranks, the zealots, the prophets, the agitators, and the unreasonable—in other words, the absolutists—that have fought for a new order."[97] Reminded by the "hard, cold facts" that it was the "unbending idealists like William Lloyd Garrison" and "men like Denmark Vesey and Frederick Douglass and women like Harriet Tubman, who recognized power would concede nothing without a fight," Obama finds his pragmatism chastened by the reality that moral urgency and even conflict are sometimes absolutely necessary for the success of democratic reforms and for the advancement of decency, equality, and human dignity. In what Kloppenberg describes as "a striking admission,"[98] Obama goes further, acknowledging the need for moral absolutes: "I am robbed even of the certainty of uncertainty—for sometimes absolute truths may well be absolute."[99] The demands of deliberative democracy (at least in the way in which Obama understands them), it would appear, leave little room to accommodate the type of moral conflict and theological partisanship that characterized the Civil War and the civil rights movement, and the appeal to inflexible and unchanging moral truths that was the hallmark of the statesmanship of both Lincoln and King. For Obama, this realization is so profound that it prompts him to begin reevaluating the uncompromising and intransigent moral absolutism of the contemporary opponents of abortion. "I can't summarily dismiss those possessed of similar certainty today," he observers, either "the antiabortion activist who pickets my town hall meeting, or the animal rights activist who raids a laboratory—no matter how deeply I disagree with their views."[100]

This admission helps us see a deeper dilemma in the philosophy of public reason that contemporary liberal theory has been unable to resolve. The noble aspiration to secure an overlapping consensus that animates both liberal theory and pragmatic politics may obscure the degree to which political liberalism depends on the contribution of theological and moral views that have historically challenged the political status quo. Thus, when Obama turns his narrative to Lincoln's Second Inaugural Address, a paradigmatic example of religiously infused but respectful and civil public reasoning about the highest constitutional priorities of the nation, he is led into a conceptual impasse. Obama stresses that more than any other politician in

American history, Lincoln understood "both the deliberative function of our democracy and the limits of such deliberation."[101] But in an attempt to cast Lincoln as a deliberative democrat in search of a "common understanding" that could be shared between the North and the South, Obama struggles to present a picture of Lincoln's moral and theological principles that is either coherent or intelligible: "I like to believe that for Lincoln, it was never a matter of abandoning conviction for the sake of expediency. Rather, it was a matter of maintaining within himself the balance between two contradictory ideas—that we must talk and reach for common understandings, precisely because all of us are imperfect and can never act with the certainty that God is on our side; and yet at times we must act nonetheless, as if we are certain, protected from error only by providence."[102] It was, Obama tells us in his surprising interpretation, Lincoln's alleged "humility" that led him to eschew unnecessary moral conflict and absolutism, and to rely on "reasoned arguments" instead.[103]

What Obama's account leaves out is that Lincoln was unhesitating in insisting that slavery was "a great moral wrong" because it violated man's God-given rights to equality and liberty, which Lincoln ultimately traced back to the Declaration of Independence and its "lofty, and wise, and noble understanding of the justice of the Creator to His creatures." Lincoln's Second Inaugural Address gives this principle a theological refraction, by asserting that slavery is incompatible with divine justice: "It may seem strange that any men should dare to ask a just God's assistance in wringing their bread from the sweat of other men's faces, but let us judge not, that we be not judged."[104] Even while acknowledging that God's judgments may ultimately be difficult (and even impossible) to discern, Lincoln quoted Psalm 19:9, "The Judgments of the Lord are true and righteous altogether," and he did not hesitate to describe the Civil War as divine punishment for the national sin of slavery: "American slavery is one of those offences" that God "now wills to remove," and he thus gives "both the North and the South this terrible war." For Lincoln, what was at stake in the great national struggle was the inviolability of the absolute moral truth of human equality, and the great emancipator rendered this idea in religious language in order to transform how Americans understood the legacy of the Declaration of Independence and the meaning of the Civil War. Obama's incomplete embrace of public reason and his hesitating doubts about pragmatism remind us that political liberalism, in spite of its theoretical aspirations, may never be able to fully transcend the need for theological and moral foundations. In the next chapter, I turn to the political philosophy of John Locke to show how this Enlightenment thinker sought to transform biblical Christianity in order to make it compatible with the theological and moral presuppositions of liberal politics. By studying this theological transformation in Locke's thought, we will better understand the Enlightenment's religious legacy on which Rawls and Obama implicitly depend but which they neither fully articulate nor defend.

CHAPTER THREE

DOES TOLERATION REQUIRE RELIGIOUS SKEPTICISM? AN EXAMINATION OF LOCKE'S TEACHING ON TOLERATION

Introduction: Religion, Skepticism, and Toleration

As we saw in the previous chapters, the leading school of liberal theory today provides a very ambiguous account of the theoretical and historical origins of religious toleration. Rawls's anti-foundationalist political philosophy, as we noticed, studiously avoided the claim that religion had to submit to the supremacy of secular reason, let alone that religion had to be transformed in light of rationalism, for political liberalism to emerge. Rawls chose, instead, to celebrate the legacy of a "reasonable faith," which he traced to post-Reformation Protestantism and also to post–Vatican II Catholicism, but he never specified what such a faith would ultimately demand of believers. Rawls's position showed cracks when it confronted illiberal objections to political liberalism, which he clearly indicated had to be either marginalized or somehow made compatible with liberalism. Obama, on the other hand, appeared more forthcoming in indicating that a faith that would be suitable for a pluralistic society would be a "faith that admits doubt, and uncertainty, and mystery." This ambiguity in contemporary liberalism points us to the need to pursue a historical and theoretical investigation that goes beyond contemporary liberal theory, and in particular it prompts us to ask the following questions about the foundations of toleration: Does toleration depend on theological skepticism?[1] Does a tolerant faith presuppose a certain kind of transformation of Christian religious presuppositions in light of modern rationalism? To answer these questions, we need to study the modern thinker who first articulated a theory of religious toleration in the Christian world: John Locke. Locke's *Letter Concerning Toleration* is rightfully regarded as one of the most influential works of modern liberalism, and by studying it (along with related works as well as its contemporary reception among Locke's religious critics) we will place into sharper focus both the foundations of toleration as well as the gulf that separates Locke's Enlightenment approach to religion from Rawls's political liberalism.[2]

On the surface, consulting this voluminous scholarship on Locke deepens the puzzle of toleration even more. A persistent but decided minority of scholars consider Locke to be a shrewd follower of the rationalism of Thomas Hobbes and interpret his religious works as rhetorical attempts to reinterpret Christianity and render it compatible with liberalism.[3] On some versions of this reading, Locke's political teaching in the *Second Treatise* ultimately abandons scriptural and theological supports,[4] whereas his religious teaching in the *Letter* depends on theological skepticism and doubt.[5] On the other end of the spectrum of scholarship, we find a diametrically opposed picture: a majority of scholars consider Locke to be a thoroughly Christian thinker.[6] Thus, while the *Letter* is broadly acknowledged to have inspired the secular doctrine of separation of church and state, Locke's appeal to the Protestant idea of liberty of conscience is thought to render his teaching on toleration inadequate for a modern world that has largely outgrown his Christian historical context.[7] For much of the scholarly community today, the *Letter*'s dependence on this premodern Christian residue renders its teaching not only politically "too narrow to provide an adequate basis for a modern doctrine" (since it excludes atheists and Catholics), but also philosophically of questionable relevance today.[8]

Some leading students of Locke have even abandoned the effort to defend a strictly rationalist Locke in favor of what could be called a "theistic Locke." The most prominent illustration of this trend is Jeremy Waldron's much-noted recent book, *God, Locke and Equality*.[9] Two decades ago, Waldron believed that it was possible to salvage a "secular" reading of Locke's teaching on toleration.[10] In the intervening years, however, he has evolved to the opposite conclusion, which is reflected in the subtitle of his book: *Christian Foundations in Locke's Political Thought*. This evolution is philosophically dramatic, since Waldron now thinks that "the main argument of the *Letter* does have to rest on its distinctively Christian foundations."[11] He seems to have abandoned the hope for a theory of toleration general and neutral enough that it can include believers and unbelievers alike, and (more generally) is drawn to the view that liberal equality requires theological foundations[12]—he has embraced what Schwartzman describes as "the sectarian" Locke.[13] This is clearly an uncomfortable conclusion for liberal theorists to accept, insofar as it renders Locke's teaching not only potentially illiberal, but also philosophically questionable in light of enduring pluralism.[14] As Michael Zuckert points out in a symposium devoted to his book, Waldron's evolution provides an important challenge to liberal theorists today: if the alleged "theological foundations" of Locke's *Letter* cannot be successfully "bracketed," then the founding father of modern liberal rationalism will have bequeathed an incoherent legacy, one in which "the knowledge of the true principles of morality depends on the Christian revelation."[15]

This chapter traces these conflicting strands of Locke scholarship to a foundational disharmony *within* Locke's own teaching about toleration, a disharmony that I highlight through a comparative study of Locke's political and philosophical works. To better understand the complexity of Locke's theological project of toleration (and its ambiguous historical results), it is necessary to compare the original *Letter Concerning Toleration* with two additional sources that help illuminate that work: the debate between Locke and his Anglican critic Jonas Proast as well as Locke's *Essay Concerning Human Understanding*. Such a comparison demonstrates that Locke presents not one but rather two accounts of the foundations of toleration, and that these accounts diverge in crucial respects. The *Letter* bases toleration on a religious argument about the sanctity of human conscience and teaches that every human being has an obligation to seek religious truth (which Locke implies is attainable). The *Essay* (as well as the debate with Proast), in contrast, grounds toleration in the limits of human knowledge. It argues that a proper demarcation of the spheres of reason and faith, and recognition of the fact that the prerequisites of a saving faith cannot be demonstrated with certainty, will defuse religiously induced violence. Locke therefore emerges as a thinker who could have promoted a nonreligious (i.e., secular) teaching of toleration, one that would have been more politically capacious at accommodating not just believing Christians but also non-Christians and nonbelievers alike, but chose instead to present it specifically as a Christian virtue in his most important theological-political work.

My study shows that while it is often thought to reflect the incoherency of Locke's thinking, or to indicate that his project is "hostage" to biblical revelation,[16] this disharmony in Locke's theological teaching is instead a sign of Locke's attempt to promote a tolerant interpretation of Christianity. Locke favored this strategy both for rhetorical reasons (since it made his liberal political order compatible with the quest for religious truth), as well as for political and psychological reasons (as an alternative to the twin dangers of orthodoxy and irreligion). In the first part of the chapter, I turn to Locke's debate with Proast to show how Locke sought to advance this synthesis between toleration and religious belief in the *Letter*. Although Locke's *Letter* never denies that true religion exists and that it is knowable, the thrust of its argument is devoted to establishing the theologically controversial proposition that salvation depends not on the "orthodoxy" of beliefs, but on "Charity" and good works.[17] Locke thus redefined the focus of "true religion" to morality, but in doing so he rendered it almost superfluous from the perspective of traditional biblical revelation, which had emphasized dogmatic orthodoxy or correct beliefs. Proast, an Oxford scholar and chaplain, sensed in these breaks with the Christian tradition glimmers of religious relativism. He claimed that Locke's position in the *Letter* would render the notion of "True Religion" (which Proast equated with Anglicanism) incoherent and inconsequential.[18] With foreboding prescience, Proast predicted that the adoption of Lockean principles of toleration would eventually lead to "skepticism in religion among us,"[19] thus precipitating the spread of atheism and moral relativism.

Over the period of a little over a decade, Locke would author three additional *Letters* responding to Proast's charges and rebuffing his claim that toleration would lead to irreligion, and these exchanges constitute the focus of the first half of this chapter.[20] Even though Locke is vehement in these defenses that his intention in the original *Letter* is to avoid the outcome that Proast predicts, Locke's rejoinders to Proast increasingly lead him to embrace an epistemological outlook about the special nature of religious truth claims, which Locke judges to be shrouded in uncertainty and doubt. In the second half of the chapter, I employ Locke's *Essay Concerning Human Understanding* for the limited purpose of illuminating these epistemological foundations of Locke's case for toleration. Because Locke insists in the *Letter* that "truth certainly would do well enough, if she were once left to shift for her self,"[21] he minimizes the obstacle that theological uncertainty poses to the quest for religious truth—an implication that he draws out much more explicitly in the *Essay*. Where some scholars have attempted to harmonize Locke's epistemology with his politics, my interpretation spotlights a tension between these two sides of Locke's corpus.[22] When the *Letter* is read in light of the *Essay*'s theological minimalism, Proast's prediction that toleration is more likely to culminate in religious relativism and skepticism than it is in the discovery of religious truth gains currency. In the conclusion, I evaluate Locke's overall theological project in light of contemporary sociological evidence on American Christianity and suggest that ongoing transformations in America's religious landscape complicate Locke's hope to promote a tolerant religion that could be insulated from skepticism in a liberal society.

The *Letter Concerning Toleration* and Locke's Debate with Jonas Proast

Scholars usually see the *Letter* as advancing three main arguments, corresponding to Locke's division of the *Letter* into three "considerations," which he claims "abundantly . . . demonstrate" the incompetence of the civil magistrate in matters of religion. The first consideration, that human beings have not consented the care of souls to the civil magistrate, Locke advances without argument, though this aspect of the *Letter* evokes the "contractualist" bent of the *Second Treatise on Government* by limiting the state exclusively to the secular purposes of "Life, Liberty, Health and the Indolency of the Body; and the possession of outward things."[23] Locke also presents two additional "considerations"—the futility of force in compelling beliefs (the *Letter*'s psychology) and the challenge posed by pluralism to the pursuit of the true religion (the *Letter*'s epistemology)—which become the focus of Locke's protracted debate with Jonas Proast. But before the *Letter* even advances these considerations, Locke actually goes out of his way to present an intricate theological argument based on his interpretation of Christian "charity," which forms the rhetorical leitmotif of the *Letter*.[24] Before evaluating his debate with Proast, in this section I will first turn to Locke's biblical argument to show how Locke develops a tolerant theology that he intends to displace the Christian Thomistic tradition and overcome the latter's posture toward heresy. This Lockean theology simultaneously minimizes the antitheological implications of the *Letter*'s overall teaching while softening the radical consequences of the *Letter*'s subsequent "considerations," especially the epistemic implications of Locke's consideration about pluralism. Because he develops such a theology through his reading of the Bible, Locke can paradoxically continue to speak of the "true religion" as that religion which is tolerant of competing orthodoxies: i.e., as a religion that is no longer concerned with theological dogma. It is therefore in the *Letter*'s biblical argument, and in Locke's manipulation of the scripture, that we can discern the germinating seeds of the epistemological questions that provoked Proast's hostile reaction to the *Letter*.

Locke's Reinterpretation of Christian "Charity" and the Attack on the Thomistic Tradition

Even though the dominant view is that Locke's argument rests on theological premises,[25] the underlying rhetorical nature of Locke's manipulation of the Bible in the *Letter* has been generally neglected. Locke rests the opening bold claim of the *Letter*—"I esteem . . . Toleration . . . to be the chief Characteristic Mark of the True Church"—on an initial surge of biblical references, citing Timothy, Luke, and Galatians a combined five times in the first three pages, laying the groundwork for his conclusion that persecution is inimical to the genuine message of Christianity.[26] This provides an entryway for Proast's critical response, which draws heavily on the traditional Thomistic and Augustinian justifications of coercion in religion. Locke's assault on that tradition on its own turf (on biblical grounds) was an innovation in his rhetorical strategy: neither the *Essay on Toleration* (1667) nor the unpublished "Critical Notes" (1681) that Locke composed on Edward Stillingfleet's antiseparationist polemics contains a defense of toleration as a Christian duty.[27] The *Letter*, in contrast, unequivocally proclaims that "if [any man] be destitute of Charity, Meekness, and Good-will in general toward all Mankind, even to those that are not Christians, he is certainly yet short of being a true Christian."[28] Waldron's dismissal (in an early interpretation) of what he calls the "Christian premises" of the *Letter* is characteristic of scholarship on Locke: acknowledging that the "immediate reaction to the publication of the *Letter* concerned this part of the Lockean case" that appealed to the scripture, he nevertheless judges it "uninteresting from a philosophical point of view."[29] Scholarship on Locke has failed to entertain the possibility that Locke's method of interpreting the Bible reveals the political (as distinguished from the religious) priorities of his teaching and sheds light on the epistemic requirements of toleration.

If Locke's theology cannot be "bracketed" from his teaching on toleration (as so many interpreters argue), then we have an even greater incentive to test whether that theology is based on an accurate portrayal of scriptural principles. The genius of Locke's opening biblical argument lies in its subtlety: in the guise of an appeal to the message of Jesus Christ as depicted in the scripture, Locke subtly elevates the principle of charity over orthodoxy of doctrine. Locke insists from the very beginning of the *Letter* that the Bible does not sanction the use of force to root out heresy or schism, because its message is limited "to the regulating of Mens Lives according to the Rules of Vertue and Piety."[30] He writes as if it were a foregone conclusion for Christians that "The Business of True Religion" consists only in instilling virtuous and moral behavior and not in promoting orthodox beliefs, even though this question was much in dispute at his time. Proast (following the traditional teaching) claims that Christian charity requires the magistrate to use force for the salvation of souls.[31] But in Locke's hands the same principle serves to expose the moral hypocrisy of persecution among Christians:

"If it be done out of a Principle of Charity . . . if all this be done meerly to make Men Christians, and procure their Salvation, Why then do they suffer *Whoredom, Fraud, Malice, and such like enormities,* which (according to the Apostle) manifestly relish of Heathenish Corruption, to predominate so much and abound amongst their Flocks and People"?[32] Surely such moral vices, Locke avers, threaten human souls more than the diversity of beliefs and the plurality of sects. This is a deliberate attempt to harness the moral message of Christian charity as an ally of toleration: sectarianism becomes the irrefutable proof of a defect of charity and of worldly ambition for "temporal dominion."[33] Myers describes this strategy as Locke's attempt to appeal to "a Christianity purified of its own historical sectarianism."[34] But, as I show below, a necessary consequence of interpreting Christian charity as a tolerant virtue is that Locke has to sever the age-old link between "True Religion" and the concern for doctrinal orthodoxy.

The *Letter* is nowadays read as resting on theological presuppositions, but in reality it is a very subtle work of theological reinterpretation, since Locke has to establish a position that was not widely shared by Christians at his time.[35] This becomes evident in the unconventional way that Locke uses the Bible to establish his account of Christian faith, a "Faith which works, not by force, but by Love," and whose chief requirements are good works and charity to fellow men.[36] The last passage that Locke invokes in a series of biblical references purportedly establishing this proposition is from the Epistle to the Galatians (5:19–20). It is worth dwelling on this reference, since it is revealing of the way in which Locke has to read the Bible in order to portray its message as supportive of toleration: "*Adultery, Fornication, Uncleanness, Lasciviousness, Idolatry, and such like things, cannot be denied to be Works of the Flesh;* concerning which the Apostle has expressly declared, *that they who do them shall not Inherit the Kingdom of God.* Whosoever therefore is sincerely solicitous about the Kingdom of God . . . ought to apply himself with no less care and industry to the rooting out of these Immoralities, than to the Extirpation of Sects."[37] But consulting the scripture reveals that Locke deliberately cuts off the list of prohibitions in order to shift the emphasis from correct belief to moral action: the passage in Galatians adds to the list of moral vices the prohibition not only of "witchcraft, hatred, variance, emulations, wrath, strife," but also of "seditions [and] heresies" (Galatians 5:20). The Bible, it would seem, did not distinguish between prohibited "moral vices," on the one hand, and "opinions," on the other, so much so that it counted *theological* deviations as "works of the flesh" that ought to be deterred through punishment. Because the Bible does not sanction such a distinction between faith and works, Locke is compelled to subtly reinterpret its meaning.[38]

As John Marshall has shown, the biblical passage on which Locke hinges so much of his opening rhetorical case for establishing the Christian duty of toleration was actually central to the Thomistic tradition's posture toward heresy.[39] In reference to the same passage from the Galatians that Locke cited, Augustine stressed that for St. Paul heresy was counted among "crimes on the same level with other fruits of iniquity" and therefore punishable under criminal law (sometimes as a capital offense).[40] In the *Summa Theologica*, Aquinas followed Augustine's definition of heretics as those "who hold mischievous and erroneous opinions" in matters of faith.[41] Just as a contagious sickness can kill an entire city, Aquinas held that heresy had the power to "corrupt" the soul of the community and accordingly urged the Church to treat it as an infectious spiritual illness. Similarly, Augustine compared heresy to a "disease" in the *City of God*, and his epistles used the image of a physician who amputates a diseased limb for the sake of the rest of the body.[42] Once heterodox opinions were identified as spiritual poison that threatened the salvation of souls, it was only natural that the Church would seek to employ the compulsive instruments of the state in its effort to suppress heresy. Thus, Aquinas insists that heretics should be not only excommunicated by the church but should also be subjected to punishment by the state: "Wherefore if forgers of money and other evil-doers are forthwith condemned to death by the secular authority, much more reason is there for heretics, as soon as they are convicted of heresy, to be not only excommunicated but even put to death."[43] As this quotation indicates, the separation of opinions and acts that Locke introduces in the *Letter*, on the basis of very tendentious scriptural exegesis, was clearly alien to the Thomistic Christian tradition. Locke does not even allude to this nearly uninterrupted Christian consensus, spanning from Augustine through Aquinas and then to Calvin, that viewed heresy as the legitimate object of state coercion, even though his real aspiration is to displace this tradition altogether.

It is this Thomistic tradition that Proast appeals to when he announces in his response to Locke's *Second Letter on Toleration* that "aversion to the true Religion is certainly and inevitably mortal to the Soul, if not cured; and so of absolute necessity to be cured."[44] In addition to comparing heresy to a disease, Locke's opponents appealed to an understanding of Christian charity that was diametrically opposed in meaning to Locke's use of that term. In the traditional Christian understanding, charity entailed the duty to love one's neighbor unconditionally, a duty that was understood to entail a categorical requirement for Christians to be actively concerned with the salvation of their fellow men's souls. In this way Christian love came to be fused with justifications of persecution, both as a means to convert the heretic as well as to protect the faithful from the corrosive influence of heresy. Thus, Augustine is famous for distinguishing between just and unjust persecution, and for insisting that "the Church persecutes out of love, the ungodly out of cruelty."[45] Similarly, Aquinas speaks of the duty of "brotherly affection" among Christians "to save those they can, even if those they cannot save die of their own accord."[46] When such communitarian zeal is combined with the certainty that one possesses the knowledge of true religion, as is the case with Proast, then the fusion between church and state is inevitable. As Proast insists, "charity requires that [men] be kept subject to Penalties, *till* they embrace the True Religion."[47]

Proast's appeal to the Thomistic tradition helps illuminate the formidable theological obstacles that Locke's tolerationist reading of the Bible confronted in his day and age. Because of that tradition, it would not suffice for Locke to simply reinterpret the principle of charity in order to defuse the Christian impulse toward persecution. Locke also needs a practical argument that can supplement his biblical exegesis. If he can demonstrate that persecution is not only un-Christian (at least on his reading of the Bible) but also ineffective at securing a saving faith, then the case for using force in the name of Christian charity and love would become impossible to sustain. So let us turn to Locke's argument about the futility of force in matters of belief.

Locke's Argument about the Futility of Force in the Letter

The *Letter's* most famous argument is that force operates only on will, and therefore the nature of belief (which is not subject to the will) makes it insusceptible to human coercion. Although this claim may appear self-evident to the modern reader, it was a matter of deep controversy in Locke's time and would be the focus of Locke's response to Proast's criticism in the *Second Letter of Toleration*. Standard interpretations hold that Locke's argument about belief is essentially a version of the Protestant liberty of conscience, and commentators have held that it shows Locke's indebtedness to post-Reformation Christianity.[48] It is true that Locke encourages this interpretation. He claims that "true and saving religion consists in the inward persuasion of the mind, without which nothing can be acceptable to God." Because "only light and evidence . . . can work a change in men's opinions," the human soul is beyond the reach of force and penalties. The use of compulsion is, at best, futile and ineffective, and, at worst, "displeasing" to God because it fosters outward conformity without internal belief—the hallmark of religious hypocrisy.[49] In his rejoinder, Proast concedes that true religion must genuinely convince the believer to qualify as a saving faith, a task that force alone "cannot do."[50] But Proast insists that precisely because true religion depends on such internal persuasion, "if force is used, not instead of reason and arguments," but in conjunction with them, then it can be of "some service": indirect compulsion can encourage men "to lend an ear" to arguments in favor of true religion and "to embrace that truth, which otherwise, either through carelessness and negligence they would never acquaint themselves with, or through prejudice they would reject and condemn unheard."[51]

Contemporary scholars are often left dissatisfied with Locke's *Letter* because, much like Proast, they focus on the argument about the inefficacy of force without reference to the broader epistemic structure that undergirds the *Letter*. Thus, just as Proast describes Locke's case for the inefficacy of force as "the single Argument by which the Author endeavors . . . to establish his Position,"[52] so also Waldron characterizes it as "the crux of the argument,"[53] "the step which dominates it and on which everything else depends,"[54] and as "the nub of the case"[55] that is intended to render persecution irrational. While it is true that the *Letter* boldly trumpets the argument about the futility of force as its primary consideration, one would search in vain throughout Locke's other *Letters*, as well as his other writings, for a demonstration or a proof of that proposition. In fact, we find Locke espousing a very different view in his *Essay Concerning Human Understanding*, where he puts forward a much more ambiguous account of the formation of beliefs: "our knowledge is neither wholly necessary, nor wholly voluntary," but instead a mixture of the two.[56] Thus Locke argues in the *Essay* that "though a man with his eyes open in the light, cannot but see, yet there be certain objects which he may choose whether he will turn his eyes to; there may be in his reach a book containing pictures and discourses, capable to delight or instruct him, which yet he may never have the will to open, never take the pains to look into."[57] If indeed beliefs depend not simply on the voluntary assent of the mind (as the original *Letter* asserts), but also on whether or not human beings have the incentive to hear out and examine the arguments of revelation, then the absolute inefficacy of coercive methods of encouraging belief becomes questionable. In the course of his debate with Proast, Locke makes a strikingly analogous concession in the *Third Letter on Toleration*:

And had you been in France some years since, who knows but the arguments the king of France produced might have been proper and sufficient to have convinced you that you ought to go to mass? I do not by this think you less confident of the truth of your religion, than you profess to be. *But arguments set on with force, have a strange efficacy upon human frailty. . . .* If you have any spell against *the force of arguments, driven with penalties and punishments,* you will do well to teach it the world.[58]

The law alone may not be able to compel men to change their beliefs, but it is striking how easily Locke is brought around to affirming the view that it can at least "lead them to the water"[59] (as Waldron puts it) or induce them to "lend an ear"[60] (as Proast argues) by prodding them to give consideration to arguments that they otherwise would not. Has Locke not retreated here significantly from his position in the original *Letter*? Richard Vernon holds that Locke has not contradicted himself. In his view, at issue between Proast and Locke is the question of whether force can be useful in shaping beliefs from the start (i.e., in educating children), and not whether force is useful in altering beliefs that are already formed (i.e., in converting heretics).[61] But as the quotation above demonstrates, this interpretation minimizes the significance of Locke's concession to Proast, since what was at stake in their dispute was precisely the possibility of conversion through force.[62] We are now able to see how Locke uses the argument about the purported futility of compulsion to mute the deeper basis of his theory in the *Letter*. But this development also brings Locke dangerously close to admitting Proast's contention that without compulsion men are not genuinely solicitous about the true religion. For as Proast stresses, if "all men were but so faithful to their own Souls, as to seek the way of Saving them, with such Care and Diligence as the Importance of the matter deserves . . . there could be no need of force to compel any man to do, what in that case every man would be sure to do voluntarily."[63] From Waldron's perspective, once "we catch the drift of this criticism, we begin to see how the rest of Locke's case falls apart," since the admission that force can alter beliefs provides "the obvious point for a rational persecutor to apply his pressure."[64]

What are we to make of Locke's concession that force may be "serviceable" for changing beliefs? Is Waldron correct in his earlier contention that conceding the efficacy of force means that Locke's case against persecution has unraveled, and does that vindicate the current consensus in scholarship that the *Letter* is "hostage" to Christian theology? Useful light is shed on this question in the opening of the *Second Letter*, where Locke insists that the argument regarding force is only one of his three "considerations" for establishing toleration. In an uncharacteristic moment of exasperation, Locke likens Proast's insistence that acknowledging the efficacy of force unravels "the whole strength of what the letter urged" to the suggestion that taking away "only one beam of the house" would collapse the whole structure "when there were several others that would support the building."[65] Even though this argument has proved to be so persuasive in the modern Western world, Locke actually goes so far as to indicate to Proast that it is not the main load-bearing beam in the *Letter* after all, especially when it is compared to the other considerations: "For the argument of the unfitness of force to convince men's minds being quite taken away, either of the other would be a strong proof for toleration."[66] While Locke featured this argument prominently in the original *Letter*, even there he acknowledged that it may be less than perfect in theory when he turned to the implications of religious pluralism for his teaching of toleration. Even if force could change men's minds, Locke insisted there, it "would not help at all to the salvation of their souls," because "in the variety and contradiction of opinions in religion, wherein the princes of the world are as much divided as in their secular interests, the narrow way [is] much straitened."[67] We see here how Locke, having momentarily spotlighted the potential deficiency of this argument, rushes to move beyond it to the consideration of pluralism, and the dialectical movement of the *Letter* never returns to the question of force. Let us then follow Locke's movement through the consideration of pluralism to see what role it plays in his justification of toleration.

Locke's "Third Consideration" in the *Letter*: Pluralism and Orthodoxy

Locke was not the first thinker to confront the intractable diversity of human beliefs, nor was he alone in recognizing that rival claims to orthodoxy within Christianity (especially in the wake of the Reformation) could present inescapable challenges to sovereignty and civic peace. We need only recall that Thomas Hobbes, no friend of persecution himself, defended absolutism in the *Leviathan* largely as a response to the civic problem of religious pluralism.[68] Disputes over the meaning of "true religion" were a problem for Locke's opponents as well, but as we saw in the example of Proast for them the concern was not so much that pluralism endangered civic peace but that it threatened orthodoxy of beliefs in the post-Reformation Christian world. In the *Letter*, Locke succeeds at turning this religious and civic suspicion of

Christian pluralism on its head. The *Letter* insists that if the accepted definition of Christian orthodoxy could be reinterpreted to deemphasize dogmas in favor of sincerity of beliefs, then Christian pluralism could be transformed into an ally not only of toleration and civic peace, but even of the quest for religious truth. The rhetorical cunning involved in this move is subtle, for it requires Locke simultaneously to affirm the existence of Christian orthodoxy without stating what such orthodoxy entails: "For there being but one Truth, one way to heaven; what Hopes is there that more Men would be let into it," Locke asks, "if they had no Rule but the Religion of the Court, and were put under a necessity to quit the Light of their own Reason . . . and blindly to re-sign themselves to the Will of their Governors?"[69] Since it would "ill sui[t] the Notion of a Deity" for men to "owe their eternal Happiness or Misery to the places of their Nativity," the freedom of the individual to examine religious opinions (and to discover those that are agreeable to his or her "conscience") must remain unobstructed by both church and state.[70]

Locke is at pains throughout the *Letter* not to encourage indifference to religious truth, and by consequence an unconcern for the salvation of souls. Accordingly, one of the challenges that Locke confronts is to show how toleration of religious diversity and heterodoxy can be reconciled with the search for religious truth. Locke's solution to this dilemma is highly puzzling: instead of providing a definition of true religion, Locke redirects our attention to the difficulty involved in adjudicating between rival claims of orthodoxy. Accordingly, one of the main refrains that Locke employs throughout the *Letter* highlights the inherent controversy in any definition of orthodoxy, and thus the difficulty in discovering which of the competing claims is the true one: "Every Church is Orthodox to it self; to others, Erroneous and Heretical. For whatsoever any Church believes, it believes to be true; and the contrary unto those things, it pronounces to be Error."[71] Locke applies the same relativistic principle to princes and individuals as well: the *Letter* opens with the proclamation that "everyone is orthodox to himself,"[72] a point that Locke later reemphasizes when he states that "the religion of every prince is orthodox to himself."[73] Because he neither denies that orthodoxy exists nor embraces explicit skepticism about the existence of religious truth as such, Locke can continue to insist "that every private mans Search and Study [can] discove[r] it unto himself."[74] But in this section of the *Letter* Locke strains to suppress the emerging implication of his argument that the consequence of religious pluralism is theological uncertainty: "in this great variety of ways that men follow, it is still doubted which is the right one,"[75] and since among the competing orthodoxies there can be no judge on earth, "the decision of that question belongs only to the supreme judge of all men."[76] Locke's treatment has kept the psychology of orthodoxy intact while employing pluralism to drain it of its theological certainty.

The question that the *Letter* conveniently avoids, however, is what will be left of the notion of orthodoxy once it has been drained by Locke's procedure.[77] Would Lockean toleration merely moderate the political ambition and the religious prejudice of those who would tyrannize others on account of faith? Or would it not necessitate (and indeed advance) more far-reaching consequences, weakening the dogmatic nature of religious beliefs and tempering the certainty with which these beliefs are embraced in the first place? An initial clue can be gleaned from the fact that Locke's treatment of orthodoxy provides the opening for Proast's explosive charge that Locke was "promoting skepticism in religion among us."[78] But even though Locke's "consideration" of pluralism entangles him in an increasingly acrimonious debate with Proast about the epistemology of faith, the limits of human understanding, and whether true religion can be known, most scholars do not regard it as putting the question of skepticism on the table. In a recent article, Richard Vernon denies that the epistemological question that gets raised in this dispute is at the core of what separates Locke and Proast: "Now it is quite true that the exchange between Locke and Proast ends with a disagreement about what is knowledge, Locke's *Fourth Letter* taking Proast systematically to task for confusing faith with knowledge."[79] But Vernon insists that the "*Fourth Letter* is unfinished and what it says is Locke's last word only in a temporal sense, not in a logical one."[80] Let us follow Proast's reaction to Locke's argument about pluralism to evaluate whether Vernon's position can be sustained.

Proast sensed that Locke's account of pluralism and its relationship to orthodoxy led Locke down a peculiarly troubling anti-theological slope, and he feared that acceptance of Locke's argument would slowly corrode the very idea of orthodoxy itself. Thus Proast responds to Locke's position with a sense of befuddled annoyance: "Now all this [i.e., diversity of religious beliefs] I acknowledge to be very true. . . . But to what sense it is here alleged I do not understand. The power I ascribe the Magistrate, is given him, to bring men, not to his *own*, but to the *true* religion."[81] In insisting that the magistrate's coercive power is to be used for the promotion of only the true religion, Proast presses Locke into confronting a question that he wanted to avoid in the original *Letter*—namely, is Anglicanism the true religion? Proast recognizes that the deeper theoretical question this consideration raises is whether human beings have the capacity to adjudicate the competing claims of orthodoxy and true religion. That Locke chose to address this objection directly in the *Second Letter* suggests that the answer to this question was of great significance to his position, even though it would lead him increasingly to retreat into a denial of the possibility of acquiring certain knowledge of religious truth. At the beginning of the *Second Letter*, Locke at first pretends to deny that the dispute has opened this controversial question of the possibility of knowing the true religion: "True religion and Christian religion are, I suppose, to you and me, the same thing."[82] But immediately after venturing this lukewarm reassurance, Locke again appeals to religious relativism to deflate Proast's claim that certainty in religious truth gives sanction to the persecutioner: "you build all you say upon *this lurking supposition*, that the national religion now in England, backed by the public authority of the law, is the only true religion, and therefore no other is to be tolerated; which being a *supposition* equally unavoidable, and equally just in other countries, . . . will in other places exclude toleration, and thereby hinder truth from the means of propagating itself."[83]

Justifying the use of political force in the name of religion becomes even more problematic, Locke suggests, in light of the overwhelming diversity of religious views: one man's true religion is another's heresy, and one nation's established faith is outlawed and suppressed elsewhere. Human beings, according to Locke's reasoning, lack certainty or scientific knowledge in religious matters, and all that they have to fall back on are, at best, "suppositions" of the truth or, even worse, mere traditions and narrow cultural prejudices that they have inherited through accident or chance of birth. "Certain demonstrative knowledge of true religion," Locke concludes, is not available to human beings.[84]

It was especially this last implication of Locke's argument that led Proast to the conclusion that Locke's theory of toleration rests on theological skepticism. Moreover, Proast discerned the ultimate direction of Locke's project (or at least its most extreme implication), predicting that it would culminate either in the denial that there is a true religion at all or, at minimum, in the view that it is inaccessible to human beings: "For 'tis obvious that there can be no other reason for this assertion . . . but either the equal truth, or at least the equal certainty (or uncertainty) of all religions."[85] Whoever considers Locke's assertion regarding the equal claim to the "supposition" of the truth of every religion, Proast argued, must necessarily come to one of the following conclusions: "either 1. That no religion is *the true religion*, in opposition to other religions: Which makes all religions *true*, or all *false*, and so either way *indifferent*. (Or, 2. That though some one religion be *the true religion*;

yet no man can have any more reason . . . than another . . . to believe his to be true . . . which . . . renders it vain and idle to inquire after the true religion)."[86] Thus, contrary to many contemporary scholars who contend that skepticism plays little or no role in Locke's defense of toleration, Proast took a different view. For Proast, what was at stake in the debate over persecution and toleration was precisely the question of whether the true religion was knowable, and Locke agreed with this characterization, pointing out in the *Fourth Letter* that the issue in their debate boiled down to the question of whether "certain demonstrative knowledge of true religion" is available to human beings.[87] In contrast, Proast insists that there exists a certain "persuasion" or "full assurance" regarding the truth of religion which, though "not grounded upon strict demonstration . . . is . . . very frequently and familiarly called in the scripture, not faith, or belief only, but knowledge."[88] The denial of the status of knowledge to such religious assurance unravels the case for persecution and, as Proast admits, "then without more adoe, the Cause is yours."[89]

The Theological Epistemology of the *Essay Concerning Human Understanding*

As becomes clear in the *Third* and *Fourth Letters*, the deepest stratum of Locke's teaching on toleration points us to his epistemology. Only on the basis of epistemology can Locke establish the distinction between belief and knowledge, which we now see serves as the foundational (though deliberately understated) basis of his case for toleration. Thus, in the *Third Letter*, Locke takes Proast to task precisely for conflating faith and knowledge: "how well grounded and great so ever the assurance of faith may be wherewith it is received; but faith it is still, and not knowledge; persuasion, and not certainty. This is the highest the nature of the thing will permit us to go in matters of revealed religion."[90] Separation of faith and knowledge—which will be the central theme of the *Essay Concerning Human Understanding*—is therefore the precondition of the regime of toleration, because the doubts that shroud our knowledge in the realm of theology are so radical that they render persecution irrational. It should be stressed, however, that this does not change the fact that Locke's original *Letter* deliberately cuts off the dialectical ascent from pluralism to the question of skepticism and the limits of human knowledge. Indeed, even after the question of skepticism is explicitly on the table in the *Third Letter*, Locke tenaciously continues to insist that Proast has failed to show that there is even "one word tending to epicurism, atheism, or scepticism in religion"[91] in the original *Letter*. Is Locke's response to Proast coherent? Can the program of toleration laid out in the *Letter* be effectively insulated from the skeptical epistemology on which it appears to depend? We turn to the *Essay* to reflect on this question.

Locke brings out the theological implications of his epistemology in Book IV of the *Essay*. Locke stresses that our knowledge is limited to our immediate senses, which necessarily confines it to "narrow"[92] boundaries. Our ignorance is "infinitely larger than our knowledge," and theology in particular confronts man with an "abyss of darkness, (where we have not eyes to see, nor faculties to perceive anything."[93] While Locke insists that reason can demonstrate the existence of a divine creator on which morality depends,[94] he also teaches that men are by nature "not imprinted" with the idea of God,[95] and that they remain in "absolute ignorance" about the "different species and properties" of spiritual beings.[96] Locke's presentation leans squarely in the direction of a natural theology, eschewing the type of reliance on or even engagement with the Bible that we discerned in the *Letter*. While the *Essay* never repudiates revealed religion, Locke elevates reason as the "last judge and guide in everything," including especially of the truth of revealed propositions.[97] The effect of this strategy is to weaken or at least to limit the unique authority of revelation insofar as it goes beyond or contradicts the principles of reason and natural theology: "whatsoever truth we come to the clear discovery of, from the knowledge and contemplation of our own ideas, will always be certainer to us than those which are conveyed to us by traditional revelation. For the knowledge we have that this revelation came at first from God can never be so sure as the knowledge we have from the clear and distinct perception of the agreement or disagreement of our own ideas."[98] In the realm of traditional revelation, Locke's strategy is to narrow the domain of theological propositions that can be called genuine knowledge. The upshot of Locke's epistemology, as Michael Ayers suggests, is to "clip the wings of revelation,"[99] by reducing it to mere "probability."[100]

Locke's argument in the *Letter* showed remarkable effectiveness in defending toleration without explicitly broaching the question of whether true religion is knowable to human beings. In the *Essay*, however, the rhetorical subtlety of the *Letter* gives way to Locke's emphatic affirmation that man's natural ignorance in theology should be employed in favor of toleration. The *Essay* seeks to elicit an attitude of forbearance on the basis of a clear-sighted understanding of the profound uncertainty that man confronts in theology (which Locke describes as the "Blindness we are in" with regard to religion).[101] Awareness of that ineradicable uncertainty, Locke indicates, can nourish a peaceable and reasonable disposition among human beings, a disposition that can be employed to neutralize those who hold religious opinions "with greatest stiffness."[102] Locke argues that those "who are most fierce and firm in their [religious] tenets" also tend to be the ones "who have least examined them."[103] But precisely because the doubts that shroud theology are inherent and radical, the *Essay* suggests that the only rational disposition between human beings is "one of mutual charity and forebearance, in the necessary diversity of opinions."[104] By emphasizing the divide between faith and knowledge, and by highlighting how little effort human beings invest in examining their own religious opinions, Locke hopes to promote such an attitude of tolerance and charity: "We should do well to commiserate our mutual ignorance," Locke argues at one point, "and not instantly treat others ill, as obstinate and perverse, because they will not renounce their own, and receive our opinions."[105] Because it explicitly elevates radical theological uncertainty as the necessary and unavoidable consequence of religious diversity, the *Essay* shows that the *Letter*'s "Christian" foundations can indeed be "bracketed."

It is generally argued that Locke's *Essay*, in spite of its goal of demarcating the limits of human knowledge, charts a careful path of epistemological restraint that aims to avoid either skepticism or relativism in matters of religion.[106] Thus, Waldron stresses that the *Essay*, just as much as the *Letter*, teaches that human beings "have a responsibility to think for themselves," even "the hard-pressed day laborer."[107] Similarly, Wolfson argues that Locke "insists that humans can inquire into the true religion."[108] These suggestions are not without merit. Just as the *Letter* taught that there are "things that every man ought sincerely to inquire into himself, and by mediation, study, search, and his own endeavours, attain the knowledge of,"[109] so the *Essay* insists that religion rightly conceived is that which "should most distinguish us from beasts, and ought most peculiarly to elevate us, as *rational creatures*."[110] According to this interpretation, short of encouraging skepticism or relativism, the *Essay* affirms the existence of religious truth and makes it the highest duty of human beings to search for it: "No man is so wholly taken up with the attendance on the means of living," Locke argues, "as to have no spare time at all to think of his soul, and inform himself in matters of religion."[111]

But while it is true that the *Essay* complements the *Letter* in affirming man's duty to search for religious truth, it also goes far beyond the *Letter* in making explicit the theological minimalism of Locke's conception of "True Religion." To put it simply, the *Essay* shows us much more clearly than the

Letter ever did that Locke's use of the idea of "True Religion" is theologically destructive: it aims not so much to ground religion and the preconditions of salvation, but to dispose of orthodoxy. Thus, insofar as the *Essay* affirms that it is man's duty to search for religious truth, it also makes explicit that Locke's God is not concerned with theological rectitude, but with the proper use of man's natural faculties: "Reason is natural revelation, whereby the eternal Father of light and fountain of all knowledge, communicates to mankind that portion of truth which he has laid within the reach of their natural faculties."[112] Moreover, Locke stresses that we should neither expect to arrive at the truth, nor despair in failing to achieve it, for what counts for salvation is only that we "sincerely" try: that man who "makes use of the light and faculties God has given him, and seeks sincerely to discover truth by those helps and abilities he has, may have this satisfaction in doing his duty as a rational creature, that, *though he should miss truth, he will not miss the reward of it.*"[113] Insofar as we follow Locke's advice in the *Essay* and rely on our natural faculties, we will have to content ourselves with very little that could be called genuine knowledge in religious matters. Even with regard to the "immateriality of the Soul," on which individual immortality and the existence of an afterlife depend, Locke warns that we "we must content . . . ourselves with faith and probability," since in this as in "many things," "our faculties cannot arrive at demonstrative certainty."[114] Anything beyond the capacity of reason to demonstrate with certainty, Locke argues, must be taken on faith.[115] By extending skepticism even to our knowledge of the afterlife, Locke's *Essay* snips the logic of the *Letter's* justification of toleration, for which salvation in the hereafter (and the certain prospect of a judging God) was the very incentive for a sincere quest for religious truth in this life.

The *Essay* also goes beyond the *Letter* in employing this skeptical epistemology to undermine what Locke describes as religious "enthusiasm," which Locke characterizes as the illusion of direct access to God's will through "pretended" immediate revelation or divine inspiration.[116] In doing so, the *Essay* makes explicit the degree to which the *Letter's* program of toleration presupposes a general attenuation of religious passions, a sociocultural transformation that the *Letter* left deliberately cloudy. Transcending both reason and revelation, enthusiasm, Locke argues, constitutes "the third ground of assent": enthusiasm "takes away both reason and revelation, and substitutes in the room of them the ungrounded fancies of man's own brain, and assumes them for the formulation both of opinion and conduct."[117] Enthusiasm, therefore, resembles Proast's "third degree of Perswuasion," which Proast described as the psychological feeling of "Full

Assurance," vouchsafed neither by reason nor by revelation, but by the intuition of the believer of the true religion.[118] As was the case with Proast, Locke shows that for the Enthusiast, this perception of an incontrovertible light from heaven "carries its own Demonstration with it" and is, moreover, constantly accompanied by the assumption of "an Authority of Dictating to others, and a forwardness to prescribe to their opinions."[119] How could it be otherwise, Locke asks, "but that he should be ready to impose on another's belief, who has already imposed on himself," and that the one who "tyrannizes over his own mind"[120] would seek to tyrannize over the minds of others? In opposition to the certainty of the Enthusiasts, Locke emphasizes the inherent ambiguity, uncertainty, and implausibility that necessarily subsumes all such claims to private inspiration: "I ask how shall any one distinguish between the delusions of Satan, and the inspirations of the Holy Ghost?"[121]

Now we are in a better position to see how far Locke's justification of toleration has come from the appeal to Christian charity and inefficacy of force that shaped the argument of the *Letter*: the deepest justification for toleration that the *Essay* advances is the insurmountable uncertainty confronting man in theology, which Locke here extends even to the afterlife. While the *Essay*'s epistemological minimalism complements the political conclusion of the *Letter*, it also stands in tension with the *Letter*'s theological teaching. Locke had argued in the *Letter* that every human being is by nature invested in caring for his or her soul, and that the concern for salvation imposes on each of us the "necessity of deliberating, and consequently allows a liberty of choosing that, which upon consideration, we prefer" among the diversity of religious opinions.[122] This view yielded the formula that religious truth would win out only if toleration were to replace persecution. In demonstrating the degree to which religious enthusiasm has to be weakened, however, the *Essay* considerably qualifies this optimistic assessment of the fate of religious truth under the regime of toleration. Indeed, one cannot help but ask whether the *Essay*'s epistemology succeeds so effectively at lowering the horizon of human knowledge in religion that it risks deflating the concerns that would animate the drive for religious truth in the first place. For once one accepts Locke's principle that we are so radically limited in our knowledge of true religion, once one accepts his injunction "to be more cautious in meddling with things exceeding [man's] comprehension" and "to sit down in a quiet Ignorance of Things, which upon Examination, are found to be beyond the reach of our Capacities,"[123] it is hard to see what incentive there may be left to engage in the necessarily challenging task of theological speculation, study, and debate. As Locke makes clear more fully in *Of the Conduct of the Human Understanding*, the pursuit of religious truth is a demanding task requiring not just freedom from persecution, but above all the great effort of self-examination, and since this task is "usually enough to take up . . . a man's . . . whole time," only few human beings seem to be suited for it.[124]

Conclusion: Has American Christianity Lockeanized?

It is often said that the American founding bears the distinctive imprint of Locke's political philosophy, and this line of influence is nowhere discernible more clearly than in Thomas Jefferson's debt to Locke in the area of religion.[125] Toward the end of his life, Jefferson expressed the hope that the struggle between orthodoxy and deism would resolve itself increasingly in the direction of what could be described as a "religion of reason," a form of faith that would eschew reliance on supernatural revelation. He predicted that Unitarianism, a liberalized form of Christianity that deemphasized theological dogma and sectarianism (much as Locke had proposed in the *Letter*), would become ascendant among Americans of his own generation: "I trust there is not a young man now living in the United States who will not die Unitarian."[126] In matters of religion and biblical revelation, Jefferson wrote in a letter to his nephew Peter Carr, we would be better off to "fix reason firmly in her seat, and [to] call to her tribunal every fact, every opinion," in order to liberate "the pure principles which [Jesus] taught" from "the artificial vestments in which they have been muffled by priests." Like Locke, Jefferson often acknowledged the utility of religion and never explicitly embraced skepticism about the existence of God. But following his Enlightenment predecessor, he also hoped that rationalism could be employed to soften the theological dogmatism of Christianity. Has Jeffersonianism triumphed over America's religious landscape, and has Locke's liberal theological vision been vindicated by this nation's political experiment with separation of church and state?

Although Unitarianism was never as popular in America as Jefferson hoped, a case can be made that a significant portion of religious denominations in America have already undergone something akin to the Lockeanization that Jefferson called for two centuries ago. For instance, in their study of America's contemporary religious landscape, Robert Putnam and David Campbell argue that Americans are surprisingly successful at combining "religious devotion with tremendous religious diversity" largely because they share a commitment to a relatively tolerant form of Christianity that transcends their denominational differences.[127] Putnam and Campbell trace the civic goods of toleration and social harmony between Americans of different faiths to the remarkable level of "religious fluidity"[128] that separation of church and state and religious pluralism nurture in this country: "Not only are religions changing, but individual Americans themselves frequently undergo religious change—finding religion, dropping out of religion, or switching from one religion to another." This religious fluidity, in turn, contributes to "interreligious mingling and marrying,"[129] which has the salutary effect of muting "interreligious tensions."

Undergirding this phenomenon of tolerance and fluidity is a particular theological outlook, one that bears striking resemblance to the principles that Locke articulated in the *Letter*. As we saw, Locke hoped that by shifting the emphasis of religious commitment from dogma and orthodoxy to "sincerity" of beliefs, he could defuse religious violence and pacify sectarianism. Many believing Americans seem to have internalized the logic of Locke's tolerationist theology, since they espouse a belief in an "equal opportunity heaven."[130] On the whole, Americans of faith "endorse the legitimacy of others' religious beliefs" and are reluctant to claim "a monopoly on truth":[131] "A whopping 89 percent of Americans believe that heaven is not reserved for those who share their religious faith."[132] Increasingly, this tolerance extends not only to Christians of competing denominations, but also to non-Christians: "According to the 2007 Faith Matters survey, nearly nine in ten (87 percent) Christians under age thirty-five believe that non-Christians can go to heaven."[133] While believing Americans are unlikely to express their religious views in these terms, it would be easy to suppose that they have simply accepted, at least for the purposes of politics, the Jeffersonian indifference in matters of religion: "It does me no injury for my neighbor to say there are twenty gods, or no god. It neither picks my pocket nor breaks my leg."[134]

But beneath this surface Lockeanization, a more ambiguous theological picture prevails, one that points to the potential limits of the Lockean project. To begin with, most believing Americans appear to straddle a tension between their embrace of religious diversity and their commitment to their own particular faith traditions—which they hope to see perpetuated by their children. As Putnam and Campbell point out, while Americans claim to "see value in religious diversity for its own sake" and regard pluralism as an "intrinsically good state of affairs,"[135] they are somewhat ambivalent about its implications for the faith of their progeny: "When Americans are asked to project into the future about the potential marriage of a child, we see a measure of ambivalence about marrying outside one's faith."[136] Over two in five Americans say that it is either "very important" or "somewhat important" that their child marry someone of the same religion. This is an important sign that some Americans, despite their intimate acquaintance with people of other faiths, are not indifferent about the religious commitments of their own children. Their desire to see their children carry on their religious beliefs reflects their confidence that they are in possession of religious truth, and that that truth matters for the salvation of souls. Believing Americans have not, in other words, entirely embraced the potentially relativistic implications of Locke's *Letter Concerning Toleration*, which taught that salvation depends not on dogma, but on mere "sincerity" of one's beliefs.

Beyond the muddled tension-riddled middle that represents the tolerant mainstream of American believers, the Lockean teaching also comes under strain on both of the opposite extremes of the theological spectrum. On the right, it is frequently alleged that mainstream American culture marginalizes religious believers from public debate, and that the beliefs and moral preferences of the religiously committed are not taken seriously in our secular, pluralistic culture. Most revealing for our purposes is the wide gulf between the attitudes of the clergy and the laity about pluralism and eligibility for salvation. Even in denominations generally thought to be liberal, the clergy are "far more likely to see a single road to heaven" than are their congregationists, and they are much more likely to treat Jesus' injunction in the New Testament—"I am the way, the truth, and the life: no man cometh unto the Father, but by me"[137]—as a literal truth that demands religious exclusivism. It would appear, therefore, that the clergy (even among liberal denominations)[138] sense that the muddled middle, or the easygoing attitude of many believing Americans about religious pluralism, is not entirely sustainable. Lurking behind the clergy's distrust of pluralism is a sentiment that we already encountered in Locke's critic Jonas Proast, who worried that Locke's central argument in the *Letter* (that "every church is Orthodox unto itself") could very easily slide into religious relativism, skepticism and, eventually, atheism.

Precisely because American Christianity has not entirely Lockeanized along the lines envisioned in the *Letter*, precisely because orthodoxy and theological dogmatism remain vibrant (and often politically powerful), the synthesis that Locke (and recently Obama) hoped for remains elusive. One additional sign that the Lockean compromise between toleration and Christianity—Locke's attempt to erect a theological "firewall" against religious skepticism[139]—has not simply worked out as envisioned in the *Letter* is reflected in the increasing secularization of American cultural life. While "old-time religion" remains resilient in parts of America, and "civil religion" often makes an appearance on the national stage, there are also increasingly pronounced currents of public secularism. We see this not only in the growing discomfort with politicized religion on the American left, but more significantly in epistemological objections to religion (usually raised in the name of modern scientific rationalism) among the cultural elite, where the "New Atheist" critiques of religion often resonate.[140] The elite rapprochement with religious skepticism and atheism has trickle-down cultural effects: studies show larger percentages of Americans who identify as religious "nones" or as lacking any institutional religious affiliation or identification with organized religion. The nones now comprise the third-largest "religious" group in America (trailing only Evangelicals and Catholics).[141] In the same speech in which Obama appealed to a religious faith that would be infused with humility and doubt, he also heralded the onset of a post-Christian epoch in America: "Whatever we once were, we are no longer just a Christian nation; we are also a Jewish nation, a Muslim nation, a Buddhist nation, a Hindu nation, and a nation of nonbelievers." Thus, the theological consensus that Locke hoped to shape through the *Letter* comes increasingly under strain by the tides of pluralism and rationalism that Locke's broader philosophical project unleashed. The result is a disharmony within our religious consciousness, and a resilient tension or an unresolved tug-of-war between the skeptical and dogmatic, the liberal and the orthodox, dimensions of America's political heritage. In the next two chapters, I will investigate this dissonance of Locke's theological legacy through the study of the religious and political statesmanship of two of the most important reformers in American history who contributed to racial equality: Abraham Lincoln and Martin Luther King, Jr.

LINCOLN'S RELIGIOUS STATESMANSHIP AND RAWLS'S "PUBLIC REASON": SLAVERY AND BIBLICAL THEOLOGY IN THE CIVIL WAR

Introduction: The Dilemma of Lincoln's Religious Statesmanship

Our encounter with Locke's religious project in the previous chapter compels us to ask whether or not Locke expected Christianity to continue to play an important role in the moral and civic life of a liberal society. As we saw, while it presents itself as a complement to Christianity, Locke's project of religious toleration depends on the erosion of religious dogmatism and the diffusion of public indifference to theological controversy. While a Lockean state itself cannot ultimately be indifferent to religion (insofar as it requires the liberalization of religious beliefs) and may even actively encourage a tolerant version of Christianity, Locke hoped that this transformation would be advanced if human beings became less invested in traditional Christian revelation and in theological questions altogether. And even though Locke refused to extend toleration to Catholics (among others) in the *Letter*, in the same work he also indicated that he anticipated his regime eventually to secure a wider level of tolerance that transcended Protestant Christianity: "neither Pagan nor Mahometan, nor Jew, ought to be excluded from the civil rights of the commonwealth because of his religion." To the extent that Catholics, Muslims, and Jews are willing to accept some version of Locke's tolerationist theology, then one can imagine that such a society could accommodate increasing levels of interreligious pluralism.[1] As I have argued, while Rawls's *Political Liberalism* takes this liberalization of Christianity for granted, and therefore depends on the historical success of Locke's religious project, Locke and Rawls agree to this extent: a liberal society can succeed (and is even better off) without the official moral support and intervention of religion in politics. Jefferson makes the full implication of this teaching crystal clear in his Virginia Bill for Religious

Freedom: "Our civil rights have no dependence on our religious opinions, any more than on geometry or physics."[2]

Does American political development bear out Locke's hope for the abatement of theological controversy, and is Rawls therefore correct to discern a certain form of "public reason" operating within American history? This chapter investigates these questions by exploring the contested role of religion in one of the greatest moral struggles in American history: the Civil War debate on the question of slavery. I turn to the speeches and actions of Abraham Lincoln to show how religion and biblical theology played a crucial role in Lincoln's political statesmanship and in his effort to challenge and reform the prevailing national opinion on the question of slavery. As Obama reminded us, the appeal to a "higher truth" was at the forefront of the Civil War conflict over slavery, which historian Mark Noll has described as a "theological crisis." In navigating this crisis, Lincoln found it necessary to intervene directly both before and during his presidency in the national debate over the meaning of the Bible and its relationship to the institution of slavery. But Lincoln's intervention, I argue, proves highly paradoxical. While he claims to base his arguments against slavery on the Bible, a deeper investigation reveals that Lincoln seeks to reshape the nation's religious consciousness in light of principles of equality that he believed were announced in the Declaration of Independence, but principles which themselves were publicly contested and required theological support if they were to be successful at reforming the political status quo. I argue that the contemporary paradigm of translation into public reason does not effectively capture this theologically reformist spirit of Lincoln's statesmanship, insofar as Lincoln was developing novel theological arguments on the basis of a contestable rational metaphysics.[3] Unlike standard critiques of public reason, therefore, I suggest that the problem posed by Lincoln's example is not merely that Rawls's paradigm is too restrictive, but instead that it has difficulty accounting for historical change and reform through theological contestation.

The complete paradox of Lincoln's religious statesmanship emerges only when it is considered in light of its evolution from his early rational deism to his mature theological position, featured most prominently in the Second Inaugural Address. Lincoln's deepest theological teaching for democracy, I argue, emerges from his immanent critique of the deficiencies of the doctrine of rational self-interest, which he concluded was incapable of resolving the moral challenge of slavery.[4] In his "Lyceum Address," a young twenty-eight-year-old Lincoln called for a "political religion" consisting of devotion to the Constitution and to a culture of law-abidingness. But this semiration-alistic civil religion, which could easily find its theoretical antecedents in Rousseau's *Social Contract*, raises more questions than it solves, since its emphasis on "cold, calculating, unimpassioned reason" seems to leave un-fulfilled the hopes for transcendent supports for republicanism that Lincoln judged in the same speech as necessary for the perpetuation of free govern-ment.[5] In his mature years Lincoln would recognize that such a political reli-gion was an insufficient response to the moral challenge of slavery, especially because defenders of slavery claimed that it was sanctioned by the Constitu-tion just as much as it was by the Bible. As a response to this theological and moral crisis, Lincoln's "political religion" would undergo an evolution, with Lincoln increasingly relying on certain theological arguments against slavery that he purported to uncover in the Book of Genesis. Public appeals to divine providence would feature very prominently in Lincoln's Civil War speeches, suggesting that for this president the resolution of the existential moral con-flict over slavery required the contribution of higher moral and theological principles that transcended mere democratic proceduralism.

But Lincoln's evolution leaves us with a dilemma about the exact source and nature of those transcendent principles of justice, and a perplexing question about their proper place in liberal democratic politics. The crux of that dilemma is discernible especially in Lincoln's Second Inaugural Ad-dress, which stands as the culmination of Lincoln's effort to inject theology into his presidential leadership by declaring the Civil War a divine punish-ment for the national sin of slavery. Can this feature of Lincoln's statesman-ship be squared with the understanding of deliberative politics that prevails among liberal theorists today? The latter view, associated with John Rawls's *Political Liberalism* but also widely echoed in popular discussions, insists on theological restraint when public officials engage in democratic deliber-ation. As Rawls himself asks, "what are we to say of the Second Inaugural with its prophetic (Old Testament) interpretation of the Civil War as God's punishment for the sin of slavery, and falling equally on North and South," an interpretation that would seem to violate both the "duty of civility" and the restrictions that "public reason" imposes on officials engaged in demo-cratic deliberation (Rawls, 2005, p. 254)? Rawls's response to this question is unsatisfactory, since he has to either deny that Lincoln was engaging in an official public speech that had direct "bearing on constitutional essentials of matters of basic justice" (254), or he has to ignore the deeply theological bent of his rhetoric.[6] While he claims to have outgrown his youthful ratio-nalism and skepticism, Lincoln's most important public speeches rely on highly idiosyncratic readings of the Bible while always maintaining a subtle ambiguity about the exact nature of God's providential involvement in the Civil War.[7] This leaves open the possibility that Lincoln employs biblical language to strengthen the moral case for an antislavery position that he himself embraced on the basis of pure rationalism, and that his model of public deliberation seeks to create a new theological and moral consensus where none existed before by fusing liberal principles with religious ones.

The Paradoxical Rationalism of the Young Lincoln's "Lyceum Address" and "Handbill Against Infidelity"

When he was only twenty-eight years old, Abraham Lincoln delivered an address to the Young Men's Lyceum, on the topic of the "The Perpetuation of Our Political Institutions." In that speech, Lincoln identified political ambition and the mobocratic spirit of lawlessness as the twin dangers confronting American democracy from within. The speech, which Lincoln gave in 1838, is famous for Lincoln's proposal that the nation should dedicate itself to the rule of law and elevate the Constitution to a "political religion" in both private and public life. Given over twenty years before he would find himself prosecuting a military campaign to preserve the union, Lincoln's speech has a strangely prophetic quality, since it argues that the greatest threat to America would emerge not from a foreign military power, but rather from internal spiritual and moral decay of the nation's political culture, signs of which Lincoln warns are already discernible in "the increasing disregard for the law which pervades the country."[8] Periodic acts of lawbreaking such as lynchings and summary executions, Lincoln observes, do not in themselves constitute the full scope of the danger: Lincoln worries about the cumulative effects of lawlessness, which he fears will undermine the nation's capacity to keep exceedingly ambitious individuals from seeking to overturn the constitutional order in their quest for political authority and glory. The solution, according to Lincoln, depends on nurturing a civic culture characterized by uncritical devotion to the nation's legal institutions and its Constitution, a devotion that Lincoln argues should be religiously instilled from childhood: "Let reverence for the laws be breathed by every American mother to the lisping babe that prattles on her lap; let it be taught in schools, in seminaries, and in colleges; let it be written in primers, spelling-books, and in almanacs; let it be preached from the pulpit, proclaimed in legislative halls, and enforced in courts of justice. And, in short, let it become the political religion of the nation" (112).

Although the Lyceum Address has been the subject of extensive commentary, scholars are divided about the exact light that it sheds on Lincoln's mature statesmanship and in particular on the evolution of his religious views. Following the suggestions made by Harry Jaffa in *Crisis of a House Divided*, a number of scholars view young Lincoln's reflections primarily through a rhetorical prism, arguing that his account of a "political religion" of law-abidingness as an antidote to the mobocratic spirit provides an inlet into understanding the religious rhetoric that Lincoln employs during the Civil War, especially in the Second Inaugural and the Gettysburg Addresses.[9] The biblical rhetoric of these latter speeches, these scholars insist, should be viewed in light of the rational solution outlined in the Lyceum Address and should therefore be interpreted as prudential or instrumental appeals to religion rather than as a reflection of Lincoln's sincere religious views.[10] On the other hand, a second group of scholars notices the rationalistic bent of the Lyceum speech, but chooses to downplay the significance of Lincoln's early position for what it regards as his embrace of biblical republicanism and the covenant tradition during the Civil War.[11] Some of these latter interpreters even suggest that Lincoln's mature position is incomprehensible if it is divorced from a framework of natural law, and perhaps even biblical revelation and divine law, as a source of transcendent standards of justice that obtain in political life.[12]

From either perspective, therefore, an understanding of the Lyceum Address seems to be essential to a correct account of the evolution of Lincoln's religious rhetoric over time: Lincoln either rejects his youthful rationalism in favor of biblical republicanism and natural law, or he moderates and mutes his rationalistic outlook through public appeals to religious language that remains instrumental to advancing his political goals. In contrast, I wish to propose that the Lyceum Address succeeds more at describing the civic and moral concerns that point to the need for a civil religion in republicanism than at offering a path for achieving one; it points more to the paradox of a rational "civil religion" than to a theoretical solution to the challenge that it poses; and it identifies an internal problem in the Founders' reliance on rationalistic politics, posed by the deep moral and civic ambivalence of their political legacy, which Lincoln comes to recognize cannot be solved merely on the basis of rationalism alone.[13] Resolution of these paradoxes will require Lincoln to move beyond a merely "political religion" of the Constitution, to a civic faith that attempts to bridge the gulf between the rational conclusions of his natural theology and the principles of biblical revelation.

This implicit critique becomes clear in the opening paragraphs of the

Lyceum Address, where Lincoln identifies the task of republican statesmanship as the preservation and transmission of the Founders' political legacy from one generation to the next. Lincoln opens the speech with the observation that Americans find themselves "under the government of a system of political institutions conducing more essentially to the ends of civil and religious liberty than any of which the history of former times tells us."[14] The blessings of these political and legal institutions presuppose the inalienable rights of the Declaration of Independence and are "a legacy bequeathed us by a once hardy, brave, and patriotic, but now lamented and departed, race of ancestors." These noble ancestors, Lincoln claims in the second half of the speech, were animated by a longing for "celebrity, and fame, and distinction," a thirst for glory that impelled them to make tremendous sacrifices of blood and life in the service of establishing free government, which they regarded as an "experiment" to be rendered successful by human nature and reason rather than as a tradition or an ancestral political inheritance (113). As Lincoln explains, their "destiny was inseparably linked" with the intellectual desire to exhibit the fruits of that rational experiment before the human race, for "their ambition aspired to display before an admiring world a practical demonstration of the truth of a proposition which had hitherto been considered at best no better than problematical—namely, the capability of a people to govern themselves" (113). Paradoxically, the success of that rational political experiment with liberty promised imperishable fame, and the Founding Fathers, in Lincoln's reading, knew that they would be "immortalized" if they brought to fruition their political undertaking. The noble and ennobling influence of that founding generation's self-sacrificial civic spirit, moreover, had a "powerful influence . . . upon the passions of the people as distinguished from their judgment," for it temporarily "smothered and rendered inactive" the self-interested motives which otherwise universally govern men (114). In Lincoln's estimation, therefore, the American Revolution succeeded at channeling the uncivic and selfish passions of human nature in the service of the noble goal of political liberty, a goal that may have been originally discovered through reason but which required the enticing hopes and the intoxicating charms of immortal glory for its success.

But Lincoln subtly implies that the political structure that emerged from the Revolution was less than successful at sustaining the self-transcendent impulses that are necessary for the perpetuation of such civic devotion among democratic citizens. This becomes clearer when Lincoln turns to assessing the task that confronts the present generation. While the Revolution offered citizens a share in the imperishable fame of a new political founding, the current generation must rest satisfied with the low distinction of ensuring that the nation can preserve and "transmit" to posterity the blessings of liberty that it did not itself acquire (108). Now that the goal of the experiment with liberty has been realized and "is understood to be a successful one," the passions on which the Revolution relied and which it promised to fulfill find themselves in a democratic and rational society that can neither successfully accommodate nor placate them (113). But what emerges from this transformation is not mere political apathy among citizens, but rather, as the mob violence that Lincoln will go on to spotlight illustrates, a pathological decay in the public's attachment to the constitution and the rule of law. The "basest principles of our human nature [which] were either made to lie dormant, or [were made] the active agents in the advancement of the noblest causes—that of establishing and maintaining civil and religious liberty"—have reasserted themselves through mobs and now threaten the rule of law only a generation after the Revolution (114). But instead of simply condemning such mob violence, Lincoln's account evinces a strange ambivalence. In each example that he marshals, Lincoln insists that those who took matters into their own hands in the service of vigilantism were animated by an admirable impulse of justice. "Abstractly considered," Lincoln notes, "the hanging of gamblers at Vicksburg was of but little consequence," and indeed "honest men would perhaps be much profited" by their death. Similarly, "the burning of the negro at St. Louis," who now Lincoln tells us had forfeited his life by an outrageous murder, was informed by "correct reasoning" (110).

Although the speech presents itself as a sermon against lawlessness and mobocracy, its deeper subject is the problem posed by slavery to the perpetuation of free government and to the Founder's legacy, a subject that Lincoln broaches only with subtlety and caution.[15] What underlies the psychology of the mobs is the passion for justice, the same passion that manifests itself in abolitionism and that seeks immediate gratification without regard for the rule of law. The Revolution took full advantage of the civic contribution of such passionate longings for justice, but it could not gratify them forever. Two months before Lincoln gave the speech, in November 1837, a proslavery mob burst into the house and office of Elijah P. Lovejoy, who ran an abolitionist printing press, murdering him in the process. This act of lawlessness, to which Lincoln vaguely refers in the speech (111), shocked the nation and spotlighted the violent animosity that simmered beneath the divisions over slavery.[16] While slavery is not the sole cause of the erosion in the civic spirit of law-abidingness that Lincoln identifies, both of the examples of mob violence that Lincoln adduces make clear that it is one of the main objectives of moral vigilantism and therefore one of the chief catalysts of lawlessness (110–111). The opportunity to demagogue and indulge the passionate longings of the mobs, in turn, can be exploited by "men of ambition" whose overweening thirst for glory cannot be fulfilled by merely upholding a decent political order or "supporting and maintaining the edifice that has been erected by others" (113–114). The moral ambivalence of America's founding legacy, therefore, points to the incomplete justice of the established law and the Constitution and demands or nurtures a hope for the type of ambitious leadership for which the Constitution cannot itself make room. In an eerily self-referential formulation that seems to anticipate the challenge that he would confront twenty years later in the Civil War, Lincoln notes that while such unrestricted ambition may lead to a humane statesman who eradicates slavery, it may just as easily also culminate in a tyrant who threatens to subvert the Constitution: "Towering genius disdains the beaten path. . . . It thirsts and burns for distinction; and, if possible, it will have it, whether at the expense of emancipating slaves, or enslaving freemen" (114). As Matthew Holbreich correctly points out, Lincoln chooses his culminating example precisely: "Slavery points to the ambivalence of the Founders' legacy: the American Constitution establishes free government while protecting what endangers it."[17]

As a solution to this problem, Lincoln proposes his famous "political religion" (112), which Michael Zuckert describes as "a passion-aided means to the reason-discerned end of civil peace through law."[18] But, paradoxically, this political religion does not depend on the Bible, nor does it point to transcendent principles of justice or divine providence for maintaining the emotional attachment to democratic institutions that Lincoln identifies as its supreme task. Instead of looking beyond this world for divine support, it looks back in history with emotional nostalgia to the Revolutionary era for its inspiration. It is to be enforced by oaths taken "by the blood of the Revolution," and every American is to "remember that to violate the law, is to trample on the blood of his father."[19] But the living memory of the Revolution and the civic influence that it radiates, Lincoln incessantly stresses throughout the speech, is already dying. Thus the religious project of the Lyceum Address is profoundly paradoxical, since as Lincoln indicates at the closing of the speech, the object of its religious attachment—the Constitution—is to find its support not in revelation, not even in tradition, but in reason alone. If in the past "the pillars of the temple of liberty" were sustained through passion, today they must be replaced "by other pillars, hewn from the solid quarry of sober reason." "Passion has helped us; but it can do so no more. It will in the future be our enemy" (115). "Reason," Lincoln concludes, "cold, unimpassioned reason, must furnish all the materials for our future support and defense" (115). Much like George Washington, of whom Lincoln reminds us in the last line of the Lyceum speech and whose Farewell Address declared "Religion and Morality [as] indispensible supports" of "political prosperity," Lincoln's speech blends together the sacred and the profane, the religious and the temporal, but it tries to bridge this gap by making the Constitution itself the object of religious longing and salvation.[20]

Lincoln's Lyceum Address leaves us with more questions than it answers, especially when it is considered in light of Lincoln's evolution. After all, while his Lyceum Address called for a reason-based "political religion," as president, Lincoln's last great speech (the Second Inaugural) proclaimed the destiny of the nation to be governed by a divine and mysterious providence over which men have no control. Was Lincoln essentially a religious skeptic (as he was sometimes depicted by his contemporaries), and should the Lyceum speech be understood as his early effort to find a rhetorical solution to the challenge of civil religion that would only fully blossom in his mature years? Or, alternatively, was Lincoln a man of deep religious conviction who struggled to resolve the disparity between his own religion views and the tragic requirements of political life? Finally, and most puzzlingly, how did Lincoln expect the "political religion" of constitutional dedication to be cultivated, nurtured, and sustained in a nation that was deeply imbued with a competing faith in the revealed word of the Bible and the Christian tradition?[21] These questions, as we will see in the second half of this chapter, are not simply antiquarian concerns about Lincoln's personal beliefs, since they go to the heart of his religious statesmanship on the question of slavery both before and during the Civil War. Understanding the evolution of Lincoln's political teaching on religion helps us see whether Lincoln was merely a passive leader whose most important decisions and public utterances were dictated by history, or whether Lincoln's statesmanship presents us with an ingenious and proactive effort of theological-political reform.

Helpful provisional light is shed on these questions by Lincoln's written pronouncements on the rules that should regulate the public disposition and utterances of political men toward the religious sensibilities of the communities that they inhabit. On August 3, 1846, Abraham Lincoln won the race for Congress in the Illinois Seventh District against Democrat Peter Cartwright. During the campaign, Lincoln was faced with public accusations that he was a scoffer of religion, and friends informed him that Cartwright "was whispering infidelity against him," threatening to turn the Bible-reading Christian electorate of Illinois against his candidacy. In spite of the smear campaign, Lincoln won the election, but lost in Marshall and Woodford counties where Cartwright's accusations had circulated most prominently. After his victory, Lincoln took the unusual step to address these charges in print through an open letter to the state electorate, which was published under the title of "Handbill Against Infidelity" in *Lacon Illinois Gazette* in Marshall County. Lincoln's law partner and biographer, William H. Herndon, believed that the charges affected the election. In his biography of Lincoln, Herndon wrote: "Another thing which operated much to Lincoln's disadvantage was the report circulated by Cartwright's friends with respect to Lincoln's religious views. He was charged with the grave offence of infidelity, and sentiments which he was reported to have expressed with reference to the inspiration of the Bible were given the campaign varnish and passed from hand to hand."[22]

Because of the political context surrounding the accusations that Lincoln's "Handbill" purports to refute, the document would appear to present us with Lincoln's version of the *Apology of Socrates*, in which Plato depicts his Athenian philosophical mentor defending himself against the charges of corrupting the youth and not believing in the city's gods. Unlike Socrates, however, Lincoln is not charged with a capital crime, which may allow him to be more frank than the already frank Athenian philosopher. Socrates' ironic defense speech, after all, proved unsuccessful at acquitting Socrates. Similarly, Lincoln's "Handbill" discloses itself not as an effort at forensic defensive rhetoric but as a highly provocative statement of the future president's views about the proper place of atheism in a religious society. Instead of refuting the charge directly, Lincoln strangely begins his "defense" by acknowledging that he is "not a member of any Christian Church," without explaining why this fact should not count as an additional strike against his already established questionable reputation with regard to religious fidelity.[23] He follows this strange and counterintuitive beginning by stating that he has "never denied the truth of the Scriptures," which manifestly falls short of an explicit and public acknowledgement of the veracity of biblical teachings. Presumably, a prudent atheist would be mindful of the social stigma associated with unbelief and would therefore exercise restraint about his personal beliefs in public, as Lincoln will appear to recommend in the second half of the Handbill. Moreover, Lincoln then continues to further brandish his record of public statements while leaving his private beliefs in the dark, adducing that he has "never spoken with intentional disrespect of religion in general, or of any denomination of Christianity in particular." But this very precise formulation is again conspicuously silent about the nature of Lincoln's own personal religious beliefs and about his own private activities, since Lincoln limits it exclusively to his sayings and doings in public.

Just like Socrates did in his "Apology" to the Athenian jury, Lincoln only deepens the mystery when he interrupts his line of argumentation to take a detour into his "early life," a detour that seems not only unnecessary, but one that also in no way helps the case that he is advancing through the Handbill. For the first time Lincoln discloses what he actually believes (or at least what he used to believe at some time in the past), by stating that in his "early life [he] was inclined to believe in the Doctrine of Necessity." As David Lowenthal (2012) notes, the word "doctrine" suggests not so much a general or vague religious outlook, but rather a developed or systematic set of positions that may follow either from philosophy or from theology. Moreover, the word "necessity" seems to distinguish this metaphysical doctrine from beliefs in mere inexplicable chance or divine or teleological purpose, suggesting the necessary character of the order discernible in the universe or the necessary rules or laws according to which that order operates. But, even more surprisingly, Lincoln next provides a definition of the doctrine in question that is startling in its philosophical candor: "the human mind is impelled to action, or held in rest by some power, over which the mind has no control."[24] While the most conspicuous aspect of this definition is its silence about the power of God over the human soul, it still forces us to ask what, if anything, it has to do with the accusation that Lincoln was a scoffer at Christianity? Is it possible that Lincoln means this doctrine as an alternative to Christian theology and perhaps to revealed religion altogether?[25] Presumably, a doctrine such as the one that Lincoln adduces would deny at least some forms of voluntary action and perhaps even free will in the human intellect or the soul. If it denies such freedom, Lincoln's doctrine would appear to be difficult to harmonize with central elements of any religious outlook that teaches the moral responsibility of human beings for their actions and choices. In a few sentences, Lincoln will go so far as to state that he has "always understood the same opinion to be held by the several of the Christian denominations," which one could interpret as a reference to the belief in predestination (a theological doctrine that could also be said to believe in a form of "necessity"). While Lincoln may appear to be reaching out to traditional religious allies, is it not the case that he has in effect constructed a subtle contrast or even a contest between the two alternatives—between a fatalistic philosophical belief in necessity and a theological belief in predestination? Which of these two doctrines does he subscribe to in the innermost parts of his mind and soul?

Hans J. Morgenthau interprets Lincoln's refusal to profess "a single positive assertion" about his religious beliefs as "a testimony both to his indifference to religious dogma and organization and to his intellectual honesty."[26] This is a rather charitable way of putting Lincoln's position, since his equivocations come very close to suggesting that he may have developed a philosophical alternative to religion consisting in a belief in Enlightenment determinism—and moreover, that he was not neutral in the contest, but viewed such "cause-and-effect" determinism as a contender against the belief in the divinely ordered necessity of predestination. While Mark Noll suggests that the two doctrines that Lincoln articulates in the Handbill "indicate how formally similar those systems of Calvinist and Enlightenment determinism are,"[27] one wonders whether Lincoln found them to be similar in anything beyond their superficial structure. Allen Guelzo, in contrast, concludes that Lincoln's professed doctrine "more nearly echoed . . . the determinism of Jeremy Bentham, whose comments on free will and necessity have, when set beside Lincoln's, an eerily familiar ring."[28] While Lincoln himself never clarifies this question, he also never repudiates either the philosophical or the theological versions of the doctrine anywhere in his life. But short of being a merely private matter as Lucas Morel (2000) and others maintain, this "doctrine of necessity" would be reflected in Lincoln's view of divine providence in the Second Inaugural. That speech, more than any other of his speeches, is formulated in such a way as to leave the ambiguity that we identified intact without ever explicitly restating the distinct two alternatives that he has fused together. Lincoln's mature "professions of faith" in providence will thus make it possible for different audiences to attribute to Lincoln either of the two beliefs—and to discern behind the Civil War either the judgment of a just and providential God or the necessary outcome of fatalistic determinism, understood as the "peculiar interest" of slavery.

Instead of rejecting the principles of determinism which he just announced, in the Handbill Lincoln simply sidesteps the question about his current beliefs by stating that in the past he "sometimes (with one, two or three, but never publicly) tried to maintain this opinion in argument."[29] He now assures us that "the habit of arguing" this position he "entirely left off for more than five years"—a timeline that would place his recovery from philosophic determinism well past beyond his "early life." But notice again that Lincoln does not say that he ceased believing in the doctrine, but that he merely ceased advancing it as an argument which he used to maintain in private company. He does not explain what induced him to abandon defending this position, but the last short paragraph of the Handbill gives a helpful indication that may illuminate the reasoning behind Lincoln's evolution. There Lincoln recommends the following disposition toward the beliefs of candidates for public office: "I do not think I could myself, be brought to support a man for office, whom I knew to be an open enemy of, and a scoffer at, religion." Lincoln has conspicuously replaced the accusation so as to set an easier threshold to overcome—while Cartwright had charged him with "scoffing at Christianity," Lincoln merely concludes that a public scoffer of "religion" in general ought not to be supported for office. Supporting such an individual would be both imprudent and antidemocratic, because no "man has the right to insult the feelings, and injure the morals, of the community in which he may live," and this includes the community's religious beliefs when such a community is both pluralistic and faithful in character. Lincoln's conclusion seems to combine the reticence of a prudent and respectful atheist with the moderation of a democrat who believes that religion can play an instrumental role in supporting the morality of a political community. His Handbill therefore seems to constitute a distillation of Locke's advice to atheists in the *Letter Concerning Toleration* and Tocqueville's prediction in *Democracy in America* that American political life would be characterized by religious "hypocrisy," with both unbelievers and believers nurturing a "public opinion" in favor of religion, especially in the public office.[30]

The remainder of this chapter argues that the challenge of the Civil War compels Lincoln to evolve beyond the rhetorically moderate, and perhaps primarily defensive, position that he articulates in the Handbill. While his early appeals to a "political religion" in the Lyceum Address and his equivocations on his personal beliefs in the "Handbill" can both be understood without references to biblical revelation, the simmering moral and theological conflict over slavery in the antebellum years would make it necessary for Lincoln to begin bridging the gulf between his rationalism and biblical revelation. A confrontation with the theological defenses of slavery that appealed to the Bible would compel Lincoln to realize that "cold, calculating, unimpassioned reason," which he had called for in the Lyceum address, could not remain aloof from the theological contest over the meaning of biblical revelation, which Lincoln would attempt to deliberately tilt through public debate in favor of his antislavery position. Furthermore, Lincoln would also evolve beyond his strictly utilitarian view of religion's role in supporting the morality of democracy. His early rationalism would recede almost entirely from his most important public speeches as president, with only subtle glimmers of his determinism remaining discernible in the form of a nonretributive, mysterious, but morally partisan view of divine providence. Lincoln would craft a new "political religion" and a novel view of divine providence in order to infuse the principles of the Declaration of Independence with religious meaning and support, and in order to defuse the morally retributive impulses on both sides of the conflict. This new political religion would feature most prominently in the Gettysburg Address and the Second Inaugural, which Lincoln hoped would consummate the moral significance of the theological conflict that he believed animated the Civil War.

Lincoln's Use of the Bible and the Response to the Theological Crisis of Slavery

Mark Noll has argued forcefully in *The Civil War as a Theological Crisis* that a proper understanding of the contest between the North and the South over the issue of slavery can only be achieved in the framework of the public religious debate among American Christians on whether the Bible sanctions slavery.[31] As his political career advanced, Lincoln would find it increasingly necessary to begin engaging in this theological debate, and both his private writings and public utterances reflect this evolution in his statesmanship. Indications of Lincoln's theological intervention in this debate are already discernible in his 1858 "Fragment on Pro-Slavery Theology," which includes a critique of the Reverend Frederick A. Ross, an Alabama Presbyterian minister and doctor of divinity, whose *Slavery Ordained of God* (1857) had made a conventional biblical defense of slavery. As other nineteenth-century Christian defenders of slavery had maintained, Ross insisted that the Bible justified slavery on humanitarian grounds. Even if the scripture in some places regarded slavery as an evil, even a curse, Ross maintained that the Bible held that it "has a corresponding and greater good," including the fact that the enslaved man "is elevated and ennobled compared with his brethren in Africa." In short, Ross concluded that "slavery is of God" and should be continued "for the good of the slave, the good of the master, the good of the whole American family, until another and better destiny may be unfolded."[32] Lincoln's mediations on revealed and natural theology, and their relationship to slavery, help us understand why he concluded that theological indifference on this question was not an option and illuminate the unique place that he would begin to occupy in this public debate over the Bible in the antebellum years.

The urgency of such an intervention was dictated by the fact that the struggle over slavery had ineluctably become a struggle over the meaning of the Bible and its moral teaching. As Sydney Alhstrom argues in his award-winning *A Religious History of the American People,* "Churchmen played lead-ing roles in the moral revolutions that swept the North and the South in opposite directions between 1830 and 1860."[33] For twenty years before the Civil War, the Northern and Southern churches buttressed their respective moral positions on slavery with increasingly intransigent theological justifi-cations. Thus, Ahlstrom concludes his account of this historical debate with the judgment that "when the cannons roared in Charleston harbor . . . two divinely authorized crusades were set in motion, each of them absolutizing a given social and political order."[34] While biblical defenses of slavery were not new, by the nineteenth century they had fallen in disrepute throughout most of the Western world outside of the United States.[35] Paradoxically, it was in America, where antitraditional and individualistic religion reigned the strongest, and where the ethos of Protestant Biblicism rested on the individual's unmediated authority to interpret the scripture on his own, that the Bible's failure explicitly to condemn the practice of slavery presented the deepest moral challenge to democracy. Indeed, Americans steeped in Bible reading had to face up to the uncomfortable fact that not only did the Bible not condemn slavery, but it explicitly condoned it, both in the Old and the New Testaments. Americans were familiar with the books of Exodus (21:20, 21:7), Leviticus (24:44–46), and St. Paul's letter to Philemon regarding an escaped slave, among other passages in the Bible, that sanctioned slavery.[36]

The Bible's troubling failure to condemn slavery posed a peculiar chal-lenge to those American Christians who wanted to base their commitment to abolitionism on the scripture. In fact, attempts to use the Bible against slavery exposed Christians to the charges of heresy. For example, on Decem-ber 9, 1860, Henry Van Dyke, minister at the First Presbyterian Church in Brooklyn, NY, delivered a sermon entitled "The Character and Influence of Abolitionism," in which he argued that abolitionism "springs from, and is nourished by, an utter rejection of the Scriptures; that it produces no real benefit to the enslaved, and is the fruitful source of division and strife, and infidelity, in both Church and State." More disturbingly, Van Dyke ac-cused those who wanted to invoke the scripture in the name of abolition-ism of subverting the plain authority of the Bible and of replacing it with the supremacy of rational human freedom as the guide for interpreting the scriptural text: "Abolitionism leads, in multitude of cases, and by a logical process, to utter infidelity. . . . One of its avowed principles is, that it does not try slavery by the Bible; but . . . it tries the Bible by the principles of freedom. . . . This assumption, that men are capable of judging beforehand what is to be expected in a Divine revelation, is the cockatrice's egg, from which, in all ages, heresies have been hatched."[37] As Noll observes, "the radicalism of all-out abolitionists like Garrison made it much harder for anyone who wanted to deploy the Bible in order to attack American slavery,"[38] especially because the plain meaning of the Bible stood in the way of emancipation, requiring abolitionists to engage in creative and highly unorthodox scriptural exegesis. Lincoln would develop a multilayered response to this challenge, embracing a more explicit skepticism about the biblical God's position on slavery in his private writings and a much more nuanced effort to articulate a scriptural foundation for self-ownership and natural rights in his public utterances during the Civil War. The latter, which Lincoln based on an idiosyncratic reading of Genesis 3:19, clearly served as a rhetorical antidote to scriptural justifications of slavery and would feature most prominently in the Second Inaugural Address.

For instance, Lincoln's rational skepticism toward the Bible is discernible in his 1848 "Fragment on Pro-Slavery" theology, in which he stringently argues that slavery violates fundamental principles of fairness and justice, but without embracing the biblical certainty and uncompromising moral idealism that characterized the conventional position of the radical Christian abolitionists like Garrison. While Thomas Krannawitter writes that "Lincoln proceeded to dismantle the pro-slavery theological arguments presented by Ross,"[39] what is most striking about Lincoln's response is the degree to which he is elusive about the Bible's precise meaning and therefore refuses to genuinely engage Ross on the same biblical turf that he shares with other theological defenders of slavery. Lincoln avers in the opening of the Fragment that "there is no contending against God's will, but still there is some difficulty in ascertaining, and applying it, to particular cases." Ross's purportedly biblical justification of slavery as a universal moral right denies not only this important issue of prudence, but, moreover, ignores the fact that the "Almighty gives no audible answer to the question" of whether slavery is divinely sanctioned, and that "his revelation—the Bible—gives none—or, at most, none but such as admit of a squabble, as to its meaning."[40] In the face of such uncertainty, or at least controversy, over the meaning of the scripture, Lincoln suggests that even Ross, when he maintains the alleged humanity of slavery as an institution, is led to assert an arbitrary and absolute authority over another human being, an authority whose justice can be evaluated on the basis of reason: "If [Ross] decides that God Wills Sambo to continue a slave, he thereby retains his own comfortable position; but if he decides that God wills Sambo to be free, he thereby has to walk out of the shade, throw off his gloves, and delve for his own bread. Will Dr. Ross be actuated by that perfect impartiality, which has ever been considered most favorable to correct decisions?" With such intransigent rational questioning Lincoln lifts the veil on sham theological defenses of slavery, exposing them to be nothing more than exploitative expressions of human self-interest. What Lincoln presents in the Fragment is therefore not so much an argument from the Bible, but rather an argument on the basis of what he describes as a "natural theology," accessible "without reference to revelation," which he would embrace more explicitly later on in his career: "I think that if anything can be proved by natural theology it is that slavery is morally wrong. God gave man a mouth to receive bread, hands to feed it, and his hand has a right to carry bread to his mouth without controversy."[41] The challenge of Lincoln's religious statesmanship, therefore, as it appears to him in antebellum years, requires bridging the gulf between the antislavery conclusions of his natural theology, accessible through reason without reliance on revelation, and the contest over the principles of the Bible that grips the imagination of American Christians. How will Lincoln achieve such a reconciliation between reason and revelation?

Both Noll and Deneen interpret the "Fragment on Pro-Slavery Theology" as Lincoln's "acknowledgment of the need for interpretative humility" with regard to the meaning of the Bible, a humility that they suggest is reflected in Lincoln's most formative wartime speeches, especially the Second Inaugural.[42] According to this line of argument, Lincoln's theology was imbued with moderation and humility, since presumably he realized that excessively zealous appeals to the Bible would only deepen controversy and animosity in a nation of believers who still remained divided over the meaning of Christianity and the status of slavery in republicanism. But there is a fundamental gap between the religious skepticism that Lincoln embraces in his private writings and the theological position that he develops for his public utterances: while the God of the "Fragment" gives "no audable answer" on whether slavery is justified, requiring a recourse to reason alone, in his public speeches Lincoln begins to offer a rationalistic appropriation of the Bible in which he purports to discover a scriptural basis for a labor theory of property rights that is antithetical to slavery. An overview of Lincoln's various appeals and references to the Bible in opposition to slavery shows that he relied primarily upon the following cluster of precepts derived directly from the scripture: The creation of man "in the image of God" (Genesis 1:27); "The Great Commandment" to "Love your neighbor as oneself" (Matthew 22: 37–40); "The Golden Rule" (Matthew 7:12); and God's command that "By the sweat of your brow you will eat your food" (Genesis 3:19).[43] With varying degrees of fidelity to context, moral message, and plain meaning of the scriptural text, Lincoln would appropriate these biblical passages for his own political and rhetorical purposes. Of these, Lincoln would place the earliest and greatest emphasis on Genesis 3:19, to which he gives a rather idiosyncratic interpretation throughout his career in order to bring the implication of the biblical teaching about man's punishment to human labor closer to the conclusions of his own natural theology about natural rights and racial equality.

Lincoln's emphasis on Genesis 3:19 was not dictated merely by the fact that defenders of slavery also favored the Book of Genesis, albeit emphasizing a different part of the text, as the source of scriptural foundation of their doctrine of human mastery. In Genesis 3:19, God announces the far-reaching meaning of Adam's loss of immortality as the consignment of the human race to the painful toil of labor, which the Bible regards as a punishment or a curse made necessary by man's original sin: "By the sweat of your brow you will eat your food until you return to the ground, since from it you were taken; for dust you are and to dust you will return." Throughout the 1850s Lincoln developed a highly idiosyncratic interpretation of this passage, which would eventually feature in the Second Inaugural Address as the scriptural basis for the condemnation of slavery as theft of other man's labor: "It may seem strange that any men should dare to ask a just God's assistance in wringing their bread from the sweat of other men's faces, but let us judge not, that we be not judged." Notice that Lincoln has reversed the meaning of biblical justice and its relationship to human labor: where the Bible regards human labor as a form of divine punishment, Lincoln has transformed it into the source of man's natural entitlement to the fruits of his labor.[44] Furthermore, Lincoln also imposes a rational standard of justice that he suggests should regulate God's disposition toward slavery: now that human labor is considered to be a source of man's ownership of the good things that he can produce, it would be "strange" for God to sanction slavery, since exploitation of other men's labor amounts to economic theft.[45] In a marvelously creative appropriation and adroit reframing of the meaning of the passage, Lincoln discerns in what the Bible regarded as the curse of human labor what amounts to a Lockean theory of a rational creature's right to self-ownership.[46] Lincoln therefore seeks to import into the biblical imagination of the American public a rational theory of the natural right to property as a foundation for human equality that is alien to the revealed text itself. While the latter principle of equality is accessible to democratic citizens without appeals to revelation, Lincoln concluded that both the historical setting and the moral challenge of slavery required it to be moored (however creatively and tendentiously) in the higher authority of the scripture.

Conclusion: The Mysterious God and Divine Providence in Lincoln's Second Inaugural

Partly because of his appeals to biblical imagery and theological language, the contemporary editorial reactions to Lincoln's Second Inaugural (often considered his "greatest speech") were full of criticism. For instance, the *New York World*, a leading Democratic paper, lambasted the theological bent of Lincoln's argument and compared his views on separation of church and state to those of Pope Pius IX: "The President's theology smacks as strong of the dark ages as does Pope Pius IX's politics." Lincoln, according to this editorial, had abandoned "all pretense of statesmanship . . . in this strange inaugural" by taking "refuge in piety" in the address.[47] But these criticisms, so similar to some contemporary objections to religiously informed speech in politics, miss the beautiful subtlety of Lincoln's theology. As we saw, Lincoln was compelled to engage in an active and rationalist reinterpretation of the Bible to graft on the revealed text the doctrine of an individual's right to property to the fruits of his labor, and the theoretical antecedents of such a reinterpretation can be found in Locke's *Second Treatise on Government*: "God, who hath given the World to Men in common, hath also given them reason to make use of it to the best advantage of life, and convenience. . . . Although the Earth, and all the inferior Creatures be common to all Men, yet every man has a *Property* in his own *Person*," and Locke goes on to stress that this means that the Earth is inherited not by the meek, but by the "Industrious and Rational," for "*Labour*, in the beginning, *gave a right of property*" (27, 34, 45). Although scholars have correctly stressed important points of overlap between Protestantism and liberalism, certain tensions unavoidably remain, and Locke's effort in Chapter 5 of the *Second Treatise* to demonstrate a foundation for man's absolute natural right to unlimited property in both "natural Reason" and "Revelation" is a timeless example of the Enlightenment's appropriation of the Bible in the service of liberal and capitalist goals.[48] Locke anticipates and charts the way for Lincoln's creative interpretation of Genesis 3:19.

The theological teaching of the Second Inaugural is anything but traditional. It is imbued with the same natural theological outlook that we discerned in the Handbill's "doctrine of necessity," and it presupposes natural determinism and culminates in a teaching of political moderation. Lincoln fuses these elements seamlessly together through biblical rhetoric and imagery, to achieve the effect of redemption and forgiveness that can heal the nation's divisions and moderate the retributive passions on both sides of the war. But to accomplish this effect, Lincoln shifts the emphasis away from moral responsibility. Glimmers of Lincoln's (nonretributive) natural theology emerge at the beginning of the address, where Lincoln identifies slavery as "a peculiar and powerful interest" that animated the conflict. While "all knew that this peculiar interest was somehow the cause of the war," the South alone is not to blame—it sought merely to "strengthen, perpetuate, and extend" an institution that served its self-interest, whereas the North aimed not so much at permanently abolishing it, but instead merely at restricting its "territorial enlargement." The North, too, was compelled to tolerate the evil institution for decades, and although it did not justify it the way Southern theologians did, it turned a blind eye to human injustice out of tragic self-interest. It is as if Lincoln is a disinterested observer describing the natural necessity of self-interest inescapably governing the moral psychology of each party to the conflict, and his strangely philosophical presentation of the two sides is distanced from conventional theological evaluation and moral judgmentalism. In a speech that is often described as a sermon, Lincoln begins with a description of the clash of interests that does not evince a belief in a world ruled by a righteous God, where the yearning for justice receives neither cosmic nor divine support: "Neither party anticipated that the cause of the conflict might cease with or even before the conflict itself should cease." Instead of seeing themselves as actors in the divine tragedy of providential justice, "each looked for an easier triumph, and a result less fundamental and astounding."[49]

However, Lincoln's view of providence also presents a model of religiously informed speech that provides a corrective to both the secular and the religious sides of the debate about liberalism today. It is true, as others have pointed out, that Lincoln's providential God is nonretributive, and his purposes are mysterious and elusive, and therefore the religious faith that Lincoln espouses in the Second Inaugural aims neither at righteous triumphalism nor at moral divisiveness.[50] However, although Lincoln's God cannot be said to be the God of the Bible, He remains an intransigent partisan on the most important moral question confronting nineteenth-century Americans: "The Almighty has His own purposes," Lincoln concedes, but these purposes are not so inscrutable to unassisted human reason as to leave men in the dark about the meaning of justice that God's providence supports. While slavery was first presented as an economic interest of the South, and then as a violation of the natural rights to property discernible in Genesis 3:19, in this passage Lincoln shifts his emphasis to depict it as a sin that makes the whole nation deserving of "the mighty scourge of war": "If we shall suppose that American slavery is one of those offenses which, in the providence of God, must needs come, but which, having continued through His appointed time, He now wills to remove, and that He gives to both North and South this terrible war as the woe due to those by whom the offense came, shall we discern therein any departure from those divine attributes which the believers in a living God always ascribe to Him." Even though Lincoln does not here indicate whether he counts himself among "the believers in a living God," he insists that any notion of "divine attributes" must include within it God's providential care for justice, which includes within it the care for human equality. Although the exact nature and operation of such providence may be unfathomable to the human mind, Lincoln insists that the standard of justice that would obtain in a world ruled by divine will would itself be discernible to human beings and therefore would not be essentially mysterious.

It is often said that John Rawls's historic hero was Abraham Lincoln.[51] Surely reflection on Lincoln's example, as well as on the religious arguments of the abolitionists during the Civil War and the theologically infused public discourse of the civil rights movement, resulted in significant modification of Rawls's original restrictive position of public reason in *Political Liberalism*. It a sign of Rawls's integrity and intellectual honesty that he made several attempts to demonstrate how the religiously motivated interventions of abolitionists and civil rights activists were compatible with his account of political liberalism and public reason. But the ambiguities in these two responses are revealing of a certain unresolved tension in political liberalism and of the perennial challenge that Lincoln's example continues to pose to Rawls's elegant political system. At the end of the chapter on public reason in the cloth-bound version of *Political Liberalism*, Rawls asks whether Lincoln's Second Inaugural Address violated public reason, settling provisionally on the following response: "I am inclined to think Lincoln does not violate public reason as I have discussed it and *as it applied in his day—*

whether in ours is another matter—since what he says has no implications bearing on constitutional essentials or matters of basic justice" (254, emphasis added). For reasons that I indicated above about Lincoln's morally and theologically infused vision of providential justice and its implications for the fate of slavery in the Civil War, the suggestion that Lincoln was not speaking about "constitutional essentials" seems unpersuasive. At the same time, Rawls hedges when he argues that Lincoln's statements did not violate public reason "as it applied in his day," insofar as we have seen the degree to which Lincoln's intention was to reshape the nation's religious and moral consciousness about the legitimacy of slavery. [52] It was precisely because Lincoln sought to challenge the conventional opinions and to expand the promise of equality he believed was inherent in the Declaration of Independence that he sought to develop novel theological concepts that could help marshal American Christianity to reinforce his case. Lincoln therefore demonstrates that because Rawls's public reason emphasizes consensus so much, it risks siding with the "status quo" (even when the status quo is unjust) and risks standing in tension with the moral and religious contestation that may be necessary for democratic progress and reform. In the next chapter I will turn to Martin Luther King, Jr.'s statesmanship to demonstrate how theological interventions continued to both challenge and inform democratic deliberation in American politics in the twentieth century.

THE THEOLOGICAL FOUNDATIONS OF MARTIN LUTHER KING, JR.'S LEGACY OF RACIAL EQUALITY AND CIVIL DISOBEDIENCE

Liberal Theory's Ambivalence about King's Theological Legacy

As I demonstrated in Chapters 1 and 2, contemporary liberalism maintains an ambiguous posture toward separation of church and state. It cannot decide whether all that liberalism requires is official disestablishment and neutrality, or whether it also demands an unofficial "culture of restraint" that imposes on citizens the duty to refrain from religious and moral arguments in public debates. We saw this paradox captured in both Obama and Rawls: both wish to celebrate the legacy of Martin Luther King, Jr., and the abolitionists before him, but the framework of public deliberation that they propose ("secular, universal" language in the case of Obama and "public reason" in the case of Rawls) has difficulty accommodating the religious reasoning that informed these historic movements. The crux of the liberal dilemma with religion to which Obama and Rawls point can be posed in the following way: are all appeals to religious principles inimical to the culture of respect and reasoned dialogue that are the hallmarks of democratic self-government, or is there such a thing as reasonable and responsible religious speech in the public sphere? Let us return to the most popular answer that liberal theory provides to this question—Rawls's *Political Liberalism* and his teaching that democracy requires citizens to draw upon "publicly accessible" arguments when engaged in deliberation.[1] Although this feature of political liberalism has received criticism for unfairly burdening religious believers,[2] Rawls in fact presents the translation requirement not as a restriction that narrows the content and character of public debate, but rather as a "duty of civility"[3] that follows from "taking to heart the depth of the irreconcilable" pluralism that characterizes modern society.[4] In Rawls's presentation, public dialogue suffused with the language of comprehensive doctrines is necessarily divisive under circumstances of enduring pluralism, because reasons conceived from within particular religious or moral world-views cannot be shared by citizens of competing outlooks. Appealing to shared political principles embodied in "public reason," on the other hand, "strengthens the ties of civic friendship" and ensures that "the commitment to constitutional democracy is publicly manifested."[5] While there is much to admire in Rawls's commonsensical position, it is not entirely clear whether he would disagree with Richard Rorty's more controversial position that religion is a "conversation-stopper."[6]

In this chapter, I evaluate whether the theological restraint that Rawls expects of democratic citizens is either theoretically feasible or practically desirable for a liberal democracy. Furthermore, I ask whether a conception of public reason that insists on theological and metaphysical neutrality can possibly do justice to the historic contribution of religion to the civic life of American liberalism. I do so by following Rawls's own invitation in "The Idea of Public Reason Revisited," his famous reappraisal and restatement of the requirements that political liberalism imposes on public speech. Rawls first introduces his translation "proviso" in that essay as a response to the objection that his version of liberalism is too restrictive, and that its limitations entail a neglect of the "social roots of democracy" and a failure to develop democracy's "religious and other supports."[7] Earlier in his *Political Liberalism*, Rawls had revealingly confessed that the friendly criticisms of Amy Gutmann and Lawrence Solum were instrumental in convincing him to revise his "exclusive view" of public reason.[8] That view, to which Rawls was initially inclined, would have rendered not only the religious arguments of the civil rights and the abolitionist movements, but arguably even Lincoln's Second Inaugural, as inadmissible public speech because of excessive dependence on comprehensive theological presuppositions.[9] Rawls's repeated attempts to overcome this difficulty are a sign of his honesty and consistency as a thinker, but they are also a reflection that these objections have him in a bind. As his rejoinders and revisions demonstrate, either political liberalism cannot accommodate the religious rhetoric of the greatest reformers in American political development, or public reason simply cannot limit the contemporary public discourse in the way that Rawls has in mind, which would constitute a serious wrinkle in the promise of political liberalism.

King's life and speeches provide an excellent litmus test for assessing Rawls's teaching of public reason. The slain civil rights leader is famous for employing religious rhetoric in public deliberation, and he grounds his teaching of racial equality on distinctly theological foundations. For that reason, King's legacy poses a peculiar challenge to political liberalism and compels us to ask whether Rawls's response to the challenge of theologically informed public speech is ultimately persuasive. Even though the solution on which Rawls ultimately settles—the translation proviso—is more inclusive of such speech, a confrontation with King's writings reveals that it is only marginally so, and only at the cost of minimizing the moral and theological seriousness of King's arguments. King aimed to achieve a spiritual transformation of American democracy through the testimony of his religious witness, and the political instrument of that transformation—civil disobedience—drew upon the Christian Thomistic conception of natural law as a standard for evaluating the justice and morality of the established segregationist legal order.[10] While the attempts to sidestep King's theological commitments fail to render justice to his legacy, they also demonstrate a tension within contemporary liberal theory, which would celebrate the political fruits of the civil rights movement while jettisoning its religious language, imagery, and conception of justice and equality.[11] The late Christopher Hitchens, for instance, provides a perfect example of such evasion, since he wishes to champion what he calls King's "humanism" while at the same time denying its theological roots: "In no real as opposed to nominal sense, then, was [King] a Christian," and "his legacy has very little to do with his professed theology."[12] Unlike Hitchens, Rawls does not deny the theological foundations of King's political principles, but he believes that King's political positions can be severed from their foundations in his theological comprehensive doctrines. This chapter challenges the notion that King's political arguments can actually be separated from his theology and argues that the excessively restricted role that Rawls envisions for religion in the public life of political liberalism risks encouraging a culture in which the Christian humanism that animated King may be impossible to sustain.[13]

Attentiveness to King's theology is especially necessary because it presents a peculiar philosophical dilemma on its own terms, since King bases many of his public arguments on a version of liberal theology in which he was immersed in graduate studies. This liberal theological approach comprises an attempt to bridge the gulf between modern natural science and democracy, on the one hand, and biblical Christianity, on the other.[14] It thus seeks to effect a combination that abandons neither modern rationalism and humanistic individualism nor the transcendent God and redemptive mission of Christianity.[15] What we therefore discover in King is a unique blending of Thomistic natural law principles and Christian theology with the natural rights philosophy of the Declaration of Independence—a synthesis that King deploys throughout his career as a civil rights leader, in both his private writings and in his public speeches. Because signs of this synthesis are discernible throughout King's speeches, a number of scholars have suggested that King provides a model example of what Rawls may have had in mind through his requirement of translation of private theological commitments into the language of public reason.[16] But as this chapter will demonstrate, it is not at all clear that King engaged in translating his religious beliefs, at least not in the way that Rawls and his supporters believe that he did, most importantly because King never distinguished or separated his religious views from his public justifications and from the moral priorities that he pursued as a civil rights leader. Instead, King's theological synthesis demonstrates the transformative influence of Lockean liberalism at work while pointing to the limits of Locke's political project—King is advancing a liberalizing and modern interpretation of the Bible while also drawing upon biblical principles as moral counterweights and correctives to liberalism.

The Political Context of the "Letter from Birmingham Jail"

In 1964, the year after Martin Luther King wrote the "Letter from Birmingham Jail," the US Senate took up civil rights legislation. Richard Russell (D-GA) led a filibuster by southern senators to prevent a vote on the bill. With regard to the civil rights legislation, in 1960 Russell had already declared to the members of the Georgia General Assembly, "I pledge to you that I will oppose them to the limits of my endurance and to the extent of my ability."[17] One of the main strategies that Russell and other opponents of the legislation employed was to dismiss the arguments of the civil rights activists on the ground that the movement was led by the clergy, and therefore violated the principle that religion should not be involved in the political affairs of the nation. For example, in his closing speech on the final day of the debate, Russell explained:

I have observed with profound sorrow the role that many religious leaders have played in urging passage of the bill, because I cannot make their activities jibe with my concept of the proper place of religious leaders in our national life. During the course of the debate, we have seen cardinals, bishops, elders, stated clerks, common preachers, priests, and rabbis come to Washington to press for the passage of this bill. They have sought to make its passage a great moral issue. But I am at a loss to understand why they are 200 years late in discovering that the right of domination over private property is a great moral issue. If it is a great moral issue today, it was a great moral issue on the day of the ratification of the Constitution of the United States. Of course, this is not, and cannot be a moral question; however it may be considered, it is a political question.[18]

Russell concludes his sermon against the prominent role of clergy leadership in the civil rights struggle by reminding his listeners of Prohibition, another instance in American history in which, according to his reading, religious movements inappropriately tried to foist their moral concerns on a political issue: "This is the second time in my lifetime an effort has been made by the clergy to make a moral question of a political issue. The other was prohibition. We know something of the results of that." Although segregation confronted the nation with clear moral challenges, Russell was not alone in voicing such sentiments against clergy activism, and in accusing them of improperly injecting their religious and moral commitments into the political arena. Speaking on the House floor, Congressman John Bell Williams of Mississippi described the clergy in the gallery as "the political parasites of our day," "peering in from their perch," while Representative Arthur Winstead complained that "a great number of liberal church people have flooded Congressmen with letters urging passage of the Civil Rights Bill." Winstead deplored this as an instance of churches "thinking only in terms of what they believe the Congress should do to right some wrongs which they consider have been placed upon the Negro race."[19] Whether out of principle or out of convenience, the defenders of segregation were led to embrace the same type of strict separationism between church and state, and between morality and politics, that we encounter among certain strands of contemporary liberal theory.

Segregationists in the Senate were not the only ones to object to the religious nature of the civil rights movement. Many Christian ministers and conservative defenders of the status quo were quick to label nonviolent protests as un-Christian displays of lawlessness and condemned the civil rights movement on the grounds that religion and politics should not mix. One source reports that white fundamentalists and evangelical clergy tried to browbeat King and other members of the Montgomery Improvement Association "with theological arguments in a futile attempt to get them to call off the boycott" in Alabama.[20] King even encountered conservative black preachers who insisted that engagement with politics degraded Christianity, and who felt that ministers and churches should "preach the gospel" and focus on "the heavenly" instead of getting involved in "earthly, temporal matters."[21] King would identify such views as reflections of a "lopsided theology" that led the church to ignore "the here and now" while promoting the dangerously docile notion that "man must lie still purely submissive" and wait on "God on His good time" to "redeem the world."[22] At the center of this religious controversy were questions of the following nature: What is the proper role of a Christian in a society? Are ministers called and commissioned by God to be social reformers and political activists, or to be merely caretakers of men's souls? Does not Jesus' admonition—"render unto Caesar the things which are Caesar's and unto God the things which are God's"—suggest a clear separation between the civil and religious spheres that every Christian should take seriously? Finally, how can one justify the campaigns of active nonviolent resistance and civil disobedience in light of Apostle Paul's assertion that the civil magistrates are ordained by God and therefore must be obeyed?

But the religious opposition to the civil rights movement was not unanimous, and a competing vision of the church's role in democratic social reform was emerging to lend support to the movement. For instance, American Protestant and Catholic clergy as well as the leaders of the Jewish community did not believe that it was either possible or desirable to bracket the question of the morality of segregation from political deliberation, nor that one could draw clear distinctions between spiritual and secular realms. Sensing that the world's focus was crystallizing around the demonstrations in Birmingham, the clergy relied on their spiritual authority to emphasize the moral urgency of the cause of equality in distinctly religious (and oftentimes unequivocally Christian) terms. Under the leadership of Father John F. Cornin of the Society of St. Sulpice, in 1958 the Catholic Bishops in the United States issued a declaration asserting that "the heart of the race question is moral and religious," and that "discrimination. . . . cannot be reconciled with the truth that God has created all human beings with equal rights and equal dignity."[23] In 1960 the northern Presbyterians, separated from the southern Presbyterian Church since the Civil War, declared that "some laws and customs requiring racial discrimination are . . . such serious violations of the law of God as to justify peaceable and orderly disobedience or disregard of these laws."[24] On July 24, 1963, Eugene Carson Blake, former president of the National Council of Churches, accompanied by Father Cornin and Rabbi Irving Black, testified before the Judiciary Com-

mittee: "The religious conscience of America," Blake said, "condemns racism as blasphemy against God. It recognizes that the racial segregation and
discrimination that flow from it are a denial of the worth which God has
given to all persons."[25] More than 5,000 churchgoers, including Blake, were
arrested for staging demonstrations in support of the bill, but the clergy
viewed these legal setbacks as the price that Christians devoted to a moral
life were expected to bear with dignity in a fallen world. "It is tragic," Blake
said after his arrest had become the focus of media coverage, "that the secular press finds so much news when a Christian does what he says."[26]

In the face of segregationist opposition to political activism by the clergy
and long-standing silence about the injustice of racism within the white
Christian ministry, King had repeatedly called on Christian leaders to embrace a more prominent role of leadership on the intractable racial issues
confronting the nation. King's effort to create the conditions for such religious activism was animated by his distinctive understanding of the
church's unique historical role in a liberal democracy, an understanding
that led him to an anti-Lockean view of what constitutes the health of organized religion under liberalism. Following Locke's teaching in the *Letter
Concerning Toleration*, modern liberal democracy had sought to privatize
religion by reforming religious institutions on the model of private voluntary associations, but King regarded such privatization to be an unhealthy
consequence of a constricted interpretation of separation of church and
state. From his perspective, a too rigid distinction between the secular and
religious spheres effectively truncated the church's capacity to contribute to
public deliberation in the civic life of liberal democracy: "If our religion is to
be real and genuine in our lives it must be experienced as a dynamic force.
Religion must be effective in the political world, the economic world, and
indeed in the whole social situation."[27] In words that may appear "totalistic"
to readers today, King intransigently insisted that religion ought to serve as
the authoritative guide for human beings, instead of reducing itself to one
of the many politically and socially insignificant commitments which adorn
the lives of individuals in the private sphere: "Religion should flow through
the stream of the whole [of] life. The easy going dicotymy [*sic*] between the
sacred and the secular, the god of religion and the god of life, the god of Sun-
day and the god of Monday has wrought havoc in the portals of religion."[28]
What hung in the balance was not simply the fate of segregation, but above
all the health and vigor of the Christian faith in America, for King sensed
that Christianity had probably been more transformed by American democracy than American democracy had been by Christianity. As he warned in

"A Knock at Midnight," American Christians had to rejuvenate the "great historic mission" of the church if they were to prevent its spiritual impoverishment and moral decline.[29] Democracy, according to King, had lulled Christianity into near inconsequentiality, and "if the church does not recapture its prophetic zeal, it will become an irrelevant social club without moral or spiritual authority."[30] "The church must be reminded," King added, "that it is not the master or the servant of the state, but rather the conscience of the state. It must be the guide and the critic of the state, and never its tool."

King seemed to arrive at his vision of the church's proactive role in a liberal society in part by becoming disenchanted with modern rationalism, a disillusionment that precipitated King's increasing anxiety about the spiritual health of liberalism. But just as similar anxieties led Alexis de Tocqueville not so much to a rejection of liberalism, but rather to a synthesis through which democracy could be moderated by the salutary influence of religion, King's diagnosis also culminated in a call for a religiously tutored liberalism. In "Pilgrimage to Nonviolence," King provides a sort of intellectual autobiography, and describes his political and philosophical disposition at the time he entered seminary as consisting of uncritical devotion to (Protestant) theological liberalism: "Liberalism provided me with an intellectual satisfaction that I could never find in fundamentalism. . . . I was absolutely convinced of the natural goodness of man and the natural power of human reason."[31] But while he was a seminary student, King immersed himself in the writings of Reinhold Niebuhr, and the encounter with neoorthodoxy, along with continued reflection on race problems in America, shattered King's hopefulness about human nature and his confidence in reason unassisted by faith. King came to confront "the complexity of human motives and the reality of sin on every level of man's existence," above all "the glaring reality of collective evil," and this led him to distrust unadulterated reason as a foundation for morality and to question "liberal theology." In grounding the promise of political salvation in man's capacity to reason, King concluded, liberalism ignored man's enduring propensity for evil and went astray by neglecting to care for the spiritual dimensions of human nature: "Liberalism failed to see that reason by itself is nothing more than an instrument to justify man's defensive ways of thinking. Reason, devoid of [the] purifying power of faith, can never free itself from distortions and rationalizations," for it is always "darkened by sin." However, as we shall see, King's solution to the crisis of modern rationalism was not to renounce human reason altogether, but rather to supplement it with a conception of justice and equality rooted in theology. I turn next to the "Letter from Birmingham Jail," in which King relies precisely on such a synthesis of rationalism and Christian Thomistic theology as a medium for moral engagement in democratic public discourse.[32] In the last section of this chapter I turn to King's theological writings, including his graduate school papers, and ask whether such a synthesis is philosophically and theologically sustainable.

The Theological Synthesis Underpinning King's Call to Civil Disobedience in the "Letter from Birmingham Jail"

In 1963 King was facing increasing pressure within the Southern Baptist Coalition against his efforts to mount a church-based movement of civil disobedience in Birmingham, Alabama. On April 12, 1963, eight white Alabama clergymen published "A Call to Unity" in the *Birmingham News* criticizing King as an "outsider" and attacking his commitment to civil disobedience, which they regarded as antithetical to constitutional government and the rule of law. After labeling King's efforts to initiate a campaign against segregation in Birmingham "unwise and untimely," the clergymen conclude their letter by calling on the Birmingham "Negro community to withdraw support form these demonstrations." Their statement was a sequel to a similar letter that the clergymen had published in January of that year, entitled "An Appeal to Law and Order and Common Sense," in which they had urged opponents of desegregation to follow legal steps for expressing their grievances. King's impatience with the legal process and his willingness to break the law, the clergymen argue, place such immediate and critical pressure on the community and its institutions that they foreclose any possibility of peaceful dialogue between the parties and therefore undermine the chances of reaching a negotiated resolution to their differences: "such actions as incite to hatred and violence, however technically peaceful those actions may be, have not contributed the resolution of our local problems" (ibid). As King acknowledges in his response, the clergymen in effect pose the following troubling questions to the members of the civil rights movement and their leadership: How can King and his supporters simultaneously urge people to obey the Supreme Court's recent decision in *Brown v. Board of Education*, which ordered the desegregation of public schools, while at the same time advocating for disobedience of duly enacted segregation statues in public accommodations in Birmingham? Was King not exhibiting a reckless disregard for the rule of law and public authority, and ultimately undermining the justice of his own cause?

As if to underscore the clergymen's criticism of his methods, at the time that their letter appeared in print, King was serving time in the Birmingham city jail for violating a court injunction against protesting without a permit. It was during his incarceration that King wrote the response to the clergymen's letter in the margins of his newspaper, which would eventually appear in print as "The Letter from Birmingham City Jail."[33] While King's "I Have a Dream" speech is better known,[34] the "Letter" is more direct in laying out the contours of King's political philosophy, both by revealing the foundations of King's approach to civil disobedience in the Thomistic natural law tradition as well as by illuminating King's understanding of the role of religion in public life. The "Letter" is also paradigmatic in presenting itself as a model of religiously informed public speech that aspires to fulfill the requirements of democratic reason-giving, since it combines arguments that are based on America's natural rights heritage with appeals both to natural law as well as to the scripture, on which King draws for his conception of personhood and justice. As we shall see, however, while King presents a synthesis of rational and natural law reasons for his argument against segregation, these reasons are in themselves insufficient to dictate immediate civil disobedience. In addition to these publicly accessible reasons, the "Letter" presupposes a theological framework in which the supremacy of divine law justifies its call to action.

King begins his response to the clergymen by addressing their charge that he is an "outsider" intruding into the local business of Birmingham, with no legitimate ties to the community that could justify his attempt to mount demonstrations in the city. King first emphasizes his official position as the president of the Southern Christian Leadership Conference, an organization that he stresses maintains a presence in every southern state and whose many affiliates include the Alabama Christian Movement for Human Rights. It was at the behest of this Alabama affiliate that King brought the civil rights movement to Birmingham. King's public or political persona, as the opening of his famous letter makes clear, is intimately interlinked with his role as the leader of a religious organization, whose stewardship imposes on him the responsibility to come to the aid of the affiliated institutions throughout the nation. Beyond the formal institutional ties that justify his presence in Alabama, King next stresses that he is "in Birmingham because injustice is here." But King immediately makes clear that he views racial injustice and the response that it demands in unequivocally biblical terms:

Just as the prophets of the eighth century B.C. left their villages and carried their "thus says the Lord" far beyond the boundaries of their home towns, and just as the Apostle Paul left his village of Tarsus and carried the gospel of Jesus Christ to the far corners of the Greco Roman world, so am I *compelled* to carry the gospel of freedom beyond my own home town. Like Paul, I must constantly respond to the Macedonian call for aid.[35]

In modeling himself after the Apostle Paul, and in comparing the promise of racial equality and freedom to the Gospel of Christ, King seems to suggest that his efforts against segregation have the character of a divinely imposed duty that he is not at liberty to disobey or ignore. From King's biblically inflected perspective, segregation is a threat to liberty wherever it may occur, and "injustice anywhere is a threat to justice everywhere. We are caught in an inescapable network of mutuality, tied in a single garment of destiny."

Furthermore, the linchpin of King's response to the charge that he is recklessly encouraging a culture of lawbreaking is an appeal to the supremacy of a higher moral law, which King ultimately conceives on the basis of the Christian natural law tradition emanating from Saint Thomas Aquinas and Saint Augustine. Acknowledging that the critics are expressing "a legitimate concern," near the midpoint of the "Letter" King reformulates their objection against civil disobedience in the following terms: "Since we so diligently urge people to obey the Supreme Court's decision of 1954 outlawing segregation in the public schools, at first glance it may seem rather paradoxical for us consciously to break laws." In responding to these objections, King provides a series of three complementary arguments that rely on religious, philosophical, and political principles to distinguish between just and unjust laws, leading to and reinforcing his famous conclusion that "one has a moral responsibility to disobey unjust laws." In each of these three different arguments, King contends that a higher moral law obliges human beings, and that men have a duty to evaluate all established human laws in light of the requirements of the higher law whenever the two conflict.

First, and most controversially, King draws upon the Christian Thomistic tradition to demonstrate that human beings have a moral obligation to engage in civil disobedience against unjust laws. "One may well ask," King inquires rhetorically, "'How can you advocate breaking some laws and obeying others?' The answer lies in the fact that there are two types of laws: just and unjust. . . . One has not only a legal, but also a moral responsibility to obey just laws." The moral responsibility to obey just laws comes with a correlative duty to disobey unjust laws: "Conversely, one has a moral responsibility to disobey unjust laws. I would agree with St. Augustine that 'an unjust law is no law at all.'" In effect, King argues that human beings are under the moral obligations of higher principles of justice that supersede their legal duty to obey conventional laws when the latter are judged to be manifestly unjust. But in light of what conception of justice does King believe that men should evaluate existing legal ordinances, and how can such a principle justify civil disobedience? In other words, King cannot avoid answering the following vexing question: "How does one determine whether a law is just or unjust?" His answer entails an appeal to a higher moral law, promulgated by a providential divine being, that equips men with a yardstick by which to evaluate existing human laws: "A just law is a man-made code that squares with the moral law or the law of God. An unjust law is a code that is out of harmony with the moral law."

After providing a formulation of a just law in terms of its harmony with the higher moral law, which he equates with "the law of God," King makes a somewhat surprising turn to natural law. This transition sheds light on the synthesis of theology and rationalism that is the hallmark of King's public reasoning. In explaining how "to determine whether a law is just or unjust," King does not suggest, as one would expect, that human laws should be evaluated in light of the word of God as it is revealed in the Bible, nor does he appeal to the theory of natural rights or to the modern conception of the sanctity of the autonomous human person. Instead, he turns to the medieval Christian Saint Thomas Aquinas for the crucial guidance on this question and applies the great Scholastic's definition of a just law to the legal apparatus of enforced segregation in America: "To put it in the terms of Saint Thomas Aquinas: an unjust law is a human law that is not rooted in eternal law and natural law." In his *Summa Theologiae*, Aquinas argued that justice is implicit in the very notion of law, which he famously described as "nothing but a certain ordinance of reason for the common good, made and promulgated by him who has care of the community."[36] Any human ordinance that deviates from these necessary characteristics of law, Aquinas claimed, is unjust, and therefore any human law that willfully aims at private advantage at the expense of the common good cannot be considered to be just. However, Aquinas insisted that while human laws would vary according to changes in circumstances and time, human beings are also equipped with the capacity to perceive the principles of an unchanging natural law, which was revealed to them by God through reason independently of divine revelation: "the light of natural reason, whereby we discern what is good and what is evil, which is the function of the natural law, is nothing else than an imprint on us of the Divine light."[37] It is above all on the basis of this Catholic Thomistic conception of natural law, which presupposes the human person as a rational creature in possession of a soul, that King establishes the injustice of segregation.[38]

But King does not restrict his appeals to Catholic doctrine alone, for he formulates his argument against segregation in three additional ways that do not rely on Aquinas's natural law teaching, even though they still point to the existence of higher principles of justice. First, King attacks segregation in terms of its effects on "the human personality," arguing that it necessarily degrades the human person by undermining man's dignity and doing violence to his soul: "Any law that degrades human personality is unjust. All segregation statutes are unjust because segregation distorts the soul and damages the personality."[39] Second, King next invokes the name and the terminology of the Jewish philosopher Martin Buber, claiming that segregation "substitutes an 'I–it' relationship for an 'I–thou' relationship and ends up relegating persons to the status of things." Finally, King also relies on the principle of democratic legitimacy, by arguing that "unjust law is a code that a numerical or power majority group compels a minority group to obey but does not make binding on itself." These appeals to Buber and democratic reciprocity supplement King's Thomistic Catholic argument with Kantian notions of human personality, but both types of argumentation presuppose controversial comprehensive doctrines—namely, the sanctity of the human person as a moral agent endowed with equal rights regardless of race.[40] As the "Letter" demonstrates, therefore, King blended together theological presuppositions with philosophical assumptions about human dignity into a synthesis that converged in his argument for racial equality. In defending a Rawlsian reading of King, Amy Gutmann insists that "King's civic genius was his ability to be his own translator between religious and civic sources of the same political positions," and that "King moved back and forth between religious and constitutional sources of the same political values."[41] But Gutmann's reading sidesteps the challenge that King presents to Rawls and risks hollowing out the full power of King's prophetic witness: what is at issue is not whether or not King provided the supposedly publicly accessible constitutional arguments as substitutes to his more controversial theological ones, but rather that he felt it necessary to deploy all of them together in a cacophony of moral and spiritual reasoning on the national stage.

What is even more revealing is that King embraces a similar blending of religion and natural rights liberalism in his more private speeches and sermons, which suggests that he is not following the Rawlsian model of translation between two alternative methods of reasoning. Contrary to the suggestions of Gutmann, Richards, and other Rawlsians who maintain that King actually separated his political positions from their theological foundations, in his less public speeches as well as his private writings King asserts that the nation's natural rights heritage *requires* a particular theology that is discernible only in the Bible. Thus, while he does not provide a detailed account of the human personality in his "Letter," elsewhere King offers a more thorough explanation of its foundations, and there King is much more explicit in stressing the theistic presuppositions of his doctrine of human equality. In "The Ethical Demands of Integration," for instance, King describes what he refers to as the "sacredness of human personality" and argues that human beings derive their dignity and moral claim to equality from the fact of the miraculous creation of man in the image of God: "Deeply rooted in our political and religious heritage is the conviction that every man is an heir to a legacy of dignity and worth. Our Hebraic-Christian tradition refers to this in the Biblical term *the image of God*. . . . Every human being has etched in his personality the indelible stamp of the Creator."[42] Remarkably, without a moment's hesitation, King next asserts that both the Declaration of Independence and Frederick Douglass's comments about the Constitution reflect this profound truth about the spiritual foundations of human equality. Regarding the Declaration, King maintains that "never has a sociopolitical document proclaimed more profoundly and eloquently the sacredness of human personality."[43]

But there is one more piece to the puzzle of King's incorporation of the Thomistic outlook into his argument in the "Letter" that further complicates this presentation of a harmonious synthesis of religion and rationalism. Despite King's invocation of Aquinas (and his reliance on Augustine), Aquinas, in fact, paradoxically counseled caution against civil disobedience. Aquinas emphatically stressed the importance of prudence and forbearance with respect to many forms of earthly injustice and warned that political disorder could unleash greater evils than the rule of even tyrants. Thus, while he held that unjust laws "do not bind in conscience" and are "acts of violence rather than laws," nevertheless Aquinas argued that one may be morally obligated to obey such laws "in order to avoid scandal or disturbance, for which cause a man should even yield his right, according to Matthew 5:40, 41: 'If a man . . . take away thy coat, let go thy cloak also unto him; and whosoever will force thee one mile, go with him other two.'"[44] Accommodation to earthly injustice, based on prudential moderation about the possibility of political salvation in this world, was therefore the hallmark of Thomistic political realism. However, Aquinas also taught that in addition to implanting in men the capacity to ascertain the natural law through human reason, God had also made human beings subject to the divine law through supernatural revelation, and this had significant political implications for the disposition that human beings should take toward politics and man-made laws. According to Aquinas, human laws may also be unjust whenever they violate God's revealed divine law, and "such are the laws of tyrants inducing to idolatry, or to anything else contrary to the Divine law." Only in the case of laws that violate God's direct commandments does Aquinas sanction immediate civil disobedience, for he stresses that such laws endangered the salvation of souls in the afterlife: laws in contravention of divine commands, he teaches, "must nowise be observed, because, as stated in Acts 5:29, 'we ought to obey God rather than man.'"[45]

What is the place of Thomistic prudence and moderation in King's public discourse, and has the latter's attempt to put Aquinas's framework of natural law in the service of civil rights reform eclipsed completely the absolute supremacy of divine law that we noticed in Aquinas? I wish to suggest that in his effort to render Thomism serviceable to his democratic ideals, King is compelled to transform the otherworldly orientation of Aquinas's natural law theology into a this-worldly gospel of social change. For according to Aquinas, the Christians who disobey laws that are "contrary to divine goodness" (e.g., as enforcing idolatry), do so to secure salvation, not to redeem society; their martyrdom is not aimed chiefly at changing laws, but rather at securing their spiritual well-being in the afterlife. King's democratic revision of Aquinas retains the Catholic saint's notion of the transcendent principles of a higher moral law, but the aim of those principles for King has become fused with American democracy's promise of political salvation through equality and freedom. Just as we owe religious freedom to the "early Christians [who] were willing to face hungry lions" instead of submitting "to certain unjust laws of the Roman Empire," King avers in the "Letter," so also "academic freedom is a reality today because Socrates practiced civil disobedience." One of the rhetorical peaks of King's argument appears in the closing sections of the "Letter," where King criticizes white clergy for their "silent . . . sanction" of the moral evil of segregation. There King hinges his criticism on what he disparagingly refers to as the "otherworldly" faith of the white clergy, which allows them to relinquish their Christian obligation to struggle against this-worldly plight and racial inequality:

In the midst of blatant injustices inflicted upon the Negro, I have watched white churchmen stand on the sideline and mouth pious irrelevancies and sanctimonious trivialities. In the midst of a mighty struggle to rid our nation of racial and economic injustice, I have heard many ministers say, "Those are social issues, with which the gospel has no real concern." And I have watched many churches commit themselves to a completely other worldly religion, which makes a strange, un-Biblical distinction between body and soul, between the sacred and the secular.

From King's perspective, if the gospel is to have any palpable meaning for human beings, it must be made to speak to present-day social challenges, and its teaching of justice must be brought to bear on concrete political problems. For King, the attempt to seek refuge in the otherworldly cita-del of religious spiritualism, under the purported imperative of separation of church and state, is both "un-Biblical" and undemocratic. If the Church and "organized religion [are] too inexplicably bound to the *status quo* to save our nation," then King counsels turning to "the inner spiritual church, the church within the Church" to "meet the challenge of this divisive hour." As becomes clear in the second half of the "Letter," King has effectively blended together two completely distinct traditions, the natural rights promise of the Declaration of Independence with "the sacred heritage of our nation and the eternal will of God." In his presentation, the two have become fused as complementary elements of a synthesis that supports the liberal democratic heritage of this country.

Conclusion: King and the Challenge of Liberal Theology

In his trenchant criticism of early twentieth-century liberal theology, *Christianity and Liberalism*, John Gresham Machen offers the following for-mulation of the ineluctable challenge that the opening to scientific ratio-nalism poses to modern-day Christianity: "if any simple Christian of one hundred years ago, or even of today, were asked what would become of his religion if history should prove indubitably that no man called Jesus ever lived and died in the first century of our era, he would undoubtedly answer that his religion would fall away."[46] Since the investigation of events in the past belongs to scientific history, Machen's hypothetical Christian "has as a matter of fact connected his religion, in a way that to him seems indissoluble, with convictions about which science also has a right to speak." If archeological and historical research can demonstrate that Jesus Christ never set foot in first-century Judea, Machen's hypothetical interlocutor confronts increasing pressure to tilt his judgment in favor of scientifically established historical facts and against assertions advanced by the biblical narrative. The modern-day Christian can either sacrifice the supremacy of biblical truth to the authority of science, or reject scientific rationalism altogether in the name of the supernatural wisdom disclosed by God's revelation. In the face of such a scientific challenge, Machen observes, the "liberal theologian" is tempted to retreat into a defensive posture through which he attempts to rescue certain general principles of religion, which "he regards as constituting 'the essence of Christianity,'" while abandoning any particular biblical claims that remain incompatible with scientific rationalism. The liberal theologian, therefore, seeks to reject neither science nor the Bible, but he can reconcile the two only by reinterpreting the Bible metaphorically so as to render its antiscientific claims if not entirely silent, then at least unimportant to the scripture's moral message.

Machen regards such a "compromise" between science and religion as amounting to a capitulation of religion to rationalism. Liberal theology, according to Machen, necessarily required the submission of theological doctrine to the demands of scientific materialism, and the reduction of the biblical message to "a way of life" or a "mere feeling" or "program of work" as distinguished from its "message" and its doctrinal "account of facts."[47] Much as we will see Tocqueville worrying about the fate of reformed Protestantism in Chapter 6, Machen worries that a middle way between faith and reason amounted not to a reformed Christianity that could guide the faithful in the modern world, but rather to an unsustainable halfway house in which science would gradually but incessantly conquer all the realms of faith:

> It may well be questioned, however, whether this method of defense
> will really prove to be efficacious; for after the apologist has abandoned
> his outer defenses to the enemy and withdrawn into some inner citadel,
> he will probably discover that the enemy pursues him even there. Modern materialism, especially in the realm of psychology, is not content
> with occupying the lower quarters of the Christian city, but pushes its
> way into all the higher reaches of life; it is just as much opposed to the
> philosophical idealism of the liberal preacher as to the Biblical doctrines
> that the liberal preacher has abandoned in the interests of peace.[48]

Liberal theology therefore had convinced itself that scientific materialism would rest satisfied with mere doctrinal concessions while leaving the spiritual core of the Christian faith and its moral message intact, but it failed to recognize that the inherent tendency of the rationalist outlook of the modern world threatened all of religion, not merely the "mythical" or "miraculous" elements of the Bible.

Not surprisingly, this liberal theological approach to the Bible was one of the points that opponents of the civil rights movement raised in their objections to King's methods. These critics pointed to what they considered to be the antipolitical and spiritually otherworldly message of the Apostle Paul and asked whether the liberal social gospel that informed King's political activism could be sustained on the basis of the biblical teaching. Shortly after King accepted the invitation to write a monthly column, "Advice for the Living," in *Ebony* magazine in 1957, a reader disturbed by King's challenge to the power structure in Montgomery raised the following criticism in a letter: "How do you reconcile Paul's statements on obeying duly constituted authorities, Romans 13:1–7, with the Negro's campaign of passive resistance in the South?"[49] King's response to this intrepid objection reflected his view that the social imperatives that modern democracy imposed on Christians demanded not only a more critical attitude toward established authorities of the state, but also a more skeptical and sociologically informed approach to reading the Bible. King wrote in response to his reader's question: "Like many Biblical affirmations, the words of the Apostle Paul must be interpreted in terms of the historical setting and psychological mood of the age in which they were written. The Apostle Paul—along with all of the early Christians—believed that the world was coming to an end in a few days . . . and accordingly . . . urged men to concentrate on preparing themselves for the new age rather than changing external conditions." Although in the Birmingham letter King would invoke both Jesus and Socrates as exemplars of civil disobedience, in his response to the reader in 1957 he seemed to be more forthcoming about the departure from the original biblical message that his method required. For King insisted in his rejoinder to the reader that in contrast to the era in which Paul and the other Apostles lived, "today we live in a new age with a different theological emphasis," one that requires that Christians adopt the spirit of social engagement, reform, and even civil disobedience.

How did King arrive at his liberalized theological viewpoint and modernized understanding of the Bible, and did he appreciate what a significant theological departure from biblical orthodoxy it entailed? Essays that King wrote during his graduate studies make vivid how he grappled with this dilemma as a young man and suggest that King seemed to share some of the same doubts and worries about liberal theology as we spotlighted in Machen's *Christianity and Liberalism.* For instance, in the late 1940s, when he was at Crozer Theological Seminary, King echoed Machen's (and, as we will see in Chapter 6, Tocqueville's) criticism that liberal theology presented a dangerous temptation to transform Christianity into a subservient hand-maiden of scientific materialism, a transformation that he regarded to be ultimately unsustainable. In an essay titled "The Weakness of Liberal Theology" that he composed for Professor Davis's class "Christian Theology for Today," King reflected on the "system of theology [that] has been gaining great recognition" since the turn of the century, and that grows out of the "attempt to wed theology to the dominant thought pattern of the day, which is science."[50] Such a synthesis, King observes, aims to imbue biblical theology with the spirit of rationalism, since it "insists that the real theologian must be as open-minded, as unbiased, and as disinterested as the scientist." Furthermore, aware of historical contingency, liberal theology aspires to structural flexibility, so as to retain relevance in changing circumstance through its capacity to evolve and adjust its teaching: "The liberal believes that the light of God is forever shining through history as the blossom shines through the bud. Therefore, there can be no set theology. Liberal theology can never be static."

While King is tremendously attracted to this theological synthesis and describes it as "the best, or at least the most logical system of theology in existence," he is also mindful of its inherent weaknesses. Above all, King judges that liberal theology necessarily tempts the believer to accept the principles of "higher criticism," the approach to biblical interpretation that was conceived during the modern Enlightenment by Thomas Hobbes, John Locke, and Baruch Spinoza, among others, and which insists that the miraculous and the supernatural are merely ancillary and inessential elements of the scripture, and can therefore be discarded while preserving the essential and genuine message of the Bible. But King avers that such a skeptical approach is not enough, for instead of serving as a stepping-stone to a purer and more convincing scriptural reading, it risks becoming the unsatisfactory terminal point of the liberal theologian's reductive intellectual journey through the Bible: "After the Bible has been stripped of all of its mythological and non-historical content, the liberal theologian must be able to answer the question—what then?" Somehow, King answers, the liberal theologian must still be able to derive moral guidance from a Bible that has undergone such a scientific reading; he must answer the question, "What relevance does Jesus have in 1948 AD?" "Too often," King notes with discouragement, "we find many of the liberal theologians dodging these questions."

On the other hand, however, almost at the same time in his intellectual development King himself seemed to be tempted precisely by the promise of such scientific reconciliation with theology. According to King, there is no natural necessity for hostility between science and religion, and, when properly understood, the two should complement each other. Consider what King wrote in one of his graduate essays on this topic: "There is widespread belief in the minds of many that there is a conflict between science and religion. But there is no fundamental issue between the two. . . . The conflict has been largely one of trespassing, and as soon as religion and science discover their legitimate spheres the conflict ceases."[51] The conflict, according to King, emerged due to the uncompromising and totalistic claims to "sovereignty" that both religion, and recently, science advance over human beings, when in fact the respective methods of these two disciplines "are dissimilar and their immediate objectives are not the same." Although "the method of science is observation, that of religion contemplation," the former aspires to the knowledge of causes and mastery over nature, while religion, according King's formulation, "interprets" and seeks "the ends" of human life. The root of science, in this account, is "the human need for knowledge and power," while the seed of religion is "the human need for hope and certitude." In spite of these profound differences in both orientation and aim, however, King does not hesitate to declare with certainty that "both [science and religion] are man-made, and like man himself, are hedged about with limitations." The impasse can be naturally resolved if and when the two disciplines voluntary accept self-restraints and moderation and limit their claims to the spheres in which they have legitimate authority. When science ceases to make "pronouncements on God, on the origin and destiny of life, and on man's place in the scheme of things," it will stop "[passing] out worthless checks" and will win respect among believers and unbelievers alike.

But what is left of the Bible in King's reformulation of the relationship between science and revealed religion, and which discipline will ultimately prevail as the master of human destiny? Will the prophetic voice of the scripture and its emphasis on the need for redemption and transcendence survive such a process of scientific reinterpretation, or will the substantive teaching of the Bible have to be reconceived as an attempt to provide moral guidelines to a premodern audience through the allegorical medium of the revealed narrative? In his essay "How to Use the Bible in Modern Theological Construction," King associates "two great advances" in the modern study of the Bible to the development of "higher criticism."[52] First, we have discovered that "the old proof text method of citing Scripture to establish points of doctrine is both unsound and inconclusive."[53] The second advance is the realization that "God reveals himself progressively through human history, and that the final significance of the Scripture lies in the outcome of the process." It is not immediately obvious whether King means by the latter advance merely a sounder understanding of the "chronological order" of the writings of the Bible, or whether he means by it that God's revelation discloses itself through human history.[54] However, in hindsight, King's attraction to "higher criticism" and "progressive revelation" is understandable, since they provide him with the necessary tools to reequip his theological approach for engagement in social transformation of democracy in the twentieth century. But the deeper puzzle with which King leaves us is whether the theological-rationalist synthesis that he anticipates in his graduate essays is ultimately sustainable. One has to wonder whether the rationalistic approach to the Bible that he appeared to embrace in graduate school can actually do justice to the moral and theological message of his mature speeches as a civil rights leader. After all, King's "Letter" asserts the sacredness of human personality and equality not on historical or scientific grounds, but instead as the distillation of the common moral and spiritual insights that are shared by both the Greek and the Judeo-Christian strands of the Western civilization. As we have seen, the divine creation of man in God's image remains the decisive element of that synthesis, and thus it would be impossible to give King's message its full moral meaning and force without its theological foundations.[55] In the next chapter, I turn to Alexis de Tocqueville and Jürgen Habermas to evaluate whether such a theological synthesis is desirable and sustainable.

CAN LIBERALISM APPROPRIATE THE MORAL CONTENTS OF RELIGION? HABERMAS AND TOCQUEVILLE ON RELIGIOUS TRANSFORMATION AND DEMOCRACY'S CIVIC LIFE

In the United States, even the religion of the greatest number is itself republican; it submits the truths of the other world to individual reason, as politics abandons to the good sense of all the care of their interests, and it grants that each man freely take the way that will lead him to Heaven, in the same manner that the law recognizes in each citizen the right to choose his government.
—Alexis de Tocqueville, *Democracy in America*, Vol. 1, Part 2, Ch. 10

Egalitarian universalism, from which sprang the ideas of freedom and social solidarity, of an autonomous conduct of life and emancipation, of the individual morality of conscience, human rights and democracy, is the direct heir of the Judaic ethic of justice and the Christian ethic of love. This legacy, substantially unchanged, has been the object of continual critical appropriation and reinterpretation. To this day, there is no alternative to it. And in light of the current challenges of a postnational constellation, we continue to draw on the substance of this heritage. Everything else is just idle postmodern talk.
—Jürgen Habermas, "A Conversation about God and the World"

Introduction: Tocqueville, Habermas, and the Transformative Agenda of Liberalism

In the preceding chapters, I have demonstrated that political actors in American history have transcended Rawlsian liberalism by drawing on religion in ways that enhance and enrich public deliberation in contentious moments in the nation's political development. At the same time, however, I have tried to show that the political theologies of Lincoln and King reveal unmistakable signs of Lockeanization, insofar as both of these actors elevate modern rationalism as the standard to which the claims of revealed theology must ultimately submit. Liberalism, therefore, does not appear to be neutral with respect to theology, but rather it reshapes and reconstitutes religion in important respects. In light of liberalism's religious transformation, we are led to ask whether the Rawlsian idea (which was echoed by Obama) of conceptualizing the contribution of religion to democracy in the form of "translation," through which religious perspectives converge with secular liberal principles while retaining the social capital that they supply to deliberative politics, is coherent. The European Court of Human Rights (ECHR), for instance, has explicitly embraced such a position: in *Lautsi v. Italy*, rejecting a challenge brought forward by a Muslim citizen, the ECHR upheld the Italian administrative court's finding that a law prescribing the display of crucifixes in state schools did not violate the European Convention of Human Rights. The Italian court's opinion (which the ECHR quoted extensively with approval) affirmed "a thread linking the Christian revolution of two thousand years ago to the affirmation in Europe of the right to liberty of the person and to the key elements in the Enlightenment (even though that movement, historically speaking, strongly opposed religion), namely the liberty and freedom of every person, the declaration of the rights of man, and ultimately the modern secular State."[1] The Italian court argued, moreover, that the crucifix "is capable of expressing . . . the religious origins" of liberal values—such as "tolerance," "mutual respect," and "the autonomy of one's moral conscience"—"which characterize Italian civilization."[2]

Is such a posture toward the genealogy of liberalism and the modern legacy of Christianity theoretically sustainable? Can liberalism appropriate the moral resources of religion for essentially secular purposes, or is something crucial in religion lost in the translation process that Rawls, Obama, and many others recommend? In this chapter, I seek to answer these questions through a comparative examination of two particularly well-formulated and crucially divergent assessments of the fate of religion in modern democracy: Alexis de Tocqueville, the French Catholic aristocrat who authored the two-volume *Democracy in America* after visiting the United States in the early 1800s, and Jürgen Habermas, arguably the most influential living political philosopher in Europe today. Habermas and Tocqueville draw our attention to what Stephen Macedo describes as the "transformative agenda" of liberal constitutionalism and what John Perry has identified in his study of John Locke as liberalism's attempt to "harmonize loyalties" between religious believers and the modern state.[3] As we will see, however, Habermas and Tocqueville offer starkly contrasting evaluations of this transformative agenda, and their differences encapsulate a deep and long-standing division over whether the Enlightenment's confidence in human reason was well-founded—a division that I show continues to animate the debates today and may explain some of our deepest anxieties about liberal democracy's civic life. Although writing from two very different vantage points and more than two centuries apart, both Tocqueville and Habermas are led to religion by way of a moral and civic critique of liberalism, and both argue that religion provides something unique that liberalism cannot replicate on its own. But where Tocqueville judges it necessary to preserve religion as a moral and civic counterweight to democracy's "savage instincts," Habermas concludes that secular reason should attempt a "critical appropriation" of the normative substance of religion as a resource that can supplement liberalism. Both thinkers, however, provide us with reasons inherent within the liberal outlook for a concern for the fate of religion in democracy.

The first part of this chapter examines these questions through an engagement with Jürgen Habermas, who has given increasing attention to the role of religion in liberalism in recent years. For much of his career, Habermas identified himself as a staunch defender of Enlightenment rationality, presenting his work as a contemporary reformulation of Immanuel Kant's normative and political philosophy. Habermas's early intellectual career is often thought to parallel some aspects of Rawls's political philosophy, since his account of liberal constitutionalism assumed only secular foundations and deliberately excluded any reference to the authority (or even contribution) of religion. But in recent years, Habermas has undergone a dramatic change of heart, having concluded shortly after 9/11 that liberalism should "not cut itself off from the important resources of spiritual explanation" afforded by religion.[4] This newfound appreciation for religion was underscored by Habermas's 2004 public discussion in Munich with then-cardinal Joseph Ratzinger on the topic of religion and democracy. Published under the title "Pre-Political Foundations of the Constitutional State?," Habermas's address is most noteworthy for broaching the controversial question of whether liberalism depends on Judeo-Christian theological inheritances, to which Habermas ultimately offers a qualified and somewhat reluctant affirmative answer. This development has perplexed and puzzled a number of leading liberal theorists, who continue to struggle to reconcile it with Habermas's long-standing commitment to communicative rationality.[5]

In the second half of the chapter, I turn to Tocqueville's diagnosis of democracy's spiritual tendencies in order to evaluate whether Habermas's evolution should be understood to entail a genuine break with liberal assumptions about religion.[6] We discover in Tocqueville a subtle but instructive corrective to Habermas's "post-metaphysical" liberalism: because he judges the religious impulse to be ingrained in human nature, for Tocqueville any political science that embraces theological and metaphysical agnosticism will leave something crucial out of its account of the human experience. Habermas's recent attempt to appropriate the moral resources of Christianity while proclaiming agnosticism about its theological (and spiritual) underpinnings may therefore be exposed to the same dangers and obstacles that Tocqueville perceived in the Enlightenment's religious strategy. Thus, for Tocqueville, while the self-transcendent impulses that animate religion can be temporarily truncated and suppressed, and to a certain extent even channeled to serve liberal political purposes, they can never be made wholly to disappear. But because these religious impulses are in tension with the secular principles of liberalism, neither can they be expected to be fully at home within a liberal society. Tocqueville helps us see that, instead of trying to translate or appropriate them through secular reason (as Habermas and others have tried to do), we would be better off to recognize religious contributions as sources of productive tensions within liberalism that are destined to continue to challenge its cultural and moral norms.

Habermas's Puzzling "Religious" Course-Correction of Liberalism

Commentators have emphasized that Habermas's thought has gone through a pronounced development, as he has become increasingly open to the contribution of religion to the liberal public sphere, but consensus about the exact scope and significance of this change remains elusive.[7] Both Philippe Portier and Maeve Cooke distinguish three major phases in Habermas's shifting position on religion.[8] The first phase covers Habermas's initial writings up to the early 1980s. In "On Social Identity" (1974) and *The Theory of Communicative Action* (1984), Habermas presents the modern hope for the disenchantment of the world as an unequivocal gain for humanity.[9] Clear influences of Weberian and Marxist theory, via the Frankfurt School, are discernible in Habermas's depiction of religion as an "alienating reality" and a powerful tool of domination. Much like Marx, Habermas hopes for the eventual "disappearance" of religion, as modern society comes to rely more and more on "communicative rationality," which is built on "principles of the secular universal ethic." In the second phase, which lasts roughly from 1985 to 2000, Habermas replaces the hope for the "disappearance" with the call for the "privatization" of religion, a move that appears to be necessitated by the failure of secularization to bear fruit.[10] In texts such as *Postmetaphysical Thinking* (1992) he begins to stress that religion is an existential necessity that is "indispensable in ordinary life."[11] While not personally "religiously motivated," Habermas now recognizes that for many people (though presumably not for him) religion offers "consolation" in the face of "unavoidable suffering and unrecompensed injustice, the contingencies of need, loneliness, sickness, and death."[12] Around this same time, in discussions with both academic philosophers and theologians, Habermas shows signs of cautious openness to the relevance of "religious language" as a depository of "semantic content" the continues to be "inspiring and even indispensable," at least until philosophical language can succeed at appropriating it.[13] Even though by this point his early antagonism to religion fades, the impenetrable wall that Habermas sees dividing religion and reason remains intact: the religiously motivated should not inject their convictions into the political domain, in which debate is expected to proceed on the basis of secular reason that is incapable of adjudicating the truth and falsity of religious claims.[14]

Beginning in the late 1990s and early 2000s, Habermas's position on religion entered its latest and most interesting stage, featured prominently in his debate with Ratzinger as well as such works as *The Future of Human Nature* and *Naturalism and Religion*. Having effectively repudiated the previous restrictions that he imposed on public deliberation in democracy, Habermas now embraces the view that "the democratic state should not overhastily reduce the polyphonic complexity of the range of public voices."[15] This lesson applies especially to religious voices in public life, which Habermas now believes "have the power to provide convincing articulations of moral sensitivities and solidaristic intuitions" on which liberal societies depend for their civic health but which, as we will see, secular reason cannot supply on its own. Even more significantly, Habermas now comes to recognize not just the symbolic and rhetorical value but also the cognitive contribution of religion, suggesting that religious perspectives may in fact contain normative truths that rationalism should seek to appropriate. Under the rubric of "publicization" that Habermas now proposes, religious arguments should not be limited to the private sphere, but instead should be given free rein to draw upon their theological traditions as they intervene in public life in an effort to refine the "moral intuitions" of society.

Most of the attention in scholarship has focused on whether or not Habermas's recent reflections on religion entail a repudiation of John Rawls's controversial "translation proviso," which held that the religiously motivated should supply secular reasons in public debate.[16] As becomes clear in what follows, I argue that Habermas is indeed led to reject the spirit, if not the exact theoretical structure, of "public reason" as Rawls had proposed it. What has not received as much attention in scholarship, however, is the broader theoretical reasoning about the limits of secular liberalism that informs Habermas's new approach to religion, which constitutes a deeper challenge to Rawlsian liberalism than has been previously appreciated. Can political liberalism as a rational *post-metaphysical* project make sense in light of Habermas's admission that democracy needs to reappropriate (at least for the time being) the moral resources of religion? Through a comparison with Tocqueville, this chapter shows that even though Habermas's own position leaves him deeply uncertain about this question, Habermas has not ultimately confronted the radical implications of this conclusion for the limits of liberalism as a political project.

It is worth underscoring that Habermas's long-standing project has been to provide a "nonreligious" and "post-metaphysical" justification of the normative foundations of constitutional democracy.[17] This is an aspiration that Habermas shares with many Western scholars who are influenced by John Rawls.[18] Interestingly, however, Habermas's recent reopening to religion has not led him to abandon the hope that liberalism can be defended on such a neutral foundation. Thus, in his recent debate with Ratzinger, Habermas begins with the assumption that this type of neutral justification is available in "political liberalism," more precisely in the form of "Kantian republicanism."[19] While now acknowledging that liberal egalitarianism has certain "antecedents" in Christian theology, he maintains that "the form of state power that remains neutral toward different worldviews ultimately derives from the profane sources of seventeenth- and eighteenth-century philosophy."[20] The Kantian strand of this Enlightenment project "insists. . . . that the basic principles of constitution have an autonomous justification and that all citizens can rationally accept the claims this justification makes."[21] Habermas's liberalism thus eschews reliance on "the 'strong' cosmological or salvation-historical assumptions of the classical and religious theories of the natural law."[22] Even if he is now willing to grant certain practical setbacks to the liberal project, Habermas appears to remain firmly committed to its theoretical assumptions about the self-sufficiency of unassisted reason vis-à-vis theology: "Post-metaphysical thought prepares to learn from religion, but remains agnostic in the process. It insists on the difference between the certainties of faith, on the one hand, and validity claims that can be publicly criticized, on the other; but it refrains from the rationalist presumption that it can itself decide what part of religious doctrines is rational and what part is irrational."[23]

The most significant setback to the liberal project that Habermas now acknowledges is the partial failure of the Enlightenment's strategy of secularization, a failure confirmed by the resurgence of religion throughout the world.[24] But even here—indeed precisely here—it is difficult to tell whether Habermas regards this revival of religious sentiments as a mere temporary detour in the necessary and irresistible march to greater secularization, or whether he sees it as a fundamental empirical development that should alter our expectations about the prospects of popular enlightenment. On the one hand, the problem is not merely the rise of politically destructive fundamentalism abroad, especially in radical strands of political Islam. Even in the West, where religion has been effectively "deinstitutionalized," Habermas recognizes that "at present" the secular society "still has to adjust itself to the continued existence of religious communities in an increasingly secularized environment."[25] But on the other hand, in certain writings Habermas suggests that the problem goes beyond the resilience of religion altogether, potentially implicating the soundness of scientific rationalism itself: he warns of recent developments in biotechnology (particularly in genetic engineering) that threaten to "instrumentalize" human nature and thus endanger the dignity of the human species.[26] He has come to regard the Enlightenment's effort to uncouple morality from theology as potentially counterproductive from the perspective of the Enlightenment project itself: in both his Frankfurt speech on "Faith and Knowledge" and in his debate with Ratzinger (as well as in other writings), Habermas raises the specter of a radical "secularism"[27] whose excessive commitment to "cultural and social rationalization"[28] threatens to culminate in the "self-annihilation" of democracy by drying up its sources of solidarity.[29] Habermas therefore appears to conclude that the two prongs of the Enlightenment strategy—the secularization of the state and the (still unsuccessful) secularization of society, which were initially joined at the hip—should now be separated, so as to make room for a "post-secular society" that can save liberal constitutionalism from its own excesses.[30]

It is important to note that in spite of his partial repudiation of secularization, in his debate with Ratzinger Habermas explicitly distances himself from such critics of liberal rationalism as Martin Heidegger, Carl Schmitt, and Leo Strauss and refuses to follow them down the troubling road that leads to a radical critique of reason itself.[31] He does not wish "to push too far the question whether an ambivalent modern age will stabilize itself exclusively on the basis of the secular forces of a communicative reason."[32] He prefers to treat the Enlightenment's hope for the decline of religion and the long-anticipated triumph of rationalism not as a certain or indubitable failure, but rather as an "open, empirical question" whose answer has not yet been disclosed by history.[33] But it is unclear if, in providing his account of the deficiencies of secularism, Habermas can ultimately escape the need for such a confrontation with the inherent limits of rationalism. In his contribution to the exchange with Ratzinger, Habermas identifies the topic that the Academy had proposed—"The Pre-Political Foundations of a Free State"—with a question that had been originally posed by Ernst Wolfgang Bockenforde in the mid-1960s: "Does the free, secularized state exist on the basis of normative presuppositions that it itself cannot guarantee?"[34] Before launching into his discussion, Habermas isolates two assumptions that undergird this question: that the liberal state depends on "ethical traditions of *a local nature*" (emphasis added), which in turn may draw on particular religious sources for their lifeblood, and that the liberal state is not capable of renewing the wellspring of these traditions.[35] He acknowledges from the very beginning that if these assumptions prove to be true, it would "be an embarrassment to a state that was committed to neutrality in terms of its world view," i.e., to the aspirations of the Rawlsian state.[36] Above all, an affirmation of these assumptions would be problematic because it would bring into doubt the fundamental goal of the liberal project: the idea that "a society of plurality of world views can achieve a normative stabilization—that is, something that goes beyond a mere *modus Vivendi*."[37]

The crux of Habermas's critique of liberalism, however, remains civic, rather than theoretical. While political liberalism is theoretically self-sufficient and rationally defensible on its own terms, i.e., it "can satisfy its own need for legitimacy in a self-sufficient manner,"[38] it suffers from a built-in motivational deficit: "When we bear in mind the role played by citizens who understand themselves to be the authors of the law, we see that the normative presuppositions for the existence of a democratic constitutional state make higher demands than would be the case if they were merely citizens of the society and 'addressees of the law.'" Because citizens of a liberal regime are expected not merely to obey the law as passive subjects, but also to partake in shaping it, rational self-interest cannot satisfy the demands that liberalism imposes on individuals. Accordingly, Habermas observes, "the obedience due to coercive laws concerning people's freedom is one thing; the motivations and attitudes expected of citizens in their role as democratic (co-)legislators are something else."[39] Because he interprets liberalism through this demanding Kantian frame, Habermas insists that citizens "make active use of their rights to communication and to participation" not only for their own self-interest (as they would in a Lockean regime), but also for "the common good," and this "demands a more costly commitment and motivation . . . that . . . cannot simply be imposed by law."[40] Crucially, citizens are expected to "accept sacrifices that promote common interests," and the cultural and civic ethos that sustains such a disposition "is nourished by springs that well forth spontaneously—springs that one may term 'pre-political.'"[41] In light of these demands, could Habermas accept the liberal bargain, whereby the civic expectations on citizenship are drastically lowered in exchange for a way of life that transcends the need for robust cultural solidarity?[42] At one point in the exchange with Ratzinger, Habermas seems strangely willing to entertain such a possibility: "the fact that we are not willing to die 'for the Treaty of Nice,' is no longer an objection to a common European constitution."[43] But for a thinker who has spent a great deal of his intellectual career ruminating on the failures of the European project and defending the notion of "constitutional patriotism," such a compromise would certainly be a strange way to sidestep the civic challenges confronting liberalism.[44]

In words that seem to echo Alexis de Tocqueville and contemporary Tocquevillian critiques of liberalism, Habermas acknowledges the depressing prospect of "the transformation of the citizens of prosperous and peaceful liberal societies into isolated monads acting on the basis of their own self-interest." But he attributes this potential for civic degeneration not to the inherent logic of liberalism as a political order, but instead to "external threats," including especially "turbo-capitalism" and "the dynamic of the global economy," which reduce "the citizen's field of action to the private realm."[45] Habermas is aware that present-day "postmodern" theorists and theological critics of liberalism regard these developments "as the logical outcome of the program of self-destructive intellectual and social rationalization"[46]—a judgment that, as we will see below, resonates with Tocqueville's critical appraisal of the effects of rationalism on modern democracy's civic tendencies. But in contradistinction to Tocqueville, Habermas does not seek to curb the civic pathologies that he has identified by questioning the self-sufficiency and the adequacy of liberal rationalism as the foundation of social life. In particular, he is resistant to the idea that "the remorseful modern age can find its way out of the blind alley only by means of the religious orientation to a transcendent point of reference": "we need not understand" the question of the limits of rationalism "in such a manner that it offers the educated defenders of religion an argument in support of their case."[47] This appears to be a remarkable statement, especially because it immediately precedes Habermas's consideration of *how* liberalism should take advantage of the capacity of religion to generate and transmit the social virtues on which democracy depends.

So what, then, is a liberal political thinker—a self-described "methodological atheist"—to do once he has acknowledged that "political virtues . . . are essential if democracy is to exist"?[48] Without virtue—without active, vigorous, and self-sacrificial virtue—citizenship, republicanism, and the common good seem to be in jeopardy. Yet where shall we find virtue amid what Habermas calls the "ethical abstinence of a postmetaphysical thinking, to which every universally obligatory concept of a good and exemplary life is foreign"?[49] Habermas recognizes that ethical values are generated, formulated, and transmitted within social groups that are loyal to something greater than themselves, greater than their constituents parts, and greater even than the state, and religious communities provide the ideal incubators for nurturing such moral and civic commitments. As he acknowledges in a different essay where he singles out Martin Luther King, Jr., and the civil rights movement for praise, "the religious roots to the motivations of most social and socialist movements in both the United States and European countries are highly impressive."[50] This realization has led Habermas to acknowledge the force of the objections to Rawlsian public reason that were advanced by Paul Weithmann and others: meeting "the yardstick set by Rawls' 'proviso,'" whereby religious individuals and organizations are compelled to translate their arguments into secular language, would entail the tragic consequences that "the churches' commitment to civil society" would weaken and perhaps even "wither away."[51] Additionally, Habermas thinks that there is an even more "compelling objection" to Rawls's strict translation "proviso," insofar as the liberal state cannot be expected legitimately to force citizens to switch from their "religiously rooted convictions onto a different cognitive basis," notwithstanding whether that basis is actually freestanding (as Rawls insists) or ultimately secular (as some critics allege).[52] Repudiating the "exclusivist" positions of Robert Audi, Stephen Macedo, and others,

Habermas proposes a modified version of Rawls's proviso, an "institutional filter" whose demand of neutrality would obligate only public officials while leaving citizens free to express themselves in religious language.[53] This will ensure that the "burdens" of tolerance are more symmetrically distributed between unbelievers and believers in a liberal society.[54]

While this dispute with Rawls has garnered attention, scholars have not stressed how much the implications of Habermas's critique go beyond a mere modification of Rawls's formal translation proviso. Habermas is abandoning the aspiration to exclude revelation as a potential source of normative truth from civic discourse, and although some restrictions on official public speech will remain, these are no longer principled objections to religion as a potential source of moral insight. In the *Dialectics of Secularization* (his debate with Ratzinger), Habermas makes this point explicit. He argues that what distinguishes his "post-secular" society from Rawls's is not merely the political question of how much "respect" is accorded religion, or the question of where liberalism can secure the necessary space for "authenticity" and "integrity" of personal beliefs. Instead, he chooses to push the debate to a more radical plane, concluding that "philosophy has good reasons to learn from religious traditions," and that reason must become "aware of its fallibility" and of its need to rely on revelation for normative supports.[55] In a number of his late works, Habermas appeals to the idea of human equality rooted in man's creation in "the image of God" as an illustration of a normative concept that reason cannot articulate with sufficient moral rigor, and that philosophy must continue to appropriate from religious traditions.[56] But on the crucial question of whether reason can actually render such "Biblical concepts" into terms that are "accessible to a general public," Habermas appears to remain deeply divided and uncertain: while he once thought that someday philosophy might "translate" the "indispensable potentials for meaning . . . from religious traditions . . . into the language of public"[57] (a position that he reiterates in his debate with Ratzinger),[58] he has also acknowledged in other writings and interviews that "philosophy cannot appropriate what is talked about in religious discourse *as* religious experience. These experiences could only be added to the fund of philosophy's resources . . . if philosophy identifies these experiences using a description that is no longer borrowed from the language of a specific religious tradition, but from the universe of argumentative discourse that is uncoupled from the event of revelation."

Habermas therefore seems to leave us with a paradox: while the goal of the more religiously accommodating liberalism that he now advocates is to learn from religion, Habermas still conceives of this learning process in terms of "a critical appropriation of the essential contents of the religious tradition." Only when the normative truths of religion have been appropriated in this way can they be rendered in universalistic and secularized terms ("into the language of the public, that is, of presumptively generally convincing reasons"), and thus shared between individuals who do not subscribe to the same faith traditions or any faith traditions at all. But however successful this translation process may be, Habermas also seems to admit that philosophy will only be able to express in secular language a pale shadow of the original normative truth that religion expresses: "I have attempted to point out this deficit [within the philosophy of modernity], or at least the clumsiness of philosophical attempts at translation."[59] But if the limits of philosophy vis-à-vis theology are as severe as Habermas now recognizes, if philosophy will never succeed at articulating a secularized replica of the moral and normative teachings of the Bible, then why should reason continue to aspire to appropriate and translate religious teachings in the first place? Does Habermas's approach pay due attention to the question of what will become of the original religious tradition (and its arguments, which are often based on biblical revelation) when it is exposed to "complementary learning process" that Habermas has in mind? Will that religious tradition remain intact once it has undergone such a process, and is this process really not unidirectional—does it not benefit only one party in the dialogue?

Tocqueville on the Ambiguous Fate of Religion in American Democracy

Habermas's attempt to appropriate theology in the service of liberalism eventually confronts an insurmountable limit that secular reason cannot overcome. This limit becomes obvious when Habermas acknowledges the difficulty involved in translating the Christian idea of man's divine creation into nontheological language: any such translation, Habermas reluctantly admits, will leave out crucial normative elements of the religious view, and "at those fracture points where a neutralizing translation of this type can no longer succeed, philosophical discourse must confess its failure."[60] This highly revealing admission prompts us to pursue a further question that Habermas himself does not raise: should philosophy even define its primary aspiration as a rationalizing translation of religion, or is there an alternative attitude that those concerned with the health of democracy should seek to adopt? Is there not another crucial role for religion within democracy, not as a supplement of secular reason, but instead as its friendly but critical interlocutor and dialectical sparring partner, a role that Habermas's approach (just as much as other "public reason"–inspired models) does not effectively capture? This is the side of faith that Ratzinger underscores in his debate with Habermas: religion and reason, according to Ratzinger, should "restrict each other and remind each other" of their mutual "limits," an approach that he emphasizes presupposes our willingness to "*doubt the reliability of reason.*"[61] Until we take this step with Ratzinger and confront this unsettling dimension of religion, and so long as we view faith as a mere repository of resources that can be appropriated to supplement rationalism, we will continue to close ourselves off from the peculiar challenge that religion poses to the adequacy of unassisted reason and the unique contribution that it can make to the civic and moral health of liberalism. In the rest of this chapter, I turn to Tocqueville's treatment of religion's role in American democracy to illuminate this important alternative to Habermas's approach.

Tocqueville is usually thought to present an overly optimistic assessment of democracy in America, and his political oeuvre is often regarded essentially as a continuation of the rationalist project of the modern Enlightenment.[62] Because of his reputation as the first "sociologist" of democracy and his tendency to stress the historical inevitability of democratic equality and its alleged foundations in Christianity, a number of scholars have concluded that Tocqueville's *Democracy in America* suffers from methodological and empirical deficiencies.[63] In 2004, Garry Wills published an essay in the *New York Review of Books* entitled "Did Tocqueville 'Get' America?" Wills faults Tocqueville for his "propensity to form instant judgments" and for ignoring the "material basis of American life," including capitalism, banking, and manufactures, and short-shrifting American literature and arts. But he reserves his harshest criticism for what he sees as Tocqueville's undue optimism regarding the future prospects for Catholicism in America, a judgment that Wills claims was informed by the "prejudices he brought with him from France."[64] The impression that Tocqueville viewed democracy through distorting lenses was originally crystallized by a French dramatist, Victorien Sardou, who accused Tocqueville of presenting an idealized or "sweetened" version of America, "l'Amerique en sucre."[65] Contemporary scholars seem to have inherited this view, and a number of them have concluded that as part of his "sweetened" presentation of American democracy, Tocqueville adopts a posture of a "religious functionalist" who misleadingly exaggerates the degree to which traditional Christianity (including especially Catholicism) is in harmony with democratic equality.[66]

More recently, the debate has been stimulated by Sheldon Wolin's magisterial study, *Tocqueville between Two Worlds* (2001).[67] In an otherwise extremely insightful interpretative work, Wolin struggles to come to grips with the full nuances of Tocqueville's assessment of the role of religion in democracy. Wolin's account has the virtue of detecting in Tocqueville a counter-Enlightenment strand, especially in his treatment of Cartesianism, with its dangerous validation of "private judgment, doubt, abstraction" and its narrow conception of "method" (84–85). By the same token, Wolin is also sensitive to the Pascalian "moment" in Tocqueville's thought—a feature that is sometimes neglected by other interpreters[68]—and this enables him to be moved by Tocqueville's worry about both the tyranny of the rationalistic method and the debilitating effects of radical doubt.[69] In spite of this, however, Wolin repeatedly argues that Tocqueville regards religion primarily as a means of "social control" and "repression"[70] He even suggests that Tocqueville supports a "Machiavellian civil religion" that is imposed on the democratic people by the "elite" ruling "class" as a quasi-Marxist "superstructure" that is legitimated by political theorists (like Tocqueville) who guide the elites.[71] Throughout his discussion, he never appears to be moved by Tocqueville's insight that religion is useful for democracy not so much because it is a means of "social control,"[72] but instead because it is an expression of a powerful and natural human longing for self-transcendence and moral concernment that democracy risks to neglect and undermine at its own peril. As we will see below, while Tocqueville accepts the triumph of equality, he is less certain that it constitutes an unqualified good for human beings, and this uncertainty is linked to his ambivalence about whether or not a democratically transformed religion can continue to ennoble democracy's civic and moral life.

America's Puritan "Point of Departure": Tocqueville's Counter-Enlightenment Narrative

The discussion of early New England Puritanism that introduces the first volume of *Democracy in America* provides an instructive point of access to the ambiguities that permeate Tocqueville's treatment of religion and to his puzzling understanding of democracy's theological foundations. Tocqueville claims in the second chapter of Volume I that the European emigrants that settled North America beginning in the 1630s were "ardent sectarians and exalted innovators," and he argues that the primary source of America's democratic principles is to be sought not in its Constitutional Founding, but instead in the covenant tradition of Old Testament Christianity.[73] According to Tocqueville, the religious zeal that animated the Puritans was of no ordinary sort, since it "was almost as much a political theory as a religious doctrine" (35). When Tocqueville elaborates on this point, he stresses that the sect in England to which Puritans belonged practiced a faith that "blended at several points with the most absolute democratic and republican theories," and that it was this feature of their religion that appeared "most dangerous [to their British] adversaries" (32; cf. 275). The Puritans therefore somehow combined a dedication to "austere principles" of orthodox biblical religion with the longing for democratic freedom, i.e., what Tocqueville describes as their desire "to live . . . in their manner and pray to God in freedom" without interference from others (32). To illustrate this strange but admirable synthesis of republicanism and orthodoxy, Tocqueville approvingly quotes from Nathaniel Morton's *New England's Memorial*, in which the author recounts that even before they reached the American shore, the first act of democratic self-governance in which the pilgrims engaged aboard the *Mayflower* was to adopt a charter establishing a political society devoted to "the glory of God, and advancement of the Christian faith" (35). It is above all this synthesis of democratic freedom and religious devotion, of republicanism and biblical law, that Tocqueville has in mind when he says that the Puritans were motivate by "a purely intellectual need: in exposing themselves to the inevitable miseries of exile, they wanted to make *an idea* triumph" (32).[74]

Although Tocqueville does not refer to the Puritans as "Calvinists," Peter Lawler has argued that he paints them as if they were "the idealistic citizens of Calvin's Geneva."[75] What Lawler means by this becomes clear when Tocqueville turns in the second half of the chapter to consider the Puritan penal legislation (37–42), of which the most "characteristic" example is the Connecticut Code of 1650, which we are promised contains "the password to the great social enigma" that is America (37). These laws begin, as does the Mayflower Compact, with reference to God: the preamble of the Connecticut Code announces that worshipping "any other God but the Lord God" will merit the death penalty (38). Turning to the body of the penal law, Tocqueville shows that in their concern to maintain "the moral order and good mores in society," the "legislators of Connecticut . . . conceived the strange idea of drawing from sacred texts." They sought guidance in particular from Exodus, Leviticus, and Deuteronomy, and constructed a penal code that Tocqueville revealingly describes as befitting a "rude and half-civilized people" (38). Their laws "constantly penetrate into the domain of conscience, and there is almost no sin that does not fall subject to the censure of the magistrate" (37–38). Laziness, drunkenness, and kissing are among the proscribed offenses that Tocqueville catalogues, and as he acknowledges somewhat regretfully, there is no "religious liberty" in the Connecticut Code (39). These "bizarre and tyrannical laws were not imposed," Tocqueville observes, but instead were adopted through "free concurrence." While Tocqueville recoils from these legal vestiges of Puritan intolerance (which he generously attributes to the legislator's "lapses"), his discussion of the Puritan law requiring compulsive public religious education makes clear his admiration for the elevated sentiments that informed the Puritan approach to democracy: "In America, it is religion that leads to enlightenment; it is the observance of divine laws that guides man to freedom."

As we are starting to see, unlike Habermas and many other liberal theorists who inherit the Enlightenment's unmitigated rationalism, Tocqueville deliberately goes out of his way to read into the origins of American democracy a pre-Enlightenment, partially illiberal (and even fundamentalist) religious strand. He thus provides what appears to be an antidote or a counterweight to the Enlightenment's rationalistic foundationlism. But Tocqueville is by no means a reactionary, and as he repeatedly stresses, he has accepted the triumph of democracy as an "accomplished fact"—as a historical inevitability (6, 13). He goes so far as to describe the gradual unfolding of equality as a "providential fact," and he warns that "to wish to stop democracy" would "appear to be to struggle against God Himself" (6–7, 673–676). After all, the "new political science" that Tocqueville argues is "needed for a world altogether new" does not have as its goal the overthrow of democracy and its replacement with any form aristocracy or theocracy (7). Instead, it seeks to elevate democracy and to make it more sustainable in the long term by moderating its most "savage instincts": "To instruct democracy, if possible to reanimate its beliefs, to purify its mores, to regulate its movements . . . such is the first duty imposed on those who direct society in our day" (7, cf. 9–10). What lessons, then, does Tocqueville hope that his account of America's Puritan origins will provide to his contemporaries, who inhabit increasingly liberalized societies where orthodox biblical religion no longer holds the unquestionable authority that it did among Puritan settlers?

A helpful indication is provided by Tocqueville's counterintuitive admission, in the middle of his catalogue of the divinely inspired penal laws of Puritan Connecticut, that the spirit of Puritan society was "enlightened and [its] mores mild" (38). While the salutary Puritan instinct to impose moral and religious restraints on freedom crossed into the absurd and the fanatical, Tocqueville also indicates that in spite of this "one never saw the death penalty laid down more profusely in the laws, or applied to fewer of the guilty" (38). At the same time, a few pages later Tocqueville observes that while the Puritans made tremendous sacrifices for "a religious opinion" when they set out on their pilgrimage from England, "one nevertheless sees them seeking with an almost equal ardor material wealth and moral satisfactions, Heaven in the other world and well-being and freedom in this one" (43). In addition to this "division of labor" between the economic and the moral-theological spheres, Tocqueville points out that Connecticut's draconian penal laws were drafted alongside and "in a way connected to a body of political laws which . . . *anticipate from very far* the spirit of freedom in our age" (39, emphasis added). It appears, then, that we may need to partially qualify Lawler's "Calvinist" reading of Tocqueville's Puritans, insofar as Tocqueville himself is beginning to indicate that they were by no means theocrats in the conventional mold.[76] Instead of a traditional fusion of divine and earthly authority, the Puritans presented a remarkable spectacle of a society that had democratically chosen to restrain individual freedoms with religious, moral, and communitarian commitments, with what Tocqueville refers to as the "duties of society" and its "obligations" of citizenship, while still somehow maintaining an almost complete freedom in the political realm (41, 43).[77] The Puritans wedded "two tendencies"—democratic and communitarian, materialistic and spiritual—which are "apparently so opposed," but which they managed to combine in such a way as "to lend each other a mutual support" (43).[78] While Tocqueville's narrative gently covers over how fragile this synthesis actually was, and how quickly it would begin to unravel, a number of scholars have argued that irreconcilable tensions within Puritanism provided especially fertile ground for a Lockean "take-over," through which the covenantal tradition became reinterpreted in terms of modern individual liberties and economic prosperity.[79]

Contrary to his insistence that the "*the spirit of religion* and *the spirit of freedom*" were in harmony from very beginning in America, Tocqueville cannot help but reveal how the peculiar Puritan combination of these two spirits required the subordination of individual freedoms to the moral and religious concerns of the community, which in turn took their bearing from the revealed word of God. But even though religion and liberalism are in subtle disharmony from the outset of *Democracy in America*, in Tocqueville's hands this tension is rendered dynamic and productive, since it demonstrates the religious prerequisites of civically responsible uses of democratic liberty.

This helps us see why Tocqueville, at crucial points in his narrative, tempts the reader with the proposition that democracy emerges organically out of Christianity, while only quietly hinting at the role of the Enlightenment. He employs this motif as an alternative to the idea of "the state of nature" and the doctrine of natural rights that were championed by modern rationalist thinkers and their closest students among the American founders.[80] For instance, after providing a compressed history of European civilization in Volume II, Part 1, Chapter 3, Tocqueville highlights the disruption of the aristocratic order of the ancient world, and the resulting moral and political leveling, that was brought about by the egalitarian teaching of New Testament Christianity: "It was necessary that Jesus Christ come to earth to make it understood that all members of the human species are naturally alike and equal" (413).[81] But while he is explicit in affirming that Jesus gave the principle of equality its historical impetus, Tocqueville does not also attribute to Christianity the triumph of democratic freedom or individual liberty, which he ultimately traces in Volume II to the Cartesian "philosophical method" of the European Enlightenment (403–407). As if to underscore this distinction, in Volume II Tocqueville will refer to Christianity as "the most precious inheritance from aristocratic centuries" (519), one that democrats should strive to preserve for the sublime benefits and the salutary restraints it provides to liberty. Much like Habermas has concluded in our day and age, Tocqueville teaches that a healthy democracy must nourish itself at the foot of two streams, one profane or rational and one sacred or religious. But unlike Habermas, Tocqueville shows that while these two streams may converge as tributaries that support equality, their contributions to democracy are fundamentally distinct.

But can the uneasy alliance of orthodoxy and republicanism that Tocqueville uncovered in New England Puritanism sustain itself in the post-Enlightenment democratic age? And, furthermore, how could a modern, commercial liberal democracy that Tocqueville encountered on his visit to America in the early nineteenth century actually be said to have emerged from Christianity? Instead of answering these questions directly, Tocqueville brings the reader into a grand historical experiment, which he himself never explicitly identifies with the Enlightenment in Volume I of *Democracy*. By showing the emergence of democracy in its incipient form from within Puritan Christianity, Tocqueville lets the reader experience its transformation *between* the two volumes of *Democracy*. In the extensive notes to Volume I of *Democracy*, Tocqueville acknowledges that "the Puritan rigor that presided at the birth of English colonies has already been much weakened" (680). In the same note, Tocqueville also draws the reader's attention to the unenforced sumptuary laws that remained on the books in the 1830s, and he highlights the degree to which Puritan austerity had been corrupted by the spirit of commercialism.[82] Similarly, Volume II begins with the very different political situation in which Christianity finds itself in nineteenth-century Jacksonian America, after the triumph of Jeffersonian and Madisonian disestablishment (a historical fact that Tocqueville's narrative conveniently suppresses or at least glides over).[83] There Tocqueville is explicit about the Cartesian rationalist method of American citizens (403–407) and about their commercial spirit, and he does not shy away from spotlighting the unmistakable effects these forces wield on American Christianity (417–426). As I show in the next section, this method of presentation allows Tocqueville to gently reveal how the Enlightenment and modern democracy transform religion. But with the Puritan founding in mind, which Tocqueville claimed contained "the key to almost the whole work," Tocqueville's indirect mode of presentation invites his readers to test the civic effects of the Enlightenment's religious project from the perspective of democracy itself.

Religious Transformation and Democracy's Harmonization of Heaven and Earth

Next to each religion is a political opinion that is joined to it by affinity. Allow the human mind to follow its tendency and it will regulate political society and the divine city in a uniform manner; it will seek, if I dare say it, to harmonize the earth with the heaven.

—Tocqueville, Democracy in America, 275

When Tocqueville reconsiders the theme of religion in the penultimate chapter of Volume I, he highlights a development that the Puritans could hardly have anticipated, and one that surely disrupted their theological-political experiment: he reports that Catholics have started arriving in America, especially Catholics form Ireland, and claims that they are prospering and winning converts to their faith within the budding religious pluralism fostered by American disestablishment (275–277). Tocqueville's discussion of American Catholicism occurs in a section entitled "On Religion Considered as a Political Institution," which lays the groundwork for his famous thesis that religion prospers in America and succeeds at contributing to its political and moral life, not in spite of but because of separation of church and state: "Religion, which, among Americans, never mixes directly in the government of society, should . . . be considered as the first of their political institutions; for if it does not give them a taste for freedom, it singularly facilities their use of it" (280). In the same chapter, Tocqueville deplores the fusion between Catholicism and French aristocracy in the old regime as an "accidental" cause through which the Catholic Church squandered its legitimate appeal by becoming a political enemy of equality. He suggests that disestablishment is the "natural state of religion" that allows faith to preserve its authority in the democratic age by drawing on the "sentiments, passions, and instincts" that are naturally inscribed in the human soul (285), an important lesson that he hopes French Catholics will take away from his analysis of America's religious harmony (286–288). These pages of Tocqueville's narrative are usually regarded as containing his fullest statement on the inherent compatibility of Christianity and (secular) democracy, and the picture that Tocqueville paints is so optimistic that both liberals and conservatives are drawn to it for arguments in defense of separation of church and state.[84]

What has garnered less attention, however, is the more ambivalent side of Tocqueville's account, which is only subtly hinted at in Volume I, but which receives a much fuller expression in Volume II. Although the latter volume contains some of Tocqueville's most famous prophetic ideas about democracy (especially on individualism, 482–489; civic associational life, 489–492; and self-interest well understood, 500–506), its discussions about democracy's effects on religion have not been fully appreciated. This is puzzling because the tendencies in American religiosity that Tocqueville foretells in Volume II anticipate with uncanny accuracy some of the key findings of contemporary social science and sociology of religion. In short, Tocqueville predicts the individualization of American religiosity, and the weakening or the erosion of theological boundaries that distinguished Christian denominations (407–410, 417–426). Although they precede present-day sociological studies by a century and a half, Tocqueville's findings are consistent with Alan Wolfe's important study of middle-class American religiosity, which found that believers in America tend to "impose their individualism on religious beliefs rather than the other way around."[85] As I show below, Tocqueville saw with surprising clarity that instead of fostering deep diversity, democratic pluralism would work to homogenize American religious beliefs by harmonizing "the earth with the heaven" (275). Tocqueville would therefore not be surprised by the recent finding by Putnam and Campbell that Americans embrace a common religious metaphysics in spite of their differing faith traditions, and that they "believe that Heaven is not reserved for those who share their religious faith."[86] This underappreciated side of Tocqueville is especially instructive for us today because, unlike many contemporary sociologists, Tocqueville does not simply celebrate these developments, and his account is complicated by his reservations about the profound spiritual and civic costs through which these changes are purchased. When Tocqueville's defense of disestablishment in Volume I is read in light of his account of religious life in America in Volume II (a theme that Tocqueville elucidates in greater detail in a shockingly revealing letter to his friend Louis de Kergorlay), there is good reason to conclude that Tocqueville had a much more reserved evaluation of this transformation than is usually thought.

It is well known that Tocqueville visited America at the height of the Second Great Awakening, a period of recurring Protestant revivals that began in the late 1790s and eventually supplied much of the moral fervor for the abolitionist cause during the antebellum and the Civil War years. No wonder, then, that Tocqueville claims in Volume I that "on my arrival in the United States it was the religious aspect of the country that first struck my eye" (282). The firsthand encounter with America's religious vibrancy, moreover, provides Tocqueville with the empirical basis for a reevaluation of Enlightenment rationalism and its secular project. Even as some of the most progressive thinkers in postrevolutionary France took for granted that Christianity was an enemy of political freedom that was destined to be vanquished by rationalism, Tocqueville argues that the assumptions undergirding the Enlightenment project were far from self-evident and its results far from conclusive: "The philosophers of the Eighteenth century," Tocqueville writes, "explained the gradual weakening of beliefs in an altogether simple fashion. Religious zeal, they said, will be extinguished as freedom and enlightenment increase" (282). The situation in America exploded this assumption: America, as Tocqueville describes it, is simultaneously "the most enlightened and the freest" of nations and "the place where the Christian religion has kept the greatest real power over men's souls, and nothing better demonstrates how useful and natural it is to man" (278). Tocqueville claims that the source of America's religious vibrancy is to be found in its religious disestablishment, a theory that he reports is proffered not only by average citizens, but also by priests of all denominations: "I did not encounter a single man, priest or laymen, who did not come to accord on this point," and "all attributed the peaceful dominion that religion exercises in their country principally to the complete separation of church and state" (283).

The paradox, however, is that by the time we reach Volume II, Tocqueville gradually discloses to the reader that the simple recipe for America's religious flourishing, through which "religion itself has so to speak set its own limits" in politics (406), has counterintuitive and troubling consequences. In Volume II, the reader encounters religion voluntarily surrendering a great deal of its direct influence to the pressures of majority opinion—not only over political affairs (as Volume I would seem to suggest), but even over the domain of morality, theology, and public opinion itself![87] Thus, while in Volume I Tocqueville optimistically hypothesized that "it could happen that in diminishing the apparent force of a religion one came to increase its real power" through disestablishment, in Volume II he paints a very different picture. What Tocqueville had initially presented as the prudent withdrawal of religion from politics, through which it preserved its power to "purify" and "restrain" democracy's dangerous passions by imposing "a salutary yoke on the intellect" (418–419), begins to come into sight as the first step in a profound and irresistible democratic transformation of religion. It turns out that "for religions to be able . . . to maintain themselves in democratic centuries, they must not only confine themselves carefully to the sphere of religious matters; their power depends even more on the nature of the beliefs they profess, the external forms they adopt, and the obligations they impose" (420). As he explains in the second chapter of Volume II, the principal source of *all* dogmatic *beliefs* in a democratic age is public opinion, and religion must necessarily confront, and ultimately compromise with, this irresistible force (407–410, 422–423). Democracy, Tocqueville will now go on to reveal, will not leave religion intact, and its tendency to reshape beliefs in its own image will mean that religion's emphasis on theological dogma, transcendent spiritualism, and moral duty become attenuated.

Nothing illustrates this transformation more effectively than Tocqueville's account of the disposition that American preachers embrace with respect to the democratic passion for material well-being. One of the chief pathologies of democracy, according to Tocqueville, and one of the main psychological engines that reinforces the drift toward democratic individualism, is its moral elevation of the quest for material well-being and prosperity (506–509). What Tocqueville finds most troubling about the "taste for material enjoyments" is not so much its moral effects, but rather its all-absorbing character: "the care of satisfying the least needs of the body . . . preoccupies minds universally" (506), and "in striving to seize them," democratic men lose "sight of the more precious goods that make the glory and the greatness of the human species" (509). Thus the threat posed by the obsessive quest for prosperity is similar to the dangers that Tocqueville uncovers in individualism—both suck human beings into a vortex that disassociates them from society, and thus both threaten to dry up "the source of public virtues" that are necessary for democratic self-government (482–484). Tocqueville stresses that "the greatest advantage of religions" is that they "inspire wholly contrary instincts," and therefore offer the hope of moderating this democratic passion for well-being: "There is no religion that does not place man's desires beyond and above earthly goods," nor one "that does not impose on each some duties toward the human species or in common with it" (419). But how effective can religion be at actually moderating democracy's materialistic and individualistic tendencies once it has to contend with democratic opinion? A few pages later, Tocqueville offers a rather underwhelming conclusion, admitting that "a religion that undertook to destroy this mother passion would in the end be destroyed by it" (422). But Tocqueville continues to insist that this does not mean that religion becomes a mere rubber stamp of democratic instincts. Instead, as Tocqueville indicates, religion in America is compelled to discover democratic means of fulfilling its moderating function: since they cannot "tear" men away from the quest for economic well-being to the contemplation of "the future life" (423), the American clergy prudently confine themselves to convincing men "to enrich themselves only by honest means" by appealing to their self-interest (cf. 275–288 with 417–424 and 504–506).

We are now in a better position to understand the paradoxical nature of the consensus that Tocqueville uncovers beneath America's religious pluralism, a consensus that many scholars refer to as an American "civil religion." Tocqueville had claimed in Volume I that disestablishment allows Americans to preserve their religious pluralism without sacrificing the distinctiveness and the religious dogmas of different sects: "There is an innumerable multitude of sects in the United States. All differ in the worship one must render to the Creator, but all agree on the duties of man toward one another. *Each sect therefore adores God in its manner, but all sects preach the same morality in the name of God*" (278, emphasis added). But now in Volume II it is becoming clear that democracy has a deeply homogenizing effect on religious sects, not only in the area of morality, but in ceremonies, practices, and even theology as well. The morality that all (or, as we will see, nearly all) religions in America share in common, Tocqueville indicates, is in essence the liberal and democratic morality, and this consensus is achieved by sacrificing ceremonial practices and institutional rigidity at the altar of public opinion and its democratic preference for simplicity: "I have not seen a country where Christianity wraps itself less in forms, practices, and [representational] figures than the United States, and presents ideas more clearly, simply, and generally to the human mind. Although Christians in America are divided into a multitude of sects, they all perceive their religion in the same light" (423). Thus, although it would be impossible to "maintain a religion without external practices" that impose an order on believers (421), Tocqueville's advice is that "in the centuries we are entering" the best course of action is for religion to simplify its practices, retaining "only what is absolutely necessary for the perpetuation of the dogma itself, which is the substance of religions" (422). This is an area where Catholicism will have to Protestantize (at least to some extent) if it is to survive in democracy: as he forebodingly predicts in a footnote, Catholicism will confront democratic pressures to make tremendous concessions that could threaten its very essence, for in the Catholic faith "ceremonies . . . are inherent in the very substance of belief" and "the form and the foundation are often so tightly united that they are one" (422).[88]

In spite of this subtle admission, throughout Volume II Tocqueville continues to present not just Protestantism, but even and especially traditional Catholicism as a sustainable religious option that can attract believers in democratic centuries (424–426).[89] Amazingly, he claims that, although "men living in democratic centuries are . . . strongly inclined to eschew all religious authority" (424), and "while several doctrines and usages of the Roman Church astonish them," they still feel a "secret admiration for its government, and its unity attracts them" (424). Scholars have interpreted this as Tocqueville's rhetorical effort to convince European Catholics to emulate their American counterparts, not only by accepting democracy's triumph, but also by evolving theologically in the direction of reformed Protestantism.[90] But when we peer behind Tocqueville's public pronouncements, we can glimpse that for Tocqueville the case of American Catholicism points to a deeper theoretical tension within the transformation of religion than *Democracy in America* presents, a tension that Tocqueville prudently obscures in his narrative but which may reveal an important but underappreciated reason why Americans may benefit from the theological and moral discipline of a traditional religion like Catholicism. In a letter to Louis de Kergorlay, Tocqueville again observes the phenomenon of the "practical exactitude that accompanies the practice of religion in America," but here he is much more explicit in spotlighting the growing religious indifference that he perceives lurking beneath America's melting pot of religious pluralism: while in America "opinion . . . compels everyone to appear at church," nevertheless, Tocqueville observes, "there is a great store of doubt and indifference hidden underneath these external forms" (48).[91] Behind this surface religiosity, Tocqueville observes, "faith is evidently inert": "enter the churches (I mean the Protestant ones) and you hear them speak of morality; of dogma not a word, nothing that could reveal the hint of dissidence" (48). Having reshaped itself in the image of Lockean Christianity, American Protestantism, in Tocqueville's estimation, is content to preach an easygoing faith that tests neither the beliefs nor the commitment of its followers, so much so that Tocqueville can say that that "religion does not move people deeply" in America (49).

In an astonishing passage in the same letter, Tocqueville admits that the liberal Protestantism of nineteenth-century America is an unsustainable halfway house on the road to deism: "It seems clear to me that reformed religion is a kind of compromise, a sort of *representative monarchy* in matters of religion which can well fill an era, serve as a passage from one state to another, but which cannot constitute a definite state itself and which is approaching its end" (50). Here, however, Tocqueville describes the place of Catholicism in the "milieu" of American religious pluralism in terms that are quite different from the presentation he gave in *Democracy in America*, for he stresses that American Catholicism is so far from being compatible with democracy and toleration that it finds itself as a reluctant participant in a regime that it is too weak to overthrow, but whose ranks are swelling with new converts who are both "poor" and "full of zeal": American Catholics, Tocqueville notes, "are making use of the tolerance of their ancient adversaries, but . . . are staying basically as intolerant as they have always been, as intolerant in a word as people who *believe*" (50, emphasis in the original). As for the future of reformed Protestantism, whose ministers he describes as "in effect businessmen of religion," Tocqueville predicts a continuing doctrinal decline into Unitarianism, followed by further degeneration, until that moment when it will collapse into outright deism: "On the borders of Protestantism is a sect which is Christian only in name; these are *Unitarians* . . . which is to say . . . those who deny the Trinity and recognize only one God, [among whom] are some who see in Jesus Christ only an angle, others a prophet, finally others a philosopher like Socrates. These are pure deists" (51). Thus, while he is never fully explicit in *Democracy in America* about the deepest theoretical reasons for his preference for Catholicism as a religion that can address the ills of the democratic age, in the letter to Kergorlay Tocqueville puts his cards on the table, indicating that the profound paradox that a religion like Catholicism presents to democracy is that its peculiar capacity to enliven the souls of democratic men may be inherently inseparable from its authoritarian and intolerant dimensions:

One religion [based on authority] works powerfully on the will, it dominates the imagination, it gives rise to real and profound beliefs; but it divides the human race into the fortunate and the damned, creates divisions on earth that should exist only in the other life, the child of intolerance and fanaticism. The other preaches tolerance, attaches itself to reason, in effect its symbol; it obtains no power, it is an inert work, without strength and almost without life.[92]

This assessment of the relative merits of Catholicism and Protestantism fundamentally distinguishes Tocqueville not only from Jefferson, but also from Rousseau. Neither of the two models of "civil religion" that latter French philosopher recommended—the civic piety of the *Social Contract* and the humanistic spiritualism of the "Confession of Faith of Sayvoyard Vicar" in *Emile*—reflect the same Tocquevillian preference for traditional (Catholic) Christianity as an antidote to democratic pathologies.[93] Indeed, while from Tocqueville's perspective deism may satisfy the open-minded curiosities of the educated elite and the upper crusts of society, it can neither address the deepest longings of the vast majority of human beings nor provide the religious foundation that a morality suited for democratic liberty requires. Tocqueville goes so far as to claim that "what is called natural religion could suffice for the superior classes of society, provided that the belief in the two or three great truths that it teaches is real and that something of an external religion mixes and ostensibly unites men in the public profession of these truth" (52). However, the Enlightenment hope that such natural religion, divorced from both revelation and from a belief in an immaterial existence beyond this life, could suffice for most human beings Tocqueville judges to be ill-founded. This may explain Tocqueville's counterintuitive but eerily accurate prediction that in democratic times people would increasingly gravitate toward the believing and the unbelieving, the religiously traditional and the secularly progressive, poles: "I am inclined to believe that . . . our posterity will tend more and more to a division into only two parts, some relinquishing Christianity entirely and others returning to the Church of Rome."

Deism, in Tocqueville's assessment, is destined to leave a spiritual void in the democratic soul, a void that cannot simply go unfilled for too long. Thus Tocqueville argues to Kergorlay that it is "indisputable that political liberty has sometimes deadened and sometimes enlivened religious passions."[94] The same reasoning also accounts for Tocqueville's fear in *Democracy in America* that modern liberal societies may increasingly confront outbreaks of spiritualism and even religious fanaticism: "If the minds of the great ma-jority of the human race were ever concentrated on the search for material goods alone," Tocqueville warns, "one can expect that an enormous reaction would be produced in the souls of some men" (510). These agitated indi-viduals, Tocqueville continues, would be moved to "throw themselves head over heels into the world of spirits" in an uncontrollable counterreaction to what they regard as the spiritual impoverishment imposed upon them by the democratic way of life. It would seem, therefore, that Tocqueville's deep-est criticism of the Enlightenment effort to liberate human beings from religiosity leads him to the conclusion that such an effort could very well backfire, producing a paradoxical increase of religious fanaticism as a reac-tion to the world that rationalism tried to bring into existence.

Conclusion

As I argued in Chapter 2, both John Locke and Thomas Jefferson envi-sioned that the triumph of liberalism and toleration would go hand in hand with the diffusion of a "religion of reason," a theologically easygoing form of Christianity in the case of Locke and a politically responsible form of de-ism in the case of Jefferson.[95] Although various forms of deism and natural religion have continued to appeal to segments of the American imagina-tion, the history of America's religious revivals both past and present should clearly qualify Jefferson's overconfidence in the prospects of an American public enlightenment. Instead of a thoroughgoing secularization or even the triumph of a pure natural religion, Tocqueville's prediction of an unre-solved tug-of-war between traditional religion and various forms of deism has continued to characterize the American religious landscape, perhaps to a greater extent than Tocqueville thought would have been possible in the post-Enlightenment age. To take just the most obvious example, although it is indisputable that American Catholicism has democratized, especially after Vatican II, whether that democratization should be understood as sim-ply a Protestantization is an open and uncertain question. But in light of Tocqueville's assessment of Protestantism, it is likely that what he would actually celebrate about twentieth-century American Catholicism is that its relatively modest successes at reconciling itself with democracy have not been purchased through the same kinds of radical concessions of theologi-cal dogma that lead Protestantism down the road to Unitarianism. This may help explain the uneasy place that even post–Vatican II Catholicism (along with Evangelicalism) continues to occupy in American politics, and why its theological and moral concerns, often thought to be too rigid and dogmatic, continue to butt heads with the secular undercurrents of American public opinion.

Although Tocqueville and Habermas both recognize the need for religion in a democracy, Tocqueville is much more effective than Habermas (or other heirs of the Enlightenment) at pointing us in the direction of a perennial tension between democracy's spiritual and moral requirements and its commitment to rationalism and tolerance. Habermas, as we saw, is too much of a thorough rationalist—in the words of Weber he describes himself as "religiously unmusical"—to accept anything but a religion that has been reinterpreted by reason. Unlike Tocqueville, he appears to be unwilling to live in the midst of the continuing dissonance that the persistence of religion may nurture in democratic life. Precisely for this reason, Paolo Flores d'Arcais has concluded that in his mature writings Habermas has been trying to square an impossible circle: "upholding liberal-democratic principles according to a demanding republican scheme . . . while, at the same time, recognizing religious 'reasons' as such (the argumentations and the political motivations that have recourse to God) not only as legitimate but, indeed, as useful and, ultimately, essential elements of liberal-democratic sociality."[96] Tocqueville reminds us that although the democratic mind may balk at such inconsistencies—"one of the most ordinary weaknesses of the human intellect is to seek to reconcile contrary principles and to purchase peace at the expense of logic"—some circles ultimately cannot be squared. He therefore points us in the direction of ineluctable trade-offs between the competing goods of human nature that democracy discloses "in plain sight," and one of these trade-offs is between the vibrancy of religious beliefs and the democratic emphasis on toleration. As Tocqueville himself declared to his friend and correspondent Arthur de Gobineau, a certain kind of intolerance may be an inherent feature of any vibrant religious outlook:

> There are . . . certain doctrines that are necessarily part and parcel of certain religions, . . . and their consequence is that a certain amount of intolerance with the contemporary absence of which you seem so satisfied. These doctrines are inherent in all religions . . . and they are necessarily inseparable from all the good they bring us. Yet I am convinced that the eventual damage to human morality thereby caused is far less than what would result from moral systems that have emancipated themselves from religion altogether. The longer I live the less I think that the peoples of the world can ever separate themselves from a

positive religion; and this growing conviction makes me less concerned with these inconveniences that are eventually inherent in every religion, including the best.[97]

As a partisan of the Enlightenment, Gobineau thought that Christianity could eventually be transcended in favor of an altogether secularized political order. But Tocqueville reminds Gobineau that the legal system regulates "matters of daily life" and so forms "the general temper of habits and ideas," a task for which he believes Christianity is especially well suited to supplement the modern society and its laws. For the purpose of shaping and sustaining society's mores, Tocqueville contends, laws, "and especially religious laws," are so necessary that "there never has been a people of any importance that could do without them." In this exchange Tocqueville unequivocally rejects the assumptions of modern secularization theory, which holds that as society becomes increasingly modernized and rationalized, its premodern religious capital will gradually diminish and eventually evaporate altogether: "I know that there are many who now think that one day they may be able to do without this regimen, and every morning they keep looking eagerly for this new day. I think they are looking in vain. I should be even more inclined to believe in the coming of some new religion than in the continuation of the prosperity and greatness of modern societies without religion." In this assessment, Tocqueville points to his abiding disagreement not only with the Enlightenment strategy of John Locke, but also with the contemporary liberalism of Jürgen Habermas and John Rawls.

TOLERATION, DEMOCRATIC RELIGION, AND AMERICA'S CIVIC LIFE

Tocqueville's political science helps us confront more clearly the central theme of this book: the inescapable trade-off that separation of church and state and toleration bring about vis-à-vis religion. Democracy, it would appear, ineluctably confronts religion with a paradoxical choice: religion can either accept the Lockean definition of orthodoxy—that "every church is orthodox unto itself"—or suffer the fate of ostracism and marginalization at the hands of majoritarian public opinion. Religion must either embrace toleration by declaring itself indifferent to theology, or be deemed an intolerant faith. To maintain its "moral empire," Tocqueville argues that religion must transform itself into the image of democracy, thus accepting not only the supremacy of individual reason (and through it the authority of the democratic majority), but also the concern for material well-being.[1] While he acknowledges that a religion so transformed will no longer pose a peculiar challenge to democracy that traditional orthodoxy (whether Puritan or Catholic) once did, Tocqueville also reminds us of the unavoidable costs of such a transformation for democracy's civic and spiritual health. As we saw, for Tocqueville, a thoroughly Lockeanized democratic religion risks being too morally easygoing to act as a civic force in democracy and too spiritually impoverished to satisfy the human longing for immortality that Tocqueville uncovered as the psychological root of human religiosity. Tocqueville's pessimism about democracy's transformation of religion should therefore prompt us to critically reconsider the costs and benefits of the Lockean project of religious reform.

Even though American Christianity shows unmistakable imprints of the transformation that Locke hoped to bring about and that Tocqueville feared, contemporary political science often operates under a blind spot to these trade-offs. Consider for instance the findings presented in Putnam and Campbell's *American Grace*.[2] In attempting to explain the puzzle of American religiosity—"How can religious pluralism coexist with religious polarization?" (4)—the authors implicitly accept the objectives of Locke's liberal project and its "reasonable" form of Christianity. According to their study, the source of America's exceptional interreligious tolerance lies in the "fluidity" of the religious habits that pluralism and separation of church and state nurture among Americans, which the authors dub the "religious churn": "Religions compete, adapt, and evolve as individual Americans freely move from one congregation to another, and even from one religion to another" (16). Americans move easily between religions, and nearly half of all Americans depart from their parents' faith traditions either through intermarriage or a lapse into nonbelief. As a result, "religious identity in America has become less inherited and fixed and more chosen and changeable" (135). "The malleable nature of American religion" contributes to interreligious mingling and harmony (5). Because it ensures that "nearly all Americans are acquainted with people of a different religious background" (5), religious fluidity increases interreligious tolerance by linking Americans in relationships that cut across theological boundaries—a phenomenon that the authors call "America's grace" (550).

While Putnam and Campbell are quick to celebrate the individualistic trends in American religiosity as drivers of increasing tolerance, their findings also point to the limits of that Lockean approach.[3] To begin with, religion remains a powerful and enduring civic force in American politics, to a degree that would surprise John Locke just as much as it would Thomas Jefferson: "in every major national survey we have found . . . religiously based social networks lead people not just inward to the church but outward to the wider secular community, in terms of giving, volunteering, and participating in civic life" (476).[4] It is this remarkably Tocquevillian finding that religious believers enjoy a civic advantage in "good neighborliness" that accounts for much of the buzz that *American Grace* has garnered: "religious Americans are up to twice as active civically as secular Americans," an edge reflected in higher levels of local political engagement, associational involvement, and club membership in both religious and secular organizations (454–457). The communitarian dimensions of faith are also reflected in dramatically higher levels of generosity and philanthropy among churchgoers: religious citizens are more than twice as likely as secular Americans to volunteer to help the needy, even after controlling for such predictors of charity as education and income; their annual giving to charitable causes is also "vastly larger," and the authors stress that this philanthropy goes beyond religious organizations, "so that religious people give more to both religious and nonreligious causes."[5] In short, *American Grace* demonstrates that religion remains a uniquely powerful source of democracy's "social capital" that secular culture has so far failed to replicate.

Is it possible that in spite of its Lockeanization, American Christianity could still retain the positive civic role that Tocqueville celebrated in nine-teenth-century America religion? Can religion maintain its communitarian advantages while becoming more and more Lockean? If we dig beneath their surface narrative we see that the picture of American religiosity is more ambiguous, and that there is less harmony than may be at first suggested by America's exceptional interreligious tolerance. For one, the civic edge that the religiously committed enjoy over their secular counterparts correlates with what the authors describe as higher levels of *moral* "intolerance" among the former, a fact that Putnam and Campbell find simultaneously troubling and hard to explain (488–500). What the authors actually succeed at showing is that although the vast majority of American believers have largely embraced Locke's tolerationist theology—they profess a belief in "an equal opportunity heaven" that includes not just Christians but Muslims and Jews as well (535–540)—they are less flexible and more judgmental than are secular citizens on certain cultural and moral issues. Thus in spite of the theological tolerance between religious groups, overall religious believers tend to take strong moral stands on such issues as gay marriage, abortion, and atheism in schools—a moral absolutism that the authors find hard to accept but which would not surprise Tocqueville. When they combine this finding with the greater civic involvement of religious believers in public life, Putnam and Campbell have arrived at the brink of a potential tension or trade-off between religiously inspired democratic engagement (which they champion) and the moral seriousness which even a relatively tolerant religion continues to demand (which they deplore).

Moreover, in their zeal to encourage a "faith without fanaticism" and a religion that is morally liberal (246–252, 257–258, 547), the authors end up neglecting the role that traditional theology may play in sustaining religion's communitarian civic edge. Thus, they are content to explain the greater civic involvement of faith communities in strictly secular terms, as a function of "the network of morally freighted personal connections," that churches offer to their members "coupled with an inclination toward altruism" (492). Remarkably, they insist that theology plays little to no role in explaining this civic side of religion. What matters is not the "flavor of religious tradition," they argue, but rather the "intensity" with which people maintain church attendance and observe religious ceremonies: "It is the religious belonging that matters for neighborliness, not religious believing," the authors explain (473). On the other hand, "theology and piety and sacraments and devotion

... do not ... matter at all" (468). This approach leaves unexplored whether there is something unique about religious devotion, something especially powerful about the theological objects of its reverence, that renders faith groups so effective at directing the concerns and energies of believers outward—to saving souls, to works of charity, and to the spiritual well-being of the political community—which in large part may also give them both their civic edge or their communitarian orientation as well as their moral intransigence. Moreover, this connection between theology and civic communitarianism would also point to the why religious traditions may resist, instead of simply sanctioning, democracy's cultural currents. As the authors themselves admit, it is the theologically easygoing Mainline Protestantism whose "share of the population has been shrinking" in recent decades (17). The evangelical and theologically conservative churches, on the other hand, both thrive in numbers and succeed at cultivating the very same social networks that Putnam and Campbell celebrate throughout their work.

Although their findings show that certain theological and moral dimensions of religion, from which democracy stands to benefit so much, are in tension with the liberal commitments to toleration and individualism, Putnam and Campbell are either reluctant or unable to recognize this conclusion explicitly. This trade-off comes into sharper focus when Putnam and Campbell's recent findings on American religiosity are considered in light of Putnam's earlier work on the decline of social capital. In *Bowling Alone*, Putnam criticized individualistic currents in American culture because they weakened institutional and communal ties.[6] Putnam lamented the tendency of Americans, and baby boomers in particular, to approach their religion in the spirit of consumerism by "surfing" from one congregation to the next until they settled on a faith suitable to their individual "preferences." The big winners in this "switching game," as Putnam called it, were the religiously unaffiliated (or what scholars today refer to as the "Religious Nones"), while the big losers were traditional religious denominations, resulting in what Putnam described as a "long-run ratcheting down of religious involvement [that] has not yet run its course" (74–75). *American Grace* identifies the same "religious churn" (6–9), especially in the form of religious intermarriage (148–159), but unlike Putnam's analysis in *Bowling Alone*, it emphasizes the competing civic goods of toleration and social harmony that this religious fluidity makes possible. But if the two works are read together, a more complicated picture emerges, and although Tocqueville anticipated it in his study of American democracy, it is less than clear that Putnam and Campbell are willing to draw this conclusion: America's distinctive religious churn may actually promote interreligious tolerance *at the cost* of depressing the social capital that religion provides.

Tocqueville left us with an apparent standoff between traditional religion and democratic tolerance, and so do Putnam and Campbell in the *American Grace*, even if they are not willing to confront this standoff head-on. Although they wish to discount the role of theology in the social good that religious identity nurtures (emphasizing "altruism" and "empathy" instead), their findings sometimes belie this conclusion, and they admit that "we occasionally find trace effects of theology on people's civic behavior." After all, what distinguishes strong believers is that they are likely to possess "fundamentalist religious convictions." Precisely because they possess such strong convictions, believers are attracted to like-minded religious groups and social networks, groups that impose moral demands on their lives and in the process increase their civic involvement in democracy. It is highly doubtful if the same civic effect could be replicated on the basis of an individualized and liberalized religion. If religion is going to play the countervailing role that Habermas, Tocqueville, and to a great degree Putnam and Campbell assign it, if it is to successfully temper the drive toward uncivic individualism, then it must have some robustness, and this may necessarily involve not only theological rigidity, but even a certain degree of moral inflexibility.[7] Such a religion will make sharp truth claims about theology and morality and will maintain a critical distance from democracy's moral and cultural currents. And while its place within a liberal society will always be uneasy and disharmonious, precisely for those reasons such a religion will be uniquely effective at filling the civic void that is often nurtured by democracy.

NOTES

CHAPTER I. RELIGION AND THE POST-ENLIGHTENMENT
LIBERALISM OF JOHN RAWLS

1. FRoss Douthat, *Bad Religion: How We Became a Nation of Heretics* (New York: Free Press, 2013), 6.

2. Ibid.

3. Ibid., 16.

4. For other influential accounts that also trace the decline of American Christianity to the secularization of American culture that was precipitated by the cultural revolutions of the 1960s and 70s, see Hugo Heclo, *Christianity and American Democracy* (Cambridge, MA: Harvard University Press, 2009), and Robert Putnam and David Campbell, *American Grace: How Religion Unites and Divides Us* (New York: Simon & Schuster, 2010).

5. John Rawls, *Political Liberalism: Expanded Edition* (New York: Columbia University Press, 2005), xix. In an earlier work, Rawls states that "government is neutral between different conceptions of the good, not in the sense that there is an agreed public measure of intrinsic value or satisfaction with respect to which all these conceptions come out equal, but in the sense that they are not evaluated at all from a social standpoint," in "Social Utility and Primary Goods," in *Utilitarianism and Beyond*, ed. Amartya Sen and Bernard Williams (Cambridge, UK: Cambridge University Press, 1982), 172. The aspiration to liberal neutrality is pervasive in contemporary liberal theory. For example, Ronald Dworkin's position echoes Rawls's neutralist view: "Government must be neutral on what might be called the question of the good life," and this means that "political decisions must be, so far as is possible, independent of any particular conception of the good life, or of what gives value to life," in *A Matter of Principle* (Cambridge, MA: Harvard University Press, 1985), 191.

6. See in general Robert Audi, *Religious Commitment and Secular Reason* (Cambridge, UK: Cambridge University Press, 2000); Stephen Macedo, "In Defense of Liberal Public Reason: Are Slavery and Abortion Hard Cases?" *American Journal of Jurisprudence* 42, no. 1 (1997): 1–29; and Richard Rorty, "Religion as a Conversation-Stopper," in *Philosophy and Social Hope* (New York: Penguin Books, 1999), 168–174.

7. P. J. Weithman, *Religion and Contemporary Liberalism* (Notre Dame, IN: University of Notre Dame Press, 1997); and Weithman, *Religion and the Obligations of Citizenship* (Cambridge, UK: Cambridge University Press, 2002).

8. Christopher Eberle expresses the inclusive alternative to Rawls's restrictive position as the view that a "citizen is morally permitted to support (or oppose) a

coercive law even if she enjoys [only] a religious rationale for that law," in *Religious Conviction in Liberal Politics* (Cambridge, UK: Cambridge University Press, 2002), 10. Eberle is joined by a growing group of scholars who could be classified in the "inclusivist" camp in challenging the view that respect between fellow citizens in conditions of moral diversity requires withholding arguments based on religious views: Jeremy Waldron, "Two-Way Translation: The Ethics of Engaging with Religious Contributions in Public Deliberation," *Mercer Law Review* 63, no. 3 (2012): 845–868; Kevin Vallier, "Against Public Reason Liberalism's Accessibility Requirement," *Journal of Moral Philosophy* 8, no. 3 (2011): 366–389; Jeffrey Stout, *Democracy and Tradition* (Princeton, NJ: Princeton University Press: 2004); Michael McConnell, "Five Reasons to Reject the Claim That Religious Arguments Should Be Excluded from Democratic Deliberation," *Utah Law Review* 49 (1999): 639–657; Michael McConnell, "Secular Reason and the Misguided Attempt to Exclude Religious Argument from Democratic Deliberation," *Journal of Law, Philosophy and Culture* 2 (2007): 159–174; Michael Perry, "Religious Arguments in Public Political Debate," *Loyola of Los Angeles Law Review* 29 (1996): 1421–1458; Michael Perry, "Why Political Reliance on Religious Grounded Morality Is Not Illegitimate in a Liberal Democracy," *Wake Forest Law Review* 36, no. 2 (2001): 217–249; and Gerald F. Gaus and Kevin Vallier, "The Roles of Religious Conviction in a Publicly Justified Polity: The Implications of Convergence, Asymmetry and Political Institutions," *Philosophy & Social Criticism* 35, no. 1–2 (2009): 51–76.

9. More strident critics of "public reason," especially those who favor greater accommodation of natural law in democratic deliberation, remain aplenty. See in general Robert P. George, *In Defense of Natural Law* (Oxford: Oxford University Press, 2001), and Christopher Wolf, *Natural Law Liberalism* (Cambridge, UK: Cambridge University Press, 2006). While natural law theorists often rely on a theistic conception of man's place in the universe, they also insist that many moral truths are accessible through human reflection even without revelation.

10. Gaus and Vallier, "The Roles of Religious Conviction in a Publicly Justified Polity." Gaus and Vallier reject what they call the "error of consensus" implicit in the exclusivist Rawlsian view. But note that even as they distinguish their "convergence" model (which is friendlier to pluralistic voices in deliberation) from the standard "consensus" model of public reasoning, they still view deliberation as a process that leads to a political consensus around "common laws": "The consensus conception of public justification is hostile to invoking religious reasoning because it is hostile to any genuinely pluralistic reasoning in public justification. Contrast this to the convergence conception according to which members of the public may arrive at common laws by reasoning based on diverse values and concerns. Here pluralistic reasoning is the very basis of justification" (58).

11. Alan Wolfe, *One Nation, After All* (New York: Viking, 1998); Wolfe, *The Transformation of American Religion: How We Actually Live Our Faith* (Chicago: University of Chicago Press, 2003); Robert P. Kraynak, *Christian Faith and Modern*

Democracy: God and Politics in a Fallen World (Notre Dame, IN: University of Notre Dame Press, 2001); and Putnam and Campbell, *American Grace.*

12. Heclo, *Christianity and American Democracy*; Stout, *Democracy and Tradition*; Patrick Deneen, *Democratic Faith* (Princeton, NJ: Princeton University Press, 2005), 50–65; Jon A. Shields, *Democratic Virtues of the Christian Right* (Princeton, NJ: Princeton University Press, 2009).

13. Putnam and Campbell, *American Grace*, 4–6, 134–160, 493–550, 504, 528–529, 534.

14. Ibid., 525–540. In their reading, pluralism generates interreligious interaction, which in turn animates the logic of religious tolerance: America's thriving pluralism has ensured that instead of "cocooning into isolated religious communities, Americans have become increasingly likely to work with, live alongside, and marry people of other religions—or people with no religion at all. In doing so, they have come to accept people with a religious background different from theirs. It is difficult to demonize the religion, or lack of religion, of people you know and, especially, those you love," in Putnam and Campbell, *American Grace*, 17.

15. Wolfe, *One Nation, After All*, 298–299.

16. Putnam and Campbell, *American Grace*, 547.

17. Ibid., 540.

18. Robert Putnam, *Bowling Alone: The Collapse and Revival of the American Community* (New York: Touchstone Books by Simon & Schuster), 2001.

19. Rawls, *Political Liberalism.*

20. Ibid., 36, 144.

21. Ibid., ix.

22. Ibid., xxvi.

23. Ibid., xviii.

24. "Which moral judgments are true, all things considered, is not a matter for political liberalism, as it approaches all questions from within its own limited point of view" (ibid., xx).

25. Richard Rorty, *Objectivism, Relativism, and Truth: Philosophical Papers*, vol. 1 (Cambridge, UK: Cambridge University Press, 1990), 181; John Rawls, "Justice as Fairness: Political Not Metaphysical," *Philosophy & Public Affairs* 14, no. 3 (1985): 230.

26. Here we see that although Rorty shares Rawls's "postmodernism" about rationalism, he concludes that Rawls's own principles dictate that liberalism should be more forthcoming about the fact that it promotes "light-mindedness" about religious and philosophical questions. *Diversity and Distrust: Civic Education in a Multicultural Democracy* (Cambridge, MA: Harvard University Press, 2000), Stephen Macedo also wants to take liberalism beyond Rawls's neutrality: he wants a "liberalism with spine" (5) and one that more explicitly embraces its religiously "transformative ambitions" (16). For Macedo, not only does liberalism reshape the nonliberal perspectives, including religion, but its political viability ultimately depends upon the success of that liberalizing process.

27. Rawls formulates the same duality between a modus vivendi and an over-lapping consensus in the Introduction to Political Liberalism: the clash between the Catholics and Protestants in the Reformation was driven by their appeal to "the conflicting authorities of Church or Bible," which meant that "there was no resolution between them, as their competing transcendent elements do not admit of compromise. Their mortal combat can be moderated only by circumstance and exhaustion, or by equal liberty of conscience and freedom of thought. Circum-stances and exhaustion lead to a modus vivendi; equal liberty of conscience and freedom of thought . . . may sometimes lead to the more hopeful possibilities of a constitutional, and then to an overlapping, consensus," xxxviii–xxxix.

28. Parts III and IV of Hobbes's *Leviathan* are titled, respectively, "Of a Chris-tian Common-wealth" and "Of the Kingdom of Darkness" and contain Hobbes's voluminous biblical exegesis aimed at demonstrating that Christianity teaches obedience to the established sovereign.

29. John Locke, *Essay Concerning Human Understanding*, IV.19.14, in *The Works of John Locke, in Nine Volumes: The Twelfth Edition*, vols. 1 and 2 (London: Riving-ton), 1824.

30. Judd J. Owen, *Religion and the Demise of Liberal Rationalism* (Chicago: Uni-versity of Chicago Press, 2001), 114.

31. Owen calls this admission "explosive": "since the liberal state must act, and since it cannot take any religious prescription as authoritative for its actions, the liberal state in principle denies that there are any true, politically relevant religious prescriptions. Liberalism rests on a theological premise," ibid., 119.

32. Rawls is similarly ambivalent about Lincoln's "Second Inaugural Address," which Jeffrey Stout describes as "perhaps the highest ethical achievement of any public speaker in U.S. history" (Jeffrey Stout, *Democracy and Tradition*, 69): "I in-cline to think Lincoln does not violate public reason as I have discussed it and as it applied in his day—*whether in ours is another matter*" (ibid., 254, emphasis added). Remarkably, in order to justify its inclusion within his restrictive view of public reason, Rawls has to embrace the unpersuasive position that "what [Lincoln] says [in his Second Inaugural] has no implications bearing on constitutional essentials or matters of basic justice" (ibid., 254). As Ronald Thiemann points out, "surely this cannot be a correct historical interpretation of this address, particularly when it is taken in the larger context of Lincoln's public discussion of slavery throughout his presidency," in *Religion in Public Life* (Washington, DC: Georgetown University Press, 1996), 87. For a more extensive account of the challenge that Lincoln poses to Rawls, see my treatment of Lincoln's religious statesmanship in Chapter 4.

33. Stout, *Democracy and Tradition*, 69.

34. Ibid., 70.

35. Rawls, *Political Liberalism*, 249–251.

36. Stout, *Democracy and Tradition*, 69.

37. Ibid.

38. Rawls, *Political Liberalism*, 217.

39. Michael Sandel, *Justice: What's the Right Thing to Do?* (New York: Farrar, Strauss and Giroux, 2009), 251.

CHAPTER 2. BARACK OBAMA'S CIVIC FAITH: A POST-CHRISTIAN
CIVIL RELIGION OR RAWLS'S PUBLIC REASON?

1. Barack Obama, Remarks by the President at National Prayer Breakfast, February 3, 2011.

2. Charlton C. Copeland, "God-Talk in the Age of Obama: Theology and Religious Political Engagement," *Denver University Law Review* 86 (2009): 664.

3. John Rawls, *Political Liberalism: Expanded Edition* (New York: Columbia University Press, 2005); and Richard Rorty, *Contingency, Irony, Solidarity* (Cambridge, UK: Cambridge University Press, 1989), 45.

4. Barack Obama "First Inaugural Address," Washington, DC, January 20, 2009. http://www.whitehouse.gov/blog/inaugural-address.

5. Robert Bellah famously argued that the American "civil religion" was "selectively derived from Christianity" and was reflected in presidential acknowledgments of a ruling God that "is actively interested and involved in history, with a special concern for America," in "Civil Religion in America," *Dædalus* 96, no. 1 (1967): 1–21. For Bellah, the archetype of American civil religion is Abraham Lincoln, whose Gettysburg Address constitutes "part of the Lincolnian 'New Testament' among the civil scriptures" that define the meaning of America's national aspirations. But the legion of leading Americans who subscribed to the civic faith that Bellah identified also includes George Washington, Thomas Jefferson, and Martin Luther King, Jr. Although they may have diverged in their private religious beliefs, all of these statesmen employed religious rhetoric to instill in Americans a shared reverence for its founding principles of liberty and equality—principles whose rational self-evidence they claimed were also reinforced by the sanctions of God. For arguments that Obama is somehow working within Bellah's "civil religion" paradigm, see David Fontana, "Obama and the American Civil Religion from the Political Left," *George Washington International Law Review* 41 (2010): 909–912; Frederick Gedicks, "American Civil Religion: An Idea Whose Time Is Past," ibid., 41 (2010): 891–908; Philip S. Gorski, "Barack Obama and Civil Religion," *Political Power and Social Theory* 22 (2011): 177–211; and Dylan Weller, "Godless Patriots: Toward a New American Civil Religion," *Polity* 45, no. 3 (2013): 372–392.

6. George Lakoff argued in his *New York Times* best seller, *Don't Think of an Elephant: Know Your Values and Frame the Debate* (White River Junction, VT: Chelsea Green Publishing, 2004), that Democrats regularly lost the religious and "value" voters to Republicans due to a failure to employ appropriate rhetorical techniques. On the attempts to bridge this "God gap" by the Democratic Party, see Corwin Smidt et al., *The Disappearing God Gap? Religion in the 2008 Presidential Election*

(Oxford, UK: Oxford University Press, 2010); Gwyneth I. Williams, "Democrats Embrace God: An Unqualified Blessing?" *Forum on Public Policy: A Journal of the Oxford Round Table* (2007), http://forumonpublicpolicy.com/papersum07.html. On Obama's relatively successful effort to bridge this gap in the 2008 presidential election, see Gastón Espinosa, *Religion, Race, and Barack Obama's New Democratic Pluralism* (London: Routledge, 2012).

7. Stephen Mansfield, *The Faith of Barack Obama* (Nashville, TN: Thomas Nelson Publishing, 2011), xix.

8. Richard Rorty, "Religion as a Conversation Stopper," *Philosophy and Social Hope* (New York: Penguin, 1999), 168–174.

9. Michael Sandel, *Justice: What's the Right Thing to Do?* (New York: Farrar, Strauss and Giroux, 2009), 251.

10. This study does not assume that Barack Obama is a political theorist. Instead, I approach his reflections on religion as an important illustration or articulation of a Rawlsian philosophical line of influence that is already present in the (liberal) popular consciousness about the best that we can hope from religion in democracy. The point is not to criticize Rawls on the basis of the inconsistencies or ambiguities that we may discover in Obama's thinking, but instead to take seriously and evaluate Obama's dual appeal to the American tradition of civil religion and to a Rawlsian vision of public deliberation.

11. James T. Kloppenberg, *Reading Obama: Dreams, Hope, and American Political Tradition* (Princeton, NJ: Princeton University Press, 2010); Jeffrey K. Tulis, "Plausible Futures," in *The Presidency in the Twenty-First Century*, ed. Charles W. Dunn (Lexington: University Press of Kentucky, 2011), 169–186; Rogers M. Smith, "The Constitutional Philosophy of Barack Obama." *Social Science Quarterly* 93, no. 5 (2012): 1251–1271.

12. As we saw in the previous chapter, the literature on the permissibility of religious reasoning in democratic deliberation is voluminous. Some scholars are not opposed to reliance on strictly religious reasons in public discussion, so long as religious arguments are accompanied by secular reasons when they are employed by both citizens and public officials in support of coercive laws: Gaus and Vallier, "The Roles of Religious Conviction in a Publicly Justified Polity," and Vallier, "Against Public Reason Liberalism's Accessibility Requirement"; see also Jeremy Waldron, "Two-Way Translation: The Ethics of Engaging with Religious Contributions in Public Deliberation," *Mercer Law Review* 63, no. 3 (2012): 845–868. Others insist on a more restrictive standard of translation and on the duty of religious self-restraint, often suggesting that both general public discussion and official political deliberation about coercive laws should be conducted in terms of secular reasons that are accessible to all individuals: Robert Audi, *Religious Commitment and Secular Reason* (Cambridge, UK: Cambridge University Press, 2000), and Stephen Macedo, "In Defense of Public Reason: Are Slavery and Abortion Hard Cases?"

American Journal of Jurisprudence 42, no. 1 (1997): 1–29; see also Amy Gutmann and Dennis Thompson, *Democracy and Disagreement: Why Moral Conflict Cannot Be Avoided in Politics, and What Should Be Done about It* (Cambridge, MA: Harvard University Press, 1996). In the second half of this chapter I show that Obama falls squarely in the latter group, settling on a restrictive standard of public reason, even though his account of the legacies of the civil rights movement and abolitionism points him toward the inclusivist camp.

13. Barack Obama, *The Audacity of Hope* (New York: Crown Publishers, 2006), 214, emphasis added. Rawls formulates the chief goal of his work as an attempt to resolve the same problem of democratic pluralism: "Political liberalism starts by taking to heart the absolute depth of [the] irreconcilable latent conflict" between viewpoints that characterizes modern pluralistic society. Rawls, *Political Liberalism*, xxvi.

14. Obama is explicit in linking increasing pluralism with a heightened risk of religious sectarianism: "Given the increasing diversity of America's population, the dangers of sectarianism have never been greater." Obama, *The Audacity of Hope*, 218.

15. As Rogers Smith points out, Obama bring a similar "anti-foundationalist" approach to his constitutional philosophy as a whole: "In Obama's reading, rather than embodying fixed moral truths, the Constitution has 'implicit in its structure' a 'rejection of absolute truth,' of 'the infallibility of any idea or ideology or theology or "ism". . . . The Founders may have trusted in God, but true to the Enlightenment spirit, they also trusted in the minds and senses that God had given them.' In so arguing, Obama plainly articulates the sort of modern 'deliberative democratic' interpretation of the Constitution urged by Sunstein and others" (internal citations omitted). Smith correctly points out that "this is an account of the Constitution that minimizes the more 'absolutist' elements in the thought of the Constitution's Framers, many of whom did believe in unchanging natural rights and fixed religious truths." Smith, "The Constitutional Philosophy of Barack Obama," 1251–1271.

16. Gorski, "Barack Obama and Civil Religion," 202–203; on the challenge that pluralism poses to civil religion, see Gedicks, "American Civil Religion." Fontana argues against Gedicks that Obama's political success demonstrates the viability of "civil religion from the political left" even in our pluralistic times. Fontana, "Obama and American Civil Religion."

17. Obama, *The Audacity of Hope*, 218.

18. Ibid., 93.

19. Barack Obama, "Keynote Address," Call to Renewal's Building a Covenant for a New America conference in Washington, DC, in 2006, http://www.nytimes.com/2006/06/28/us/politics/2006obamaspeech.html. Hereafter cited as Obama, "Call to Renewal."

20. In the discussion that follows, I will focus on the version of Obama's comments on faith that appear in his speech. I will quote Obama's *The Audacity of Hope* where its formulations add to or substantively improve on the details of the speech.

21. See E. J. Dionne, Jr., "Obama's Eloquent Faith," *Washington Post*, April 2006, http://www.washingtonpost.com/wp-dyn/content/article/2006/06/29/AR 2006062901778.html; E. J. Dionne, Jr., "Full Faith—Despite Jeremiah Wright, Obama Gets Religion," *New Republic* 238, no. 6 (2008): 23–24; and Sandel, *Justice*, Chapter 10.

22. While on a presidential trip in Turkey in April 2009, Obama declared that America is not a Christian nation, and that its "ideals" and "values" transcend any one particular religion: "Although as I mentioned, we have a very large Christian population, we do not consider ourselves a Christian nation or a Jewish nation or a Muslim nation; we consider ourselves a nation of citizens who are bound by ideals and a set of values." The statement in the "Call to Renewal Address," which I analyze below, highlights the growing element of "nonbelievers" within America's broader religious pluralism: "Whatever we once were, we are no longer just a Christian nation; we are also a Jewish nation, a Muslim nation, a Buddhist nation, a Hindu nation, and a nation of nonbelievers."

23. Obama, "Call to Renewal."

24. Ibid.

25. Ibid.

26. Ibid.

27. Michael Barone, for example, has written that the "demographic factor most highly correlated with voting behavior in 2000 and 2004 was religion, or depth of religious belief." Michael Barone, "Throw Out the Maps in 2008," Realclearpolitics.com, 2008, http://www.realclearpolitics.com/articles/2008/03 /throw_out_the_maps_in_2008. Similarly, Alan Abramowitz and Kyle L. Saunders conclude that the divide on the electoral map between "red states" and "blue states" really does reflect a deepening cleavage between the secular, progressive, and urban coasts, and the more religious and traditionalist "Middle America." Alan Abramowitz and Kyle Saunders, "Is Polarization a Myth?" *Journal of Politics* 70, no. 2 (2008): 542–555. See also Robert D. Putnam and David E. Campbell, *American Grace: How Religion Divides and Unites Us* (New York: Simon & Schuster, 2010), 1–36.

28. In part as a response to the politicization of religion, the tendency among some public intellectuals to dismiss religion as inherently irrational and dangerous for politics has only increased in the years since Obama gave his speech. Consider, for instance, the recent writings of the self-proclaimed "New Atheists," who see themselves as carrying to completion the once stalled antireligious project of the modern Enlightenment: Richard Dawkins, *The God Delusion* (London: Bantam Press, 2008); Christopher Hitchens, *God Is Not Great: How Religion Poisons*

Everything (Crows Nest, UK: Allen & Unwin, 2007); Sam Harris, *The End of Faith: Religion, Terror, and the Future of Reason* (New York: Norton, 2005).

29. For influential accounts of "civic liberalism" that eschew a reliance on religion, see Stephan Macedo, *Diversity and Distrust: Civic Education in a Multicultural Democracy* (Cambridge, MA: Harvard University Press, 2000), and Gutmann and Thompson, *Democracy and Disagreement*. On the other hand, Robert Putnam's *Bowling Alone: The Collapse and Revival of American Community* (New York: Touchstone Books by Simon & Schuster, 2000) and Putnam and Campbell's *American Grace* both marshal powerful sociological evidence demonstrating religion's unique role as a civic resource in American democracy.

30. Stephen L. Carter, *Culture of Disbelief: How American Law and Politics Trivialize Religious Devotion* (New York: Anchor Books, 1993), and Jim Wallis, *God's Politics: Why the Right Gets It Wrong and the Left Doesn't Get It* (San Francisco, CA: Harper San Francisco, 2006).

31. Obama, "Call to Renewal."

32. Michael Sandel, "The Procedural Republic and the Unencumbered Self," in *Public Philosophy: Essays on Morality in Politics* (Cambridge, MA: Harvard University Press, 2005), 156–173; see also Michael Sandel, *Liberalism and the Limits of Justice* (Cambridge, UK: Cambridge University Press, 1998), and *Democracy's Discontent: America in Search of a Public Philosophy* (Cambridge, MA: Harvard University Press, 1996).

33. For communitarian criticisms of liberalism that also see religion as having a central role in counteracting the drift toward atomistic individualism, see especially Robert N. Bellah, *Habits of the Heart: Individualism and Commitment in American Life* (New York: Harper and Row, 1986); Alasdair MacIntyre, *After Virtue: A Study in Moral Theory* (Notre Dame, IN: Notre Dame University Press, 1981); Putnam, *Bowling Alone*; and Sandel, *Democracy's Discontents*.

34. Obama, *The Audacity of Hope*, 213.

35. Ibid.

36. Ibid.

37. Obama, "Call to Renewal."

38. Ibid.

39. Obama, *The Audacity of Hope*, 199.

40. Obama, "Call to Renewal," emphasis added. Of course, a thoughtful secularist may object to Obama's stark formulation. They may contend that it is at best a gross exaggeration, and at worst simply inaccurate, to interpret the demands of public reasonableness that secularists make as an attempt to establish outright exclusion of religiously informed arguments from the public sphere. See Andrew F. March, "Rethinking Religious Reasons in Public Justification," *American Political Science Review* 107, no. 3 (2013): 523–539.

41. Obama, "Call to Renewal."

42. Ibid.

43. Alexis de Tocqueville, *Democracy in America*, ed. Harvey C. Mansfield and Delba Winthrop (Chicago: University of Chicago Press, 2000), 284. Contrast Tocqueville's account of religion as having its roots in the hope for immortality with Thomas Hobbes's definition of religion as an outgrowth of fear: "Fear of power invisible, feigned by the mind, or imagined from tales publicly allowed, religion; not allowed, superstition," in Hobbes, *Leviathan*, ed. Richard Tuck (Cambridge, UK: Cambridge University Press, 1991), 42.

44. Obama, *The Audacity of Hope*. In an influential study of Obama's intellectual history, James T. Kloppenberg interprets this passage not as Obama's diagnosis of the self-transcendent spiritual longings of Americans, but rather as an allusion to the erosion of social or civic capital in American democracy. "Obama began with Putnam's argument in Bowling Alone and Robert Bellah's in Habits of the Heart," in *Reading Obama*, 142. Obama, Kloppenberg continues, "diagnosed the problem of purposelessness by using arguments from the scholarship on civil society, and . . . recommended a solution—tapping into the religious values most Americans espouse—straight out of the communitarian playbook," 143. Michael Sandel sees these statements as a sign of Obama's more thorough repudiation of the liberal aspiration to a neutral public sphere and a more thorough affirmation of the religious dimension of American civic and political life: "The key to [Obama's] eloquence was not simply that he was adept with words. It was also that his political language was infused with a moral and spiritual dimension that pointed beyond liberal neutrality." Sandel, *Justice*, 130.

45. Obama, "Call to Renewal."

46. Obama, *The Audacity of Hope*, 204.

47. Ibid.

48. Ibid., 205. In the same passage in *The Audacity of Hope*, Obama also uncovers in his mother's deeply spiritual outlook a moral concern for economic justice: "And yet for all her professed secularism, my mother was in many ways the most spiritually awakened person that I've ever known. . . . She raged at poverty and injustice, and scorned those who were indifferent to both."

49. Obama, "Call to Renewal."

50. Ibid.

51. Obama, *The Audacity of Hope*, 206.

52. Ibid., 208. In later interviews Obama sometimes used more spiritual language to speak of his conversion, stressing that he has "a personal relationship with Jesus Christ," and that he believes "in the redemptive death and resurrection of Jesus Christ. . . . that faith gives me a path to be cleansed of sin and have eternal life."

53. Mansfield, *The Faith of Barack Obama*, 54. The same passages lead Kloppenberg to conclude that "Obama's conversion narrative rests on no metaphysical or theological foundation but only on his own felt experience," and that in this

it resembles William James's *Varieties of Religious Experience: A Study in Human Nature* (Boston, MA: Bedford/St. Martin's Press, 2012). Kloppenberg, *Reading Obama*, 223. Obama seems to confirm this interpretation, for he stresses that while his religious conversion offered him spiritual belonging, it "came about as a choice and not an epiphany," and it did not alleviate his skepticism: "the questions I had did not magically disappear," in *The Audacity of Hope*, 208.

54. Obama, "Call to Renewal."

55. Obama, "First Inaugural."

56. Interview by David Brody, Christian Broadcasting Network, July 30, 2007, http://www.cbn.com/cbnnews/204016.aspx. The claim that "we're no longer just a Christian nation" is repeated in both Obama's "Call to Renewal" as well as *The Audacity of Hope*, 218.

57. Laura Meckler, "Obama Walks Religious Tightrope Spanning Faithful, Non-believers," *Wall Street Journal*, March 24, 2009.

58. David Axelrod, a senior adviser to the president, said that Obama personally inserted the nonbeliever references into his inaugural speech. "He is a person of deep faith and also a person who has a profound belief in the Constitution and the nature of this country," Axelrod said in an interview.

59. Copeland "God-Talk in the Age of Obama," Fontana, "Obama and American Civil Religion," Gorski, "Barack Obama and Civil Religion," and Gedicks, "American Civil Religion."

60. Gedicks, "American Civil Religion," 901.

61. Gedicks hopes that we can develop an explicitly secular civil religion, not dependent on revelation or the Christian tradition, that can provide the same solidarity over civic purposes that Christianity used to supply in our not-too-distant past: "there is nevertheless a portion of American civil religion worth saving, that really can function to bind us together as a people and a nation. That would be the *civil* component of the civil religion. . . . It is this 'civil' of the civil religion that we must preserve in the United States, even as we leave behind the 'religion' of this self-same civil religion," emphasis in the original. Ibid., 908.

62. Obama, "Call to Renewal."

63. Gorski, "Barack Obama and Civil Religion," 202.

64. Obama, "Call to Renewal."

65. Rawls, *Political Liberalism*, xix–xx, 62–63, 150–154.

66. Ibid., 247.

67. Ibid.

68. Ibid., 247–254.

69. Ibid., 250–251.

70. Ibid., 462.

71. P. J. Weithman, *Religion and Contemporary Liberalism* (Notre Dame, IN: University of Notre Dame Press, 1997); and Weithman, *Religion and the Obligations of*

Citizenship (Cambridge, UK: Cambridge University Press, 2002). See also Christopher Eberle, *Religious Conviction in Liberal Politics* (Cambridge, UK: Cambridge University Press, 2002); and Waldron "Two-Way Translation"; and March, "Rethinking Religious Reasons."

72. Paul Horwitz, "Religion in American Politics: Three Views of the Cathedral," *University of Memphis Law Review* 39 (2009): 973–1035.

73. Jeffrey Stout, *Democracy and Tradition* (Princeton, NJ: Princeton University Press: 2004), 66.

74. Ibid., 89–90.

75. Waldron, "Two-Way Translation," 858; Hugo Heclo, *Christianity and American Democracy* (Cambridge, MA: Harvard University Press, 2009), 132.

76. For a helpful discussion, see in general Waldron, "Two-Way Translation." For Catholic social justice arguments, consider the National Conference of Catholic Bishops, *Economic Justice for All: Pastoral Letter on Catholic Social Teaching and the US Economy* (1986), where the US Catholic bishops argue that "themes of human dignity and the preferential option for the poor are at the heart of our approach; they compel us to confront the issue of poverty with a real sense of urgency." The bishops also assert that they "share [the] conviction that most of the policy issues generally called economic are, at root, moral and therefore require the application of moral principles derived from the Scriptures and from the evolving social teaching of the Church and other traditions." For the US Catholic bishops' condemnation of torture, see *Torture Is a Moral Issue: A Catholic Study Guide* (2008).

77. March, "Rethinking Religious Reasons," 15.

78. "It is precisely at these moments of founding and refounding within a polity, when obligations of justice are extended to previously excluded groups, that religious, philosophical, and extrarational modes of persuasion are most urgently needed," in March, "Rethinking Religious Reasons," 13. Kent Greenawalt argues that debates over welfare assistance, punishment, military policy, abortion, euthanasia, and environmental policy all fall into this category of divisive issues that cannot be resolved through appeals to commonly accepted principles of justice. Greenawalt, *Religious Convictions and Political Choice* (Oxford, UK: Oxford University Press, 1988).

79. Rawls stakes a great deal on this promise of neutrality, for he claims that any approach that sacrifices impartiality fails to secure true tolerance and a genuinely rich diversity of comprehensive views: if political liberalism promoted "skepticism or indifference" about truth, it "would put political philosophy in opposition to numerous comprehensive doctrines, and thus defeat from the outset its aim of achieving an overlapping consensus." Rawls, *Political Liberalism*, 15. As we have seen, from Rawls's point of view, a liberalism that demands or promotes theological and metaphysical indifference makes too strong a foundationalist claim, for it effectively seeks to replace the competing conceptions of the good life with rational skepticism as the foundation of political liberalism.

80. Obama, *The Audacity of Hope*, 9.

81. Barack Obama, interview by Kathleen Falsani, *Chicago Sun Times*, March 27, 2004, http://www.patheos.com/blogs/thedudeabides/obama-on-faith-the-exclusive-interview/.

82. Barack Obama, "Testing the Waters," interview with David Remnick of *The New Yorker*, http://www.newyorker.com/magazine/2006/11/06/testing-the-waters.

83. Ibid. This view of religion has curious implications for Obama's understanding of prayer and the existence of the afterlife. Responding to a question about his prayer life, Obama described it as "an ongoing conversation with God," but also hinted that this conversation was actually with himself: "I am constantly asking myself questions about what I'm doing, why I am doing it." Similarly, when his daughter asked about what happens after death—"I don't want to die, Daddy," Obama recalls her saying—he was unable to assure her about heaven: "I wondered if I should have told her the truth, that I wasn't sure what happens when we die, any more than I was sure of where the soul resides or what existed before the Big Bang" (Obama, *The Audacity of Hope*, 226). These pronouncements lead John Q. Wilson to conclude that the "afterlife is neither believed nor disbelieved by Obama; it's ignored because it's an unknowable factor that shouldn't affect what we do on earth." Mansfield discerns in this "evidence of Obama's postmodern picking and choosing" approach to religion and the Bible. Mansfield, *The Faith of Barack Obama*.

84. Obama, "Testing the Waters."

85. Putnam and Campbell, *American Grace*, 246–252, 257–258, 547.

86. Obama, *The Audacity of Hope*, 219.

87. Ibid.

88. Ibid.

89. Ibid.

90. Rawls, *Political Liberalism*, 442.

91. Obama, "Call to Renewal."

92. John Locke, *A Letter Concerning Toleration*, ed. James Tully (Indianapolis: Hackett Publishing, 1983), 26; Locke, IV.19.4, in *An Essay Concerning Human Understanding*, ed. Peter H. Nidditch (Oxford, UK: Clarendon Press, 1975).

93. Obama, *The Audacity of Hope*, 224.

94. Ibid., 224, emphasis added.

95. Obama, "Remarks by the President in Commencement Address at the University of Notre Dame," May 17, 2009, http://www.whitehouse.gov/the-press-office/remarks-president-notre-dame-commencement.

96. Obama, *The Audacity of Hope*, 93.

97. Ibid., 97.

98. Kloppenberg, *Reading Obama*, 244.

99. Obama, *The Audacity of Hope*, 97. Rogers Smith is led to uncover in this admission of the need for moral absolutes a sign of Obama's "Constitutional faith,

one defined to be consistent with the moral imperatives Obama embraces as a matter of religious conviction," namely "the equal worth of every individual" and "universal rights." Smith concludes provocatively that Obama's "beliefs" in these values *rest on religious faith, not philosophic proofs*—the faith that for him centers on his embrace of the 'battle for economic and social justice' pursued by America's black churches and allied religious and secular activists," in Smith, "The Constitutional Philosophy of Barack Obama," 1261 and 1263, emphasis added.

100. Obama, *The Audacity of Hope*, 97.

101. Ibid.

102. Ibid., 98.

103. Ibid.

104. Abraham Lincoln, *The Writings of Abraham Lincoln*, ed. Steve B. Smith (New Haven, CT: Yale University Press, 2012).

CHAPTER 3. DOES TOLERATION REQUIRE RELIGIOUS SKEPTICISM?
AN EXAMINATION OF LOCKE'S TEACHING ON TOLERATION

1. Throughout this chapter, I use the terms "skepticism" and "theological skepticism" to denote the view that certain (demonstrative) knowledge is unattainable in religious matters.

2. Peter Myers calls the *Letter* "the founding document of modern political liberalism." Peter C. Myers, *Our Only Star and Compass* (New York: Rowman & Littlefield, 1998), 180.

3. Leo Strauss, *Natural Right and History* (Chicago: University of Chicago Press, 1953), chapter 5; Thomas L. Pangle, *The Spirit of Modern Republicanism: The Moral Vision of the American Founders and the Philosophy of Locke* (Chicago: University of Chicago Press, 1988); Michael S. Rabieh, "The Reasonableness of Locke, or the Questionableness of Christianity," *Journal of Politics* 53, no. 4 (1991): 933–957; Michael Zuckert, *Launching Liberalism: On Lockean Political Philosophy* (Lawrence: University Press of Kansas, 2002), chapter 6; Ross Corbett, "Locke's Biblical Critique," *Review of Politics* 74, no. 1 (2012): 27–51.

4. Strauss, *Natural Right and History*, 202–203, 226–227; Ross Corbett, "Locke's Biblical Critique," in *Review of Politics*, 74, no. 1 (2012): 27–51.

5. Robert Kraynak, "John Locke: From Absolutism to Separation," in *American Political Science Review* 74, no. 1 (1980): 53–69; Adam Wolfson, *Persecution or Toleration: An Explication of the Locke-Proast Quarrel, 1689–1704* (Lanham, MD: Lexington Books, 2010); Adam Wolfson, "Toleration and Relativism: The Locke-Proast Exchange," *Review of Politics* 59, no. 2 (1997): 213–231.

6. John Dunn, *The Political Thought of John Locke: An Historical Account of the Argument of the Two Treatises of Government* (Cambridge, UK: Cambridge University Press, 1969), xi, 29, 80, 259; cf. Richard Ashcraft, "Faith and Knowledge in Locke's Philosophy," in *John Locke: Problems and Perspectives*, ed. John Yolton

(Cambridge, UK: Cambridge University Press, 1969), 214; Jeremy Waldron, *God, Locke and Equality: Christian Foundations in Locke's Political Thought* (Cambridge, UK: Cambridge University Press, 2002).

7. Micah Schwartzman, "The Relevance of Locke's Religious Arguments for Toleration," *Political Theory* 33, no. 5 (2005), esp. 695; Paul Bou-Habi, "Locke, Sincerity and the Rationality of Persecution," *Political Studies* 51, no. 4 (2003): 611–626.

8. Alex Tuckness, "Rethinking Intolerant Locke," *American Journal of Political Science* 46, no. 2 (2002): 288–298. See also John Dunn, "What Is Living and What Is Dead in the Political Theory of John Locke?" in *Interpreting Political Responsibility: Essays 1981–1989* (Princeton, NJ: Princeton University Press, 1990), 9–25; for a critical reappraisal of Dunn's "obituary" of Locke's theory of toleration, see Richard Vernon, *The Career of Toleration: John Locke, Jonas Proast, and After* (Montreal: McGill-Queen's University Press, 1997), 143–154 ("Conclusion").

9. Jeremy Waldron, *God, Locke and Equality: Christian Foundations in Locke's Political Thought* (Cambridge, UK: University of Cambridge Press, 2002).

10. In *God, Locke, and Equality*, Waldron claims that earlier in his career he had thought that "theology could be bracketed out of Locke's theory" of toleration, 44. But in a well-known essay analyzing the debate between Locke and his critic Jonas Proast, Waldron concluded that Locke was ultimately compelled to concede the efficacy of force in forming beliefs, a concession that "opens up a first and fatal crack in the framework of Locke's argument for toleration," leaving only its Christian foundations intact. Jeremy Waldron, "Locke, Toleration and the Rationality of Persecution," in *Justifying Toleration*, ed. Susan Mendus (Cambridge, UK: Cambridge University Press, 1988), 81.

11. Waldron, *God, Locke and Equality*, 211.

12. Ibid., 13–14, chapters 3, 7, and 8.

13. Schwartzman, "The Relevance of Locke's Religious Arguments," 682.

14. For thoughtful assessments of Waldron's book, see the symposium in *Review of Politics* 67, no. 3 (2005).

15. Michael Zuckert, "Locke: Religion: Equality," *Review of Politics* 67, no. 3 (2005): 429. Thus, in spite of Waldron's "religious turn," the driving question of Locke scholarship has remained whether we can reconstruct Locke's teaching using a secular toolkit in order to salvage a doctrine of toleration suitable for our day and age: John William Tate, "Dividing Locke from God: The Limits of Theology in Locke's Political Philosophy," *Philosophy and Social Criticism* 29, no. 2 (2013): 133–164; Sam Black, "Locke and the Skeptical Argument for Toleration," *History of Philosophy Quarterly* 24, no. 4 (2007): 355–375. While abstaining from the claim "that nothing in Locke is essentially Protestant," Richard Vernon tries to show "that there is something valuable in it that is not" dependent on Protestantism. Richard Vernon, "Lockean Toleration: Dialogical Not Theological?" *Political Stud-*

ies 61 (2013): 215–230. Locke's case for toleration "is indeed supported by theological considerations," but in contrast to Waldron, Vernon concludes that "it does not require them" for its theoretical coherence (ibid., 216).

16. Waldron, *God, Locke and Equality*, 210.

17. All references to Locke's original *Letter* (1689) are to the Tully edition: John Locke, *A Letter Concerning Toleration*, ed. James Tully (Indianapolis: Hackett Publishing, 1983).

18. Jonas Proast's critique of Locke's teaching on toleration is presented in three separate letters (available in *The Philosophy of John Locke*, ed. by Peter A. Schouls [New York: Garland, 1984]): *The Argument of the Letter Concerning Toleration Consider'd and Answer'd* (1690); *A Third Letter Concerning Toleration* (1691); and *A Second Letter to the Author of the Three Letters on Toleration* (1704), subsequently cited as P.I, P.II, and P.III.

19. Proast, P.II.35.

20. Locke's subsequent three *Letters*—*A Second Letter on Toleration* (1690); *A Third Letter on Toleration* (1692); and *A Fourth Letter on Toleration* (unfinished, 1704)—are available in *The Works of John Locke* (London, 1823), vol. 5. The following abbreviations have been adopted in the text for Locke's four letters, L.I, L.II, L.III, and L.IV, followed by page numbers.

21. Locke, L.I.46.

22. Several thoughtful studies have emphasized how Locke's "deconstructive" rational epistemology in the *Essay Concerning Human Understanding* complements the *Letter*'s policy of toleration: Nicholas Jolley, *Locke: His Philosophical Thought* (Oxford, UK: Oxford University Press: 1999); Myers, *Our Only Star and Compass*. Judd Owen goes even further by showing that the *Essay* supplies a natural theology (as a replacement of revelation) that complements the *Letter*'s argument, Owen, "Locke's Case for Religious Toleration: Its Neglected Foundations in the *Essay Concerning Human Understanding*," *Journal of Politics* 69, no. 1 (2007): 156–168. While I agree with these studies that the *Letter*'s argument for toleration depends on the *Essay*'s epistemology, I seek to highlight an often-overlooked tension between these two works: the *Essay*'s theological minimalism risks to undermine the *Letter*'s emphasis on man's duty to search for religious truth.

23. This formulation echoes Locke's classical statement on the secular purposes of civil government in *Two Treatises of Government*, ed. Peter Laslett (Cambridge, UK: Cambridge University Press, 1988), §87.

24. Because the core of this argument is that toleration is a Christian duty, imposed by Christ's message in the New Testament, it is regarded as the chief defect that renders Lockean toleration too constricted for the modern pluralistic world. Waldron quotes John Dunn's claim that there is a "yawning chasm between the implications of Locke's argument for tolerating varieties of Christian belief and practice within a Christian state and society and the implications . . . for freedom of thought and expression more broadly within a secular state or a more intracta-

bly plural religious culture" (Dunn, "What Is Living," 19, quoted in Waldron, *God, Locke and Equality*, 209).

25. Mark Goldie writes that "the *Letter* remains an essay in evangelical tolerance, penned by a devout Christian, albeit one whom contemporaries suspected of theological heterodoxy." Goldie, "The Theory of Religious Intolerance in Restoration England," in *From Persecution to Toleration*, ed. Ole Peter Grell, Jonathan I. Israel, and Nicholas Tayacke (Oxford, UK: Clarendon Press, 1991). Similarly, Waldron argues that "the first point to notice is that [Locke's] argument for toleration does not rest on any religious doubt, religious scepticism, or epistemic misgivings in relation either to the orthodox position Locke is considering or to the beliefs and practices that are being tolerated" (Waldron, "Rationality of Persecution," 69). Goldie does grant that Locke's silence on skepticism may be dictated by rhetorical considerations, but he does not explain how that may affect our overall interpretation of the *Letter*: "Arguably [Locke's] avoidance of a skeptical position is in part tactical. If he seeks to persuade the devout persecutor that force is improper, it makes more sense to dwell on reasons why force is inappropriate than on reasons why devoutness is ill-grounded."

26. Locke, L.I.5–6.

27. Locke's *Essay on Toleration* (1667) and *Critical Notes* (1681) are available in *John Locke: A Letter Concerning Toleration and Other Writings*, ed. Mark Goldie (Indianapolis: Liberty Fund, 2010). For a more comprehensive account of the evolution in Locke's arguments for toleration, see in general John Marshall, *John Locke: Resistance, Religion and Responsibility* (Cambridge, UK: Cambridge University Press, 1994), 367–370.

28. Locke, L.I.6.

29. Waldron, "Rationality of Persecution," 111. Waldron has since then evolved to the opposite conclusion that "the main line of argument in Locke's case for toleration that survives Proast's critique . . . depends on . . . the specific biblical evidence of the life and teaching of Jesus," in Waldron, *God, Locke and Equality*, 211.

30. Locke, L.I.6.

31. Proast, P.II.43–44.

32. Locke, L.I.7.

33. Ibid., L.I.27.

34. Myers, *Our Only Star and Compass*, 46.

35. Consider how John Horton and Susan Mendus introduce the *Letter* in their influential collection of essays on toleration: the unfortunate neglect of the *Letter* is partly explained by the fact that it "was written for an age when Christian belief was the norm rather than the exception." (Horton and Mendus, *John Locke: A Letter Concerning Toleration in Focus* (London: Routledge: 1991), 2.

36. Locke, L.I.23–24.

37. Ibid., L.I.24–25.

38. For Locke's more sustained effort to reinterpret the Bible so that it can be

made to sanction the distinction between faith and works, see his *Reasonableness of Christianity*, in *The Works of John Locke*, vol. 6., sections 222–227. Based on his idiosyncratic interpretation of the Bible's portrayal of God's judgment of man, Locke argues that "we may observe, none are sentenced or punished for unbelief, but only for their misdeeds" (Locke, ibid., 222). The "guilt on which the punishment is laid," according to Locke, is "not for want of faith" but for violation of the moral law (ibid., 227). Cf. Aaron Herold, "The Chief Characteristic Mark of the True Church: John Locke's Theology of Toleration and His Case for Civil Religion," *Review of Politics* 76 (2014): 195–221.

39. See in general the very helpful discussion of Christian Thomism and heresy in John Marshall, *John Locke, Toleration and Early Enlightenment Culture* (Cambridge, UK: Cambridge University Press, 2006), 215–218.

40. Augustine, *Contra Epistulam Parmeniani*, I, X, 16, quoted in Marshall, *John Locke, Toleration and Early Enlightenment Culture*, 216. For a more comprehensive account of the complexity of Augustine's position, see Rainer Frost, *Toleration in Conflict* (Cambridge, UK: Cambridge University Press, 2013), 47–70, and especially the discussion of Augustinian justification of temporal coercion in the name of religion at 52–54.

41. Saint Thomas Aquinas, *Summa Theologica*, II-II, Question 11, Article 2.

42. Augustine of Hippo, *City of God*, trans. Henry Betterson (New York: Penguin Classics, 2004); Augustine, *Epistles*, 1.5.

43. Aquinas, *Summa Theologica*, II-II, Question 11, Article 3. See also Joseph Lecler, *Toleration and the Reformation*, trans. T. L. Westow, vol. 1:55 (New York: Association Press, 1960), 1 and 94.

44. Proast, P.II.52 and P.II.43–44.

45. Augustine, Epistle 185, 11, quoted in Lecler, *Toleration and the Reformation*, 85. See also Frost, *Toleration in Conflict*, 67–69.

46. While Aquinas advises the Church to practice "mercy which looks to the conversion of the wanderer," this clemency has it limits, and the heretic should ultimately be condemned to death, but "only after the first and second admonition" had failed. Aquinas, *Summa Theologica*, Question 11, Article 3, "Whether heretics ought to be tolerated?"

47. Proast, P.II.51; see also P.I.20.

48. Waldron, "Rationality of Persecution," 81; Waldron, *God, Locke and Equality*, 210. James Tully, "Introduction," in Locke, *A Letter Concerning Toleration*, 6–7; Dunn, "What Is Living"; Joshua Mitchell, "John Locke and the Theological Foundation of Liberal Toleration: A Christian Dialectic of History," *Review of Politics* 52, no. 1 (1990): 64–83.

49. Locke, L.I.27.

50. Proast, P.I.5.

51. Ibid., 5 and 11. That such force is necessary, Proast argues, is evident from human experience, which demonstrates that men have utterly failed in their duty

to examine and pursue the true religion: "There is nothing more notorious, than that men have fought out many inventions, and contrived a great variety of religions for themselves," which explains "all the false religions now on foot in the world" (7).

52. Ibid., 4.

53. Waldron, "Rationality of Persecution," 67.

54. Ibid., 79.

55. Ibid.

56. Locke, *Essay*, 4.13.1. Hereafter cited as E. followed by the book number, chapter number, and section number.

57. Ibid.

58. Locke, L.III.400, emphasis added. Locke makes an even more shocking acknowledgment of the effectiveness of religious persecution in the *Second Letter*: "The gallies, it is like, might reduce many a vain, loose protestant to repentance, sobriety of thought, and a true sense of religion: and the torments they suffered in the late persecution might make several consider the pains of hell, and put a due estimate of vanity and contempt on all things of this world," L.II.70.

59. Waldron, "Rationality of Persecution," 81.

60. Proast, P.I.11.

61. To rescue Locke from self-contradiction, Vernon distinguishes between "how people initially make up their minds," which force can influence, and "how minds are changed," which Vernon interprets Locke as exempting from the efficacy of force: "Locke can maintain the view" that "only light and evidence can work a change in men's opinions" while "accepting everything his critics say about the complex and murky ways in which people come to have opinions in the first place" (Vernon, *The Career of Toleration*, 30).

62. See Locke, L.III.297.

63. Proast, P.I.6.

64. Waldron, "Rationality of Persecution," 81–82.

65. Locke, L.II.2.

66. Ibid., 2.

67. Ibid., L.I.27–28.

68. Thomas Hobbes, *Leviathan*, ed. Edwin Curley (Indianapolis: Hackett Publishing, 1994), Chapter 18. Hobbes's infamous solution to the problem of religious diversity was to grant the sovereign the authority "to be Judge of what Opinions and Doctrines are averse, and what conducing to Peace" in order to control their public promulgation accordingly.

69. Locke, L.I.27.

70. Ibid.

71. Ibid., 32.

72. Ibid., 23.

73. Ibid., 42.

74. Ibid., 36.

75. Ibid.

76. Ibid., 32.

77. Kraynak characterizes Locke's procedure as aiming "to preserve the possibility of orthodoxy, while creating doubt but not total cynicism about discovering it" (Kraynak, "From Absolutism to Separation," 64). Similarly, Wolfson argues that Locke's treatment of orthodoxy is intended to instill the attitude that "that religious truth is hard to find" (Wolfson, "Toleration and Relativism," 217).

78. Proast, P.II.35.

79. Vernon, "Lockean Toleration," 219.

80. Ibid.

81. Proast, P.I.25–26.

82. Locke, L.II.63; cf. L.III.144.

83. Ibid., L.II.65, emphasis added.

84. Ibid., L.IV.562; see also L.II.144 and L.IV.566.

85. Proast, P.II. 47.

86. Ibid.

87. Locke, L.IV.62.

88. Proast, P.III, 6.

89. Ibid., P.II, 47.

90. Locke, L.III, 144.

91. Ibid., L.III, 415.

92. Ibid., E.IV.3.22.

93. Ibid., IV.3.21.

94. Ibid., I.3.6, II.28.6, IV.3.21.

95. Ibid., I.4.17.

96. Ibid., IV.3.27.

97. Ibid., IV.19.4.

98. Ibid., IV.18.4.

99. Michael Ayers, *Locke: Volume I: Epistemology* (London: Routledge, 1991), 121–124; see also Nicholas Jolley, "Locke on Faith and Reason," in *The Cambridge Companion to Locke's "Essay Concerning Human Understanding,"* ed. Lex Newman, 436–455 (New York: Cambridge University Press, 2007).

100. Ayers, *Locke: Volume I: Epistemology,* 122.

101. Locke, E.IV.16.4.

102. Ibid., 3.

103. Ibid.

104. Ibid., 4.

105. Ibid.

106. Nicholas Wolterstorff, *John Locke and the Ethics of Belief* (Cambridge, UK: Cambridge University Press, 1996), 71–72; Richard Ashcraft, *Locke's Two Treatises*

of Government (New York: Routledge, 1987), 250–251; Waldron, *God, Locke, Equality*, 87–89.

107. Waldron, *God, Locke, Equality*, 87.

108. Wolfson, "Toleration and Relativism," 221.

109. Locke, L.I.36.

110. Locke, E.IV.18.11, emphasis added

111. Ibid., E.IV.20.3. Ashcraft sees in this "the assertion of moral egalitarianism as an aspect of Locke's theory of knowledge," requiring all individuals to search for religious truth (Ashcraft, *Locke's Two Treatises*, 250). Wolterstorff reaches a similar conclusion: "Truth on [religious] matters concern[s] everyone; and everyone, no matter how much a 'beast of burden' he or she may be, has talent and time" to pursue it with seriousness (Wolterstorff, *The Ethics of Belief*, 72).

112. Locke, E.IV.19.4.

113. Ibid., E.IV.17.24, emphasis added.

114. Ibid., E.IV.3.6.

115. Although Locke would reject such an association, this conclusion puts him in the same theological circle as Thomas Hobbes, since the latter argued that "there is no natural knowledge of man's estate after death" (Hobbes, *Leviathan*, ed. Edwin Curley, 15.8). Moreover, much like Hobbes, whose materialism rules out the existence of spirits, Locke is equally pessimistic about the possibility of demonstrative knowledge of spiritual beings: "But that there are degrees of spiritual beings between us and the great God, who is there, that, by his own search and ability, can come to know? Much less have we distinct ideas of their different natures, conditions, states, powers, and several constitutions wherein they agree or differ from one another and from us. And, therefore, in what concerns their different species and properties we are in absolute ignorance" (Locke, E.IV.3.27).

116. Ibid., IV.19.5.

117. Ibid., IV.19.3.

118. Proast, P.III.6.

119. Locke, E.IV.19.2, see also IV.19.8.

120. Ibid., IV.19.2.

121. Ibid., IV.19.10.

122. Locke, L.I.30.

123. Locke, E.I.1.4.

124. Locke, *Of the Conduct of the Understanding*, Section 19, "Universality," in *The Works of John Locke*, vol. 2, 354.

125. Sanford Kessler, "Locke's Influence on Jefferson's 'Bill for Establishing Religious Freedom,'" *Journal of Church and State* 25 (1983): 231–252; Judd Owen, "The Struggle between 'Religion and Nonreligion': Jefferson, Backus, and the Dissonance of America's Founding Principles," *American Political Science Review* 101, no. 3 (2007): 493–503.

126. Thomas Jefferson, *The Writings of Thomas Jefferson*, vol. 15, ed. Albert Ellery Bergh and Andrew A. Lipscomb (Washington, DC: Thomas Jefferson Memorial Association, 1904), 385.

127. Robert D. Putnam and David E. Campbell, *American Grace: How Religion Divides and Unites Us* (New York: Simon & Schuster, 2010), 2 and 516–550.

128. Ibid., 4–5, 11, 36, 523–524.

129. Ibid., 550.

130. Ibid, 535–540.

131. Ibid., 535.

132. Ibid. This is true not just of members of liberal denominations (Mainline Protestants), but even those who belong to more traditional churches: "Large majorities of even stricter religious traditions believe in an equal opportunity heaven. Eighty-three percent of evangelicals, for example, say that other religions can bring salvation; eighty-seven percent of black Protestants believe so." Ibid.

133. Ibid., 538.

134. Thomas Jefferson, *Notes on the State of Virginia* (New York: Harper and Row, 1964), 152 (Query XVII).

135. Putnam and Campbell, *American Grace*, 522.

136. Ibid., 533.

137. Ibid., 536.

138. "For example, 63 percent of clergy in the Evangelical Lutheran Church in America agree that Jesus is the only way (in spite of its name, the theology of the ELCA puts it in the mainline Protestant camp). This was also true for 59 percent of United Methodist clergy and 57 percent of clergy from the Presbyterian Church, USA," ibid., 539.

139. Wolfson, "Toleration and Relativism," 215–217, 228.

140. See in general Richard Dawkins, *The God Delusion* (London: Bantam Press, 2008).

141. Putnam and Campbell, *American Grace*, 18, 20, 121–127.

CHAPTER 4. LINCOLN'S RELIGIOUS STATESMANSHIP AND
RAWLS'S "PUBLIC REASON": SLAVERY AND BIBLICAL THEOLOGY
IN THE CIVIL WAR

1. The political implication of Locke's religious strategy is neatly captured by Thomas Jefferson in this famous saying: "It does me no injury for my neighbour to say there are twenty gods, or no god. It neither picks my pocket nor breaks my leg." To the extent that religious believers become Jeffersonian in their attitudes, then Locke's project has effectively succeeded, and one can imagine that in such a regime atheists would also enjoy political protection.

2. In spite of this bold statement about the political irrelevance of religious opinions, Jefferson himself appeared to be ultimately ambivalent about whether religion was altogether irrelevant for the perpetuation of freedom. Thus, in the

Notes on Virginia (in the context of his discussion of the injustice of slavery), Jefferson acknowledges the need for something like a civil religion, or a popular belief or "conviction" that there exists divine supports for natural rights: "Can the liberties of a nation be secure when we have removed a conviction that these liberties are the gift of God?" Similarly, although in the *Letter* Locke promoted a secular state that he claimed had no competence in the "care of men's souls," throughout his corpus he also argued that a belief in a providential deity was a necessary precondition for the broad success of a liberal morality: see in general Thomas L. Pangle, *The Spirit of Modern Republicanism: The Moral Vision of the American Founders and the Philosophy of Locke* (Chicago: University of Chicago Press, 1988), Chapter 17, and Locke, *Essay*, I.3.6.

3. This study therefore makes a contribution to the debate over the "accessibility" requirement of public reason, which stipulates that "novel" arguments can be introduced into public debate in political liberalism if they are "widely accessible or available" at the time. John Rawls, *Political Liberalism: Expanded Edition* (New York: Columbia University Press, 2005). See also Jeremy Waldron, "Religious Contributions in Public Deliberation," *San Diego Law Review* 30 (1993): 817–848; Lawrence B. Solumn, "Novel Public Reasons," *Loyola of Los Angeles Law Review* 29 (1996): 1459–1486; Gerald F. Gaus and Kevin Vallier, "The Roles of Religious Conviction in a Publicly Justified Polity: The Implications of Convergence, Asymmetry and Political Institutions," *Philosophy & Social Criticism* 35, no. 1–2 (2009): 51–76; Andrew F. March, "Rethinking Religious Reasons in Public Justification," *American Political Science Review* 107, no. 3 (2013): 523–539. I show that Lincoln's novel theological arguments cannot be considered to have either been widely "accessible" or "available" at the time, since Lincoln developed them through rationalism but presented them through a novel biblical framework.

4. Scholars are divided on whether slavery was a high priority on Lincoln's agenda throughout his career, but the dominant interpretation sees Lincoln as either a lifelong pragmatist or a gradualist undergoing a pronounced evolution in favor of emancipation only late in the course of his life. For "Lincoln the pragmatist," see especially John Burt, *Lincoln's Tragic Pragmatism: Lincoln, Douglas, and Moral Conflict* (Cambridge, MA: Harvard University Press, 2013), and David Donald, *Lincoln* (New York: Simon & Schuster, 1996). Proponents of the "evolving Lincoln" include Eric Forner, who argues that "the hallmark of Lincoln's greatness was his capacity for growth," in *The Fiery Trial: Abraham Lincoln and American Slavery* (New York: W. W. Norton, 2010), xix, and Allen Guelzo, who concludes that slavery was not a major agenda issue for Lincoln until well into his presidency, in *Abraham Lincoln: Redeemer President* (Cambridge, UK: Cambridge University Press, 1999).

5. Joseph Fornier, who in general discounts the importance of the "Lyceum Address" for understanding Lincoln's mature religious statesmanship, nevertheless interprets it as an "early expression of Lincoln's biblical republicanism." Joseph

R. Fornier, *Abraham Lincoln's Political Faith* (DeKalb: Northern Illinois University Press. 2005), 91. On the other hand, Steven B. Smith and Robert Bellah both trace the "political religion" of the Lyceum Address to Enlightenment influences, in particular to Rousseau's *Social Contract:* Smith, "How to Read Lincoln's Second Inaugural," *The Writings of Abraham Lincoln*, ed. Steven B. Smith (New Haven, CT: Yale University Press, 2012), 177–178, and Bellah, "Civil Religion in America," *Dædalus* 96, no. 1 (1967): 1–21. While my interpretation will be closer to Smith and Bellah's approach, I attempt to show that the Lyceum Address also contains Lincoln's subtle critique of Enlightenment rationalism (and of the American Founders), which prefigures his turn to theological rhetoric during the Civil War.

6. Jeremy Waldron refers to this as Rawls's "Abraham Lincoln exception" to the restrictions of public reason: "[Rawls] seems to suggest that it is acceptable to introduce religious reasons (for example) into public debate, provided you promise to redeem their introduction with a nonreligious paraphrase later," i.e., Rawls's translation "proviso" (cf. *Public Liberalism*, 254), in "Public Reason and 'Justification' in the Courtroom," *Journal of Law, Philosophy and Culture* 1, no. 1 (2007): 107–134; cf. Waldron, "Two-Way Translation: The Ethics of Engaging with Religious Contributions in Public Deliberation," *Mercer Law Review* 63, no. 3 (2012): 845–868. Jeffrey Stout similarly judges Rawls's "modified" view insufficient, suggesting that the requirement of translation amounts to a "promissory note" that religious speakers must fulfill to obtain legitimacy, in *Democracy and Tradition* (Princeton, NJ: Princeton University Press. 2004), 69–70. Compare these criticisms to the very unpersuasive account that Christopher Hitchens offers of the contribution of religion to abolitionism—a contribution that Hitchens judges to be minimal: *God Is Not Great: How Religion Poisons Everything* (New York: Allen & Unwin, 2007), 179.

7. A confrontation with Lincoln's speeches and his use of the Bible also compels us to raise a controversial question about the sincerity of his own position. Although a number of scholars have interpreted his position as an example of "Biblical republicanism," Lincoln himself had a reputation for unorthodox religious beliefs and, at least as a young man, for his commitment to a Spinozistic philosophical doctrine of necessity. For a helpful overview of the debate about Lincoln's personal beliefs and the sincerity of his public religious pronouncements, see Samuel W. Calhoun and Lucas E. Morel, "Abraham Lincoln's Religion: The Case for His Ultimate Belief in a Personal, Sovereign God," *Journal of the Abraham Lincoln Association* 33, no. 1 (2012): 38–74. Calhoun and Morel conclude that Lincoln evolved from his early religious skepticism to a sincere belief in a personal and providential Christian God in his Civil War speeches.

8. Abraham Lincoln, "The Perpetuation of Our Political Institutions: Address before the Young Men's Lyceum of Springfield Illinois," in *Collected Works of Abraham Lincoln*, vol. 1, ed. Roy P. Basler (New Brunswick, NJ: Rutgers University Press, 1953), 109. Hereafter cited as Lincoln, *Collected Works*.

9. Harry Jaffa, *Crisis of a House Divided* (Chicago: University of Chicago Press, 1959), 244–245, 316.

10. As Michael Zuckert (2005) observes, "this speech, and a companion statement made five years later, reveals more about Lincoln's thinking on civil religion than the later speeches in which he actually preached it, because in the earlier speeches he focused far more explicitly on the reasons for, and the nature of, civil religion," "Lincoln and the Problem of Civil Religion," in *Lincoln's American Dream*, ed. Kenneth L. Deutsch and Joseph R. Fornieri (Washington, DC: Potomac Books, 2005), 350–366. Glen E. Thurow also suggests that the political religion "of the Lyceum speech is not developed in the speech; to understand it we will have to view it in full flower in the Gettysburg Address and the Second Inaugural," in *Abraham Lincoln and American Political Religion* (Albany, NY: State University of New York Press, 1976), 36.

11. "The Lyceum Address constitutes neither a formal guide to understanding Lincoln's subsequent thought nor the definitive statement of his civil theology. . . . scholars invest the Lyceum Address with far greater significance than it actually merits," in Fornier, *Abraham Lincoln's Political Faith*, 92. In particular, Fornier denies that there is any evidence in the Lyceum Address or in Lincoln's later speeches of esotericism or lack of forthrightness, and he especially rejects the notion that Lincoln "devised a 'popular religion' to accommodate the cultural prejudices of a Bible-reading nation," 96–97. Mark Neely also criticizes what he regards as the Straussian overreliance on the Lyceum speech for evidence of Lincoln's esotericism: "Lincoln's Lyceum Speech and the Origins of a Modern Myth," *Lincoln Lore* 1776, no. 3 (1987): 1–3. Contrast Calhoun and Morel, "Abraham Lincoln's Religion," who, while not addressing the question of Lincoln's potential esotericism explicitly, also conclude that Lincoln's mature professions of faith are sincere.

12. Fornier argues that during the Civil War Lincoln evolved to the view that "a legitimate republican government was bound to and limited by the universal moral law revealed by God in the Bible, known through human reason, and promulgated by the Declaration," in *Abraham Lincoln's Political Faith*, 5. In this reading, Lincoln was the champion of "Biblical republicanism" and regarded the principles of the Declaration as constituting "a rational expression of humankind's participation in the divine law that governs the universe" (ibid.). Similarly, Herman Belz has proposed that "in the sectional conflict over slavery, Lincoln affirmed, clarified, and vindicated the unique amalgam of classical natural law and modern natural rights that defined American republicanism," in "Abraham Lincoln and the Natural Law Tradition," The Witherspoon Institute, http://www.nlnrac.org/american/lincoln (2013). See also Guelzo, *The Redeemer President* (1999), Richard Cowardine, *Lincoln: A Life of Power and Purpose* (New York: Penguin Random House, 2007), and Stewart Winger, *Lincoln, Religion, and Romantic Cultural Politics* (DeKalb: Northern Illinois University Press, 2002).

13. Lincoln's "aim (in this speech, but perhaps not in some later ones) seems to have been more theoretical than practical—to indicate a weakness in our system that it can never fully eliminate," in David Lowenthal, *The Mind and Art of Abraham Lincoln: Philosopher Statesman* (Lanham, MD: Lexington Books, 2012), 22.

14. Lincoln, *Collected Works*, vol. 1, 108.

15. The subtle allusions to the problem of slavery that underpin the Lyceum Address often go unnoticed. For instance, Ronald C. White suggests that "Lincoln did not speak of slavery in his Young Men's Lyceum Lecture of 1838, but nearly every speech he delivered in the 1850s dealt with America's 'peculiar institution' head-on," "Lincoln and the Rhetoric of Freedom," in *Lincoln and Freedom: Slavery, Emancipation, and the Thirteenth Amendment*, ed. Harold Holzer and Sara Vaughn Gabbard (Carbondale: Southern Illinois University Press, 2007), 134.

16. The other example that Lincoln adduces is also related to the question of slavery: Francis McIntosh, a freedman who killed a constable, was burned and lynched by a proslavery mob in St. Louis in 1836. Elijah Lovejoy was one of the abolitionists who condemned McIntosh's lynching. See Matthew Holbreich, "In the Valley of Dry Bones: Lincoln's Biblical Rhetoric and the Coming of the Civil War," *History of Political Thought* 35, no. 1 (2013): 121–146, and Lowenthal, *The Mind and Art of Abraham Lincoln*, 21.

17. Holbreich, "In the Valley of Dry Bones," 126.

18. Zuckert, "Lincoln and the Problem of Civil Religion," 356.

19. Abraham Lincoln, "The Perpetuation of Our Political Institutions," in *Collected Works*, vol. 1, 112.

20. Cf. Jaffa, *Crisis of a House Divided*, 238–240.

21. For a helpful exploration of similar questions about Lincoln's religious statesmanship, see Steven Smith's "How to Read Lincoln's 'Second Inaugural,'" in *The Writings of Abraham Lincoln*, ed. Steven B. Smith (New Haven, CT: Yale University Press, 2012), 476–492.

22. William H. Herndon and Jesse W. Weik, *Herndon's Life of Lincoln: The History and Personal Reflections of Abraham Lincoln* (New York: Da Capo Press, 1983), 218.

23. Abraham Lincoln, "Handbill Replying to Charges of Infidelity," July 31, 1846, in *Collected Works*, vol. 1, 383.

24. Ibid. Lincoln's formulation resembles Benedict de Spinoza's denial of free will in Propositions 48 and 49 of his *Ethics*: "In the mind there is no absolute or free will; but the mind is determined to wish this or that by a cause, which has also been determined by another cause, and this last by another cause, and so on to infinity." Spinoza draws the following moral and theological conclusion from his denial of free will that Lincoln never openly states but puts into practice in his Second Inaugural: "This doctrine teaches us to hate no one, to despise no one, to mock no one, to be angry with no one, and to envy no one." In *The Essential*

Spinoza: Ethics and Related Writings, ed. Michael L. Morgan, trans. Samuel Shirley (Indianapolis: Hackett Publishing, 2006).

25. Lowenthal, *The Mind and the Art of Abraham Lincoln*, also sees Lincoln's "doctrine of necessity" as a potential philosophical alternative to religion, but he does not focus on its implications for moral responsibility or on its presuppositions in Spinozistic rationalism, 51–56.

26. Hans J. Morgenthau, *The Mind of Abraham Lincoln*, ed. Kenneth W. Thompson (Lanham, MD: University Press of America, 1983), 8.

27. Mark Noll, "Lincoln's God," *Journal of Presbyterian History* 82, no. 2 (2004): 77–88, 85.

28. Guelzo, *The Redeemer President*, 119. Lucas E. Morel, in *Lincoln's Sacred Effort* (Lanham, MD: Lexington Books, 2000), suggests that Lincoln's private beliefs do not influence his statesmanship: "Lincoln's belief in the doctrine of necessity was a private matter not intended for the public ear and one that did not threaten Christian orthodoxy because none existed on the subject," 89.

29. Lincoln, "Handbill," 383.

30. "It is permissible to think that a certain number of Americans follow their [political] habits more than their convictions in the worship they render to God. In the United States, moreover, the sovereign is religious, and consequently hypocrisy ought to be common," in Alexis de Tocqueville, *Democracy in America*, ed., trans. Harvey C. Mansfield and Delba Winthrop (Chicago: University of Chicago Press, 2000), 278. Locke comes to very similar conclusions about the rhetorical requirements and constraints that a liberal society of believers unofficially imposes on atheists in the public sphere in his *Letter Concerning Toleration* (ed. James H. Tully [Indianapolis: Hackett Publishing, 1983]): "Lastly, those are not at all to be tolerated who deny the being of a God. Promises, covenants, and oaths, which are the bonds of human society, can have no hold upon an atheist. The taking away of God, though but even in thought, dissolves all." Richard Rorty finds the type of religious "hypocrisy" that Tocqueville and Lincoln seem to recommend highly objectionable from the perspective of atheists: "We atheists . . . think it bad enough that we cannot run for public office without being disingenuous about our disbelief in God; despite the [liberal] compromise [with religion], no uncloseted atheist is likely to get elected anywhere in the country," in "Religion as a Conversation Stopper," *Philosophy and Social Hope* (New York: Penguin Books, 1999), 169.

31. Mark Noll, *The Civil War as a Theological Crisis* (Chapel Hill: University of North Carolina Press, 2006).

32. Frederick Augustus Ross, *Slavery Ordained of God* (Philadelphia: J. B. Lippincott, 1857), 4. Jack P. Maddex writes: "In their controversy with the Northern abolitionists, Southern Presbyterian theologians insisted that the Bible recognized slavery as a legitimate system without hinting that it was bad or transient. . . . That argument did not serve only to rebut the abolitionist belief that holding slaves was

a sin. It also enabled Southern Presbyterians to discard the Northern conservatives' axiom that slavery was a temporary and undesirable system," in "Postslavery Millennialism: Social Eschatology in Antebellum Southern Calvinism," *American Quarterly* 31, no. 1 (1979): 46–68, 49.

33. Sydney Alhstrom, *A Religious History of the American People* (New Haven, CT: Yale University Press, 2004), 673.

34. Ibid., 672.

35. Thomas Thompson published *The African Slave Trade for Negro Slaves, Shewn to Be Consistent with the Principles of Humanity, and with the Laws of Revealed Religion* in the 1770s. But in Britain, such biblical arguments were on the losing end of history, since the British Parliament outlawed slave trade in 1803 and eventually banned slavery in British territories by 1833.

36. Noll, *The Civil War as a Theological Crisis*, 3, 33–34, 38.

37. In his *Slavery Ordained of God*, Frederick Ross made a similar accusation of biblical heresy and infidelity against abolitionists: "The development has been twofold in the North. On the one hand, some antislavery men have left the light of the Bible, and wandered into the darkness until they have reached the blackness of the darkness of infidelity. Other some [sic] are following hard after, and are throwing the Bible into the furnace,—are melting it into iron, and forging it, and welding it, and twisting it, and grooving it into the shape and significance and goodness and gospel of Sharpe's rifles. Sir, are you not afraid that some of your once best men will soon have no better Bible than that?" Ross, *Slavery Ordained of God*, 37.

38. Noll, *The Civil War as a Theological Crisis*, 32.

39. Thomas L. Krannawitter, *Vindicating Lincoln: Defending the Politics of Our Greatest President* (New York: Rowman & Littlefield, 2008), 243.

40. In contrast to my interpretation, Patrick Deneen notices Lincoln's dismissive attitude toward revelation, but suggests that this is informed by Augustinian humility: "At first glance, this statement appears to be nothing other than a cheeky dismissal of any actual applicable 'wisdom' in the Bible—a work that, six years later, he locates as the source of human morality," in *Democratic Faith* (Princeton, NJ: Princeton University Press, 2005). Similarly, Mark Noll sees in the "Fragment" evidence of Lincoln's sense of "providential mystery," which would develop even further during the war, *The Civil War as a Theological Crisis*, 88.

41. Elsewhere Lincoln was even more explicit that the conclusions of natural theology were accessible entirely without reliance on revelation: "We think slavery is morally wrong, and a direct violation of that principle. We all think it wrong. It is clearly proved, I think, by natural theology, *apart from revelation*. Every man, black, white or yellow, has a mouth to be fed and two hands with which to feed it—and that bread should be allowed to go to that mouth without controversy" (emphasis added), in Lincoln, *Collected Works* (1953), vol. 4, 9.

42. Deneen, *Democratic Faith*, and Noll, *The Civil War as a Theological Crisis*.

43. Kenneth L. Deutsch and Joseph R. Fornieri, eds., *Lincoln's American Dream* (Washington, DC: Potomac Books, 2005), 27–28. Lincoln's most famous use of biblical text involved his references to "a house divided" (Matt. 12:22–28, Mark 3:22–26, Luke 11:14–20). Earl Schwartz points out that Lincoln used that metaphor "in literary settings wholly disassociated from its biblical context. Herndon maintained that this was intentional. 'I want to use some universally known figure [of speech],' Herndon recalled Lincoln telling him, 'expressed in simple language as universally well-known, that may strike home to the minds of men in order to raise them up to the peril of the times,'" in "A Poor Hand to Quote the Scripture: Lincoln on Genesis 3:19," *Journal of the Abraham Lincoln Association* 23, no. 2 (2002): 37–49. Whatever one makes of the accuracy of Hendon's account, Lincoln's employment of Genesis 3:17 went beyond mere appropriation: he attempted to reinterpret the Bible's meaning to develop a biblical theory of natural rights that condemned slavery as theft.

44. Standard interpretations suggest that Lincoln is presenting slavery as an attempt to shirk the divine curse of human labor, and indeed Lincoln encourages this view in his other statements. But Lincoln also shows that he is infusing this biblical perspective with a spirit of capitalist free labor that is alien to the scripture. In his 1854 "Fragment on Free Labor," the two alternative postures toward labor— as a biblical curse and as a capitalist blessing—that Lincoln is blurring together are discernible more in their dissonance than in their harmony, suggesting that Lincoln was aware how wide of a theological gulf he was bridging: "*Advancement— improvement in condition—is the order of things in a society of equals.* As labor is the *common burden of our race,* so the effort of some to shift their share of the burden on to the shoulders of others is *the great durable curse of the race. Originally a curse* for transgression upon the whole race, *when, as by slavery, it is concentrated on a part only,* it becomes *the double-refined curse of God* upon his creatures. *Free labor has the inspiration of hope; pure slavery has no hope,*" emphasis added, in Lincoln, *Collected Works* (1953), vol. 3, 462.

45. This may explain why a contemporaneous report in the *New York Herald* describes the audience reacting to this section of the president's speech as "a satirical observation," which "caused a half laugh." See in general Susan Jacoby, *Freethinkers: A History of American Secularism* (New York: Metropolitan Books, 2005), 120–123, and Ronald C. White, *Lincoln's Greatest Speech: The Second Inaugural* (New York: Simon & Schuster, 2002), 181–182.

46. Ronald Hendel's *The Book of Genesis: A Biography* (Princeton, NJ: Princeton University Press, 2012) neglects to emphasize how radically capitalist and innovative Lincoln's reading of this passage from Genesis turns out to be. Morel also tries to cover over the dissonance between the two views of labor, in *Lincoln's Sacred Effort,* 187.

47. A more serious charge was advanced by a Connecticut Democrat: "The inaugural is a mixture of Bible quotations made blasphemous in a degree by his use

of them and bloody anathema well suited to the times of corruption and lunacy in which we live," quoted in Michael Burlingame, *Abraham Lincoln: A Life*, vol. 2 (Baltimore, MD: Johns Hopkins University Press, 2008), 771.

48. Thomas L. Pangle, *The Spirit of Modern Republicanism: The Moral Vision of the American Founders and the Philosophy of Locke* (Chicago: University of Chicago Press, 1988), Chapter 14.

49. Smith interprets this differently: "Both texts present the war as the outcome of events that human intention could not and did not fully control, something that not even the most far-seeing statesman could have directed. Both texts express a profound sense of the limits of reason to discern the causes of the war, to understand its purpose, or to predict its outcome. *The will of God may prevail, but God's will is inscrutable to the human mind. The language throughout seems almost Augustinian or Pascalian—the inability of reason to penetrate or to make sense of human affairs*," emphasis added, in Smith, "How to Read Lincoln's Second Inaugural."

50. Burt, *Lincoln's Tragic Pragmatism*, 684–707.

51. Nagel, "John Rawls and Affirmative Action," in *Journal of Blacks in Higher Education* 39 (2003): 82–84. See also Percy B. Lehning, *John Rawls: An Introduction* (Cambridge, UK: Cambridge University Press, 2006): "His paradigm of injustice was slavery as it had existed in the southern states of the USA. Some judgments Rawls viewed as fixed points: ones we never expect to withdraw, as when Abraham Lincoln said: 'If slavery is not wrong, nothing is wrong.' Lincoln was, next to Immanuel Kant, a permanent source of inspiration," 1.

52. Waldron says that this sets public reason on the side of the status quo, and therefore does not allow for novel arguments conducive to social reform and change. Because it insists on using arguments that are shared and noncontroversial, Rawls's public reason "conception seems to rule out . . . the novel or disconcerting move in political argumentation: the premise that no one has ever thought of before, but which, once stated, sounds plausible or interesting. Rawls' conception seems to assume an inherent limit in the human capacity for imagination and creativity in politics, implying as it does that something counts as a legitimate move in public reasoning only to the extent that it latches onto existing premises that everybody already shares," in "Religious Contributions in Public Deliberation," 838.

CHAPTER 5. THE THEOLOGICAL FOUNDATIONS OF MARTIN LUTHER KING, JR.'S LEGACY OF RACIAL EQUALITY AND CIVIL DISOBEDIENCE

1. John Rawls, *Political Liberalism: Expanded Edition* (New York: Columbia University Press, 2005), 462–465.

2. Jeffrey Stout, *Democracy and Tradition* (Princeton, NJ: Princeton University Press, 2004); P. J. Weithman, *Religion and the Obligations of Citizenship* (Cambridge, UK: Cambridge University Press, 2002); Nicholas Wolterstorff, "The Role

of Religion in Decision and Discussion of Political Issues," in *Religion in the Public Square: The Place of Religious Convictions in Political Debate* (1997), 67–120, and "Why We Should Reject What Liberalism Tells Us about Speaking and Acting in Public for Religious Reasons," in *Religion and Contemporary Liberalism*, ed. Paul Weitham (Notre Dame, IN: Notre Dame University Press, 1997), 162–181.

3. Rawls, *Political Liberalism*, 464.

4. Ibid., xxvi.

5. Ibid., 785.

6. Richard Rorty, "Religion as a Conversation Stopper," in *Philosophy and Social Hope* (New York: Penguin Books, 1999), 158–174. What Rorty states openly (put simply, that religion is a "conversation stopper"), Rawls seems only to imply through the superstructure of public reason—that public dialogue is more genuinely tolerant when it is conducted in language that does not appeal exclusively to religious principles.

7. Rawls, *Political Liberalism*, 463n.

8. Ibid., 247.

9. Ibid.

10. As Charles Larmore correctly points out, "William Ellery Channing argued for the emancipation of the slaves just as Martin Luther King, Jr., argued against racial segregation by appealing to the belief that all human beings are equally God's creatures. Clearly they did not do so simply to indicate where they stood personally and to persuade others to share their faith. Their aim was to encourage others to take this religious view to heart as they dealt with those questions in their capacities as voters, legislators, officials, and judges. Did Channing and King therefore overstep the boundaries of public reason? On a straightforward understanding of that concept, they did," in "Public Reason," *The Cambridge Companion to Rawls*, ed. Samuel L. Freeman (New York: Cambridge University Press), 385.

11. For example, in replying to critics of their influential work *Democracy and Disagreement: Why Moral Conflict Cannot Be Avoided in Politics, and What Should Be Done about It* (Cambridge, MA: Harvard University Press, 1996), Amy Gutmann and Dennis Thompson want to enlist King in favor of a modern pragmatist notion of deliberative politics, one that aims at avoiding conflict or deep disagreement. But they do so only by minimizing the moral and theological intransigency of King's public testimony: "Martin Luther King Jr. certainly challenged the deepest convictions of committed racists, but he did so consistently while economizing on moral disagreement. In some cases, the economizing process may sharpen the disagreement that remains, but it will usually also narrow it," "Democratic Disagreement," in *Deliberative Politics: Essays on Democracy and Disagreement*, ed. Stephen Macedo (Oxford, UK: Oxford University Press, 1999), 262.

12. Christopher Hitchens, *God Is Not Great: How Religion Poisons Everything* (Crows Nest, UK: Allen & Unwin, 2007), 179, 180.

13. The question of whether or not political conceptions of justice are severable

from their comprehensive foundations is a thorny issue in scholarship on Rawlsian liberalism, since Rawls's "translation proviso" presupposes the citizens can bracket off the comprehensive doctrines on which their political values are actually based while still relying on the latter political values (now in "freestanding" form) to inform their public deliberations. See in general Kevin Vallier, "Against Public Reason Liberalism's Accessibility Requirement," *Journal of Moral Philosophy* 8, no. 3 (2011): 366–389.

14. Because I uncover this modern rationalist strand in King's theology that stands in uneasy combination with his Thomistic outlook, my interpretation is distinguished from those studies that see King as a straightforward embodiment of Thomas Aquinas's principles of natural law in modern society. For a more thoroughly Thomistic interpretation of King, see in general Justin Dyer and Kevin Stuart, "Rawlsian Public Reason and the Theological Framework of Martin Luther King's 'Letter from Birmingham Jail,'" *Politics and Religion* 6, no. 1 (2013): 145–163.

15. Liberal theology aims "to create a progressive Christian alternative to established orthodoxies and a rising tide of rationalistic deism and atheism," an alternative that will require the abandonment of neither the authority of modern knowledge and its humanistic individualism nor the transcendent God and redemptive mission of Christianity. See Gary J. Dorrien, *The Making of American Liberal Theology: Crisis, Irony, and Postmodernity, 1950–2005* (Louisville, KY: Westminster John Knox Press, 2006), 2.

16. Amy Gutmann refers to King's ability to engage in "self-translation" (911) between his religious and civic views, in Gutmann, "Religious Freedom and Civic Responsibility," *Washington and Lee Law Review* 56 (1999): 907–922; David Richards goes even further in claiming that "at no point in the argument [of King's Letter] is there an appeal to anything that would conventionally be understood as religious dogma, ritual or theology" (2140), in David A. J. Richards, "Ethical Religion and the Case for Human Rights: The Case of Martin Luther King, Jr.," *Fordham Law Review* 72 (2003): 2105–2152.

17. Richard B. Russell, Speech to the "Georgia General Assembly 8 February 1960," in *Voice of Georgia: Speeches of Richard B. Russell, 1928–1969*, ed. Calvin McLeod Logue and Dwight L. Freshley (Macon, GA: Mercer University Press, 1997), 352.

18. *Congressional Record*, Senate, June 10, 1964, 13309.

19. Cited in James Reichley, *Religion in American Public Life* (Washington, DC: The Brookings Institute, 1985), 248.

20. Michael B. Friedland, *Lift Up Your Voice Like a Trumpet: White Clergy and the Civil Rights and Antiwar Movements, 1954–1973* (Chapel Hill: University of North Carolina Press), 27.

21. Martin Luther King, Jr., *Stride toward Freedom: The Montgomery Story*, edited by Clayborne Carson (Boston: Beacon Press: 2010), 116–117.

22. Lewis V. Baldwin, *The Voice of Conscience: The Church in the Mind of Martin Luther King, Jr.* (Oxford, UK: Oxford University Press, 2010), 78.

23. Cited in James Reichley, *Faith in Politics* (Washington, DC: Brookings Institution Press, 2002), 234.

24. Ibid., 235.

25. Blake continued, framing the question of segregation in unequivocally moral terms: "As churches, synagogues, and religious leaders, our concern is with the purpose of civil rights legislation and with the moral principles that indicate the necessity of such legislation."

26. Hubert Humphrey estimated that the role of the clergy in the passage of the Civil Rights Act was indispensable: "We needed the help of the clergy, and this was assiduously encouraged," Humphrey noted. "I have said a number of times, and I repeat it now, that without the clergy, we couldn't have possibly passed this bill." http://www.congresslink.org/civilrights/1964.htm.

27. Martin Luther King, Jr., "A Religion of Doing," Sermon at Dexter Avenue Baptist Church, July 4, 1954, Montgomery, AL, in *The Papers of Martin Luther King, Jr.*, vol. 6, ed. Clayborne Carson (Berkeley: University of California Press, 2007), 171.

28. Ibid,. 172.

29. Martin Luther King, Jr., "A Knock at Midnight," in *A Knock at Midnight: Inspiration from the Great Sermons of Reverend Martin*, ed. Clayborne Carson and Peter Holloran (New York: Warner Books, 2000).

30. Martin Luther King, Jr., "Guidelines for a Constructive Church," in ibid.

31. Martin Luther King, Jr., "Pilgrimage to Nonviolence" (1960), in *A Testament of Hope: The Essential Writings and Speeches of King*, ed. James W. Washington (New York: Harper Collins, 1991), 35–40.

32. "An adequate understanding of man is found neither in the thesis of liberalism nor in the antithesis of neo-orthodoxy, but in a synthesis which reconciles the truths of both."

33. Martin Luther King, Jr., "A Letter from Birmingham Jail" (1963), in *A Testament of Hope*, 289–302.

34. Martin Luther King, Jr., "I Have a Dream" (1963), in ibid., 217–220.

35. King, "Letter from Birmingham Jail."

36. Thomas Aquinas, *Summa Theologiae*, ed. R. W. Dyson (Cambridge, UK: Cambridge University Press, 2002), I-II, Question 90, Article 4.

37. Ibid., I-II, Question 91, Article 2.

38. This umbilical cord connecting King to the Catholic natural law tradition is an important element that defines his civil theology and gives it its capacity to act as a prophetic voice of social reform. It is also what distinguished King from the modern theologians who are usually thought to have influenced him—in particular Reinhold Niebuhr and Paul Tillich. Niebuhr and Tillich both take a dim view of natural law. Tillich, a towering figure of midcentury US theology and a

subject of King's dissertation, associated natural law theory with the Roman Catholic Church's legalistic explication of the Ten Commandments and the Sermon on the Mount. While he affirms the values of equality and freedom he finds in natural law theory, Tillich argues that these concepts, when applied to the existing world, "become indefinite, changing, [and] relative," with the result that "natural law theory cannot answer the questions of the contents of justice." Niebuhr, a renowned public intellectual and theological proponent of "Christian realism," is even more critical, pointing to "the perils of moralism and self-righteousness in the rigidities of the natural law." See Reinhold Niebuhr, *The Nature and Destiny of Man: A Christian Interpretation* vol. 1 (Louisville, KY: Westminster John Knox Press, 1996 [1941]), 221.

39. King, "Letter from Birmingham Jail."

40. Gutmann, "Religious Freedom and Civic Responsibility," 910. While Amy Gutmann describes this as "King's translation of the Christian and Thomist argument into purely civic terms in the very same letter" (910), as I have been stressing the more accurate interpretation is that King sees the civic and theological dimensions of his witness to be intertwined and inseparable from each other. As Robert Kraynak points out, "in reading Martin Luther King's description of higher moral law, one can see another version of Christian personalism. It combines the Augustinian and Thomistic concept of eternal law with Kant's ethical imperative to treat human beings as 'persons' rather than as 'things.'. . . Buber's formulation . . . distinguishes an 'I–thou' relationship from 'I–it' in exactly the same way that Kant distinguishes the treatment of 'persons' from the treatment of 'things,'" in Robert Kraynak, *Christian Faith and Modern Democracy: God and Politics in a Fallen World* (Notre Dame, IN: University of Notre Dame Press, 2001), 158.

41. As Gutmann herself acknowledges, part of the moral power of King's Birmingham Letter is that it fused the theological and constitutional arguments together: "surely King's letter to his fellow citizens would have been *less morally compelling*, not more, had King limited himself *to only the religious discourse*, or *to only the nonreligious discourse*," in Gutmann, "Religious Freedom and Civic Responsibility," 911, emphasis added.

42. Martin Luther King, Jr., "The Ethical Demands of Integration," in *A Testament of Hope*, 117–125.

43. Ibid.

44. Aquinas, *Summa Theologiae*, 96.4.

45. Ibid.

46. John Gresham Machen, *Christianity and Liberalism* (Grand Rapids, MI: Eerdmans Publishing, 2009), 4.

47. Ibid., 15.

48. Ibid., 5.

49. Martin Luther King, Jr., "Advice for Living" (1957), in *The Papers of Martin Luther King, Jr.*, vol. 4, 279–281.

50. Martin Luther King, Jr., "The Weakness of Liberal Theology" (1948), Chester, PA, in ibid., vol. 6, 78–80.

51. Martin Luther King, Jr., "Science and Religion" (September 1948–May 1951), Chester PA, in ibid., vol. 6, 108–109.

52. Martin Luther King, Jr., "How to Use the Bible in Modern Theological Construction," in ibid., vol. 1, 253.

53. Ibid., 253–254.

54. Ibid., 254.

55. "When the social gospelers spoke of the authority of Christian experience, they took for granted their own deep grounding in Bible study, family devotions, personal prayer, and worship. Today the loss of the transcendental, biblical voice in liberal theology is one important reason that much of it gets little notice," Gary J. Dorrien, "American Liberal Theology: Crisis, Irony, Decline, Renewal, Ambiguity," *Cross Currents*, http://www.crosscurrents.org/dorrien200506.htm.

CHAPTER 6. CAN LIBERALISM APPROPRIATE THE MORAL CONTENTS OF RELIGION? HABERMAS AND TOCQUEVILLE ON RELIGIOUS TRANSFORMATION AND DEMOCRACY'S CIVIC LIFE

1. *Case of Lautsi and Others v. Italy* (2011), European Court of Human Rights, 5.

2. Ibid., 9. Lautsi therefore presents a watershed moment in European religious jurisprudence, insofar as the decision explicitly embraced the idea that liberalism derives its normative character from what was (at least until very recently) a religious ethos: "Singularly, Christianity—for example through the well-known and often misunderstood 'Render unto Caesar the things which are Caesar's, and unto . . . '—through its strong emphasis placed on love for one's neighbour, and even more through the explicit predominance given to charity over faith itself, contains in substance those ideas of tolerance, equality and liberty which form the basis of the modern secular State, and of the Italian State in particular," ibid., 5.

3. Stephen Macedo, "Transformative Constitutionalism and the Case of Religion: Defending the Moderate Hegemony of Liberalism," *Political Theory* 26, no. 1 (1998): 56–80; John Perry, *The Pretenses of Loyalty: Locke, Liberal Theory, and American Political Theology* (Oxford, UK: Oxford University Press, 2011).

4. Habermas, "Faith and Knowledge," an acceptance speech for the Peace Prize of the German Publishers and Booksellers Association, Paulskirche, Frankfurt, October 14, 2001. In *The Future of Human Nature* (Cambridge, UK: Polity, 2003), 101–115.

5. See Stanley Fish, "Does Reason Know What It Is Missing?" http://opinionator.blogs.nytimes.com/2010/04/12/does-reason-know-what-it-is-missing /?_php =true&_type=blogs&_r=0, and Peter Berger, "What Happens When a Leftist Philosopher Discovers God?" http://www.the-american-interest.com/berger/2011/09 /21/what-happens-when-a-leftist-philosopher-discovers-god/. The debate between Habermas and Ratzinger has been published under the title "Pre-political Foun-

dations of the Democratic Constitutional State?" in *The Dialectics of Secularization: On Reason and Religion*, ed. with a foreword by Florian Schuller and trans. Brian McNeil (San Francisco: Ignatius: 2006).

6. Several notable studies have argued that Habermas's turn to "post-secularism" should not be interpreted as a repudiation of modern rationalism: "There has indeed been a real transformation in Habermas' thought. But it has occurred within a modern body of ideas that remains committed to the principle of the autonomy of politics," Philippe Portier, "Religion and Democracy in the Thought of Jürgen Habermas," *Culture and Society* 48 (2011): 427. See also Christina Lafont, "Religion in the Public Sphere: Remarks on Habermas's Conception of Public Deliberation in Postsecular Societies," *Constellations* 14, no. 2 (2007): 239–259, and Simone Chambers, "How Religion Speaks to the Agnostic: Habermas on the Persistent Value of Religion," *Constellations* 14, no. 2 (2007): 210–223. This chapter does not quibble with this finding, but it seeks to question whether Habermas's postsecular middle way can be consistently understood within the frame of modern thought through an encounter with Tocqueville.

7. Chambers, "How Religion Speaks to the Agnostic"; Lafont, "Religion in the Public Sphere"; see also: Pablo C. Jimenez Loberia, "Liberal Democracy: Culture Free? The Habermas-Ratzinger Debate and Its Implications for Europe," *Australian and New Zealand Journal of European Studies* 2, no. 2 (2011): 44–57; Patrick Neal, "Habermas, Religion, and Citizenship," *Politics and Religion* 7, no. 2 (2014): 318–338; Melissa Yates, "Rawls and Habermas on Religion in the Public Sphere," *Philosophy & Social Criticism* 33 (2007): 880–891.

8. Portier, "Religion and Democracy"; Maeve Cooke, "Salvaging and Secularizing the Semantic Contents of Religion: The Limitations of Habermas's Postmetaphysical Proposal," *International Journal for Philosophy of Religion* 60 (2006): 187–207.

9. Jürgen Habermas, "On Social Identity," *Telos* 1974, no. 19 (1974): 91–103, and *The Theory of Communicative Action*, trans. Thomas McCarthy (Boston: Beacon Press, 1984), especially 77.

10. Portier, "Religion and Democracy."

11. Jürgen Habermas, *Postmetaphysical Thinking*, trans. W. M. Hohengarten (Cambridge, MA: MIT Press, 1992), 51.

12. Jürgen Habermas, "To Seek to Salvage an Unconditional Meaning without God Is a Futile Undertaking," *Religion and Rationality* (Cambridge, UK: Polity: 2002), 108.

13. Religious reason would survive in the West only "as long as no better words for what religion can say are found in the medium of rational discourse," Habermas, *Postmetaphysical Thinking*, 52.

14. In Peter Berger's view, this stage marks Habermas's evolution "from Marxism to the French ideal of *laicite*—the public life of the republic kept antiseptically

clean of religious contamination," in "What Happens When a Leftist Philosopher Discovers God?"

15. Jürgen Habermas, *Europe: A Faltering Project* (Cambridge, UK: Polity, 2009), 76.

16. Scholars are divided on whether Habermas has genuinely repudiated Rawls's public reason position. Those who stress the difference between Habermas and Rawls emphasize Habermas's claim that liberal citizens can learn from religious reasons, which embody important moral insights that cannot be accessed by secular reason alone: Chambers, "How Religion Speaks to the Agnostic." Others argue that Habermas does not present a genuine alternative to the leading liberal theory of public reasoning because he still insists on a "translation proviso" that requires religious reasons to be rendered into nonreligious language, albeit only at the institutional stage: Lafont, "Religion in the Public Sphere," and James W. Boettcher, "Habermas, Religion and the Ethics of Citizenship," *Philosophy and Social Criticism* 35, no. 1–2 (2009): 215–238.

17. Habermas, "Pre-political Foundations," 24.

18. Robert Audi, *Religious Commitment and Secular Reason* (Cambridge, UK: Cambridge University Press, 2000); Macedo, "Transformative Constitutionalism and the Case of Religion."

19. Ibid.

20. Ibid.

21. Ibid., 28.

22. Ibid., 24.

23. Jürgen Habermas, "Religion in the Public Sphere," *European Journal of Philosophy* 14, no. 17 (2006): 17.

24. Ibid. For a recent statement, see Habermas's *Europe: A Faltering Project* (Cambridge, UK: Polity, 2009): "Ever fewer sociologists support the long unchallenged hypothesis that there is close connection between social modernization and the secularization of the population," 60. There Habermas argues that the United States, which for a long time appeared as the exception to the secularization thesis due to the "undiminished vibrancy" of its religious communities, "appears today more like the normal case," given the recent religious revival in the rest of the non-European world.

25. Jürgen Habermas, "Notes on a Post-Secular Society," 2008, available at: http://www.signandsight.com/features/1714.html.

26. Jürgen Habermas, "The Debate on the Ethical Self-Understanding of the Species," in *The Future of Human Nature* (Cambridge, UK: Polity, 2003), 16–100, especially 19, 24–25, 40–41, 48, 98.

27. In "Faith and Knowledge," Habermas warns the West against being "perceived as crusaders of a competing religion or as salespeople of instrumental reason and destructive secularization" and instead recommends "translation" of

religious traditions as the "nondestructive [form] of secularization," in *The Future of Human Nature*, 103, 114.

28. Jürgen Habermas, *Between Naturalism and Religion* (Cambridge, UK: Polity, 2008), 6.

29. Habermas, *Dialectics of Secularization*, 22–23.

30. Ibid., 46.

31. Ibid, 38–39.

32. Ibid., 38.

33. Ibid.

34. Ibid., 21.

35. Ibid.

36. Ibid.

37. "It still remains the case that liberal societal structures are dependent on the solidarity of their citizens," Habermas acknowledges, and if such solidarity can be supplied only by a morality that derives from a specific religious tradition, then the liberal project effectively unravels, ibid., 22.

38. Ibid., 29.

39. Ibid., 30.

40. Habermas points to the ubiquitous example of the civic challenge of voting: "For example, in a democratic constitutional state, a legal obligation to vote would be just as alien as a legal requirement to display solidarity. All one can do is suggest to the citizens of a liberal society that they should be willing to get involved on behalf of fellow citizens whom they do not know and who remain anonymous to them," 30.

41. Ibid., 30–31.

42. Ibid., 32–34.

43. Ibid., 33.

44. Christina Lafont does not fully confront this massive challenge that Habermas identifies to the civic health of liberalism as a political project, a challenge that he suggests can only be overcome by religion. Lafont, "Religion in the Public Sphere." As Habermas states in his Peace Prize speech in Frankfurt: "Giving due consideration to the religious heritage of its moral foundations, the liberal state should consider the possibility that it may not be able to meet the completely new challenges it faces simply by relying on the formulations it developed earlier to meet those attending its origins," in "Faith and Knowledge." Hugh Baxter is closer to the truth when he stresses that "the crisis tendencies Habermas identifies are not just economic and environmental. He sees also a crisis in the solidarity among citizens that sustained the democratic constitutional state. No analogous solidarity, in his view, can yet be drawn on at the transnational or supranational level," in *Habermas: The Discourse Theory of Law and Democracy* (Stanford, CA: Stanford University Press: 2011), 229.

45. Habermas, "Pre-political Foundations," 35–36, 45.

46. Ibid., 37.

47. Ibid.

48. Ibid., 30.

49. Ibid., 43.

50. Jürgen Habermas, "Religion in the Public Sphere," *European Journal of Philosophy* 14, no. 17 (2006): 1–25.

51. Ibid., 8. To support this assertion about the positive contribution of religion to civil society, a contribution that secularism would endanger if it were hostile to religious arguments in the public sphere, Habermas quotes the following passage from Paul Weithmann's 2002 study: "churches contribute to democracy in the United States by fostering realized democratic citizenship. They encourage their members to accept democratic values as the basis for important political decisions and to accept democratic institutions as legitimate. The means by which they make their contributions, including their own interventions in civic argument and public political debate, affect the political arguments their members may be inclined to use, the basis on which they vote, and the specification of their citizenship with which they identify. They may encourage their members to think of themselves as bound by antecedently given moral norms with which political outcomes must be consistent. The realization of citizenship by those who are legally entitled to take part in political decisionmaking is an enormous achievement for a liberal democracy, one in which the institutions of civil society play a crucial role," in Weithmann, *Religion and the Obligations of Citizenship* (Cambridge, UK: Cambridge University Press, 2002), 91.

52. Habermas, "Religion in the Public Sphere."

53. Ibid., 5.

54. Ibid., 18, and *Dialectics of Secularization*, 49–50. This has extremely curious un-Rawlsian implications. For instance, in his Peace Prize speech in Frankfurt, Habermas laments the attempt made by pro-life Protestant and Catholic advocates in Germany to translate their position into scientific and secular terms. Rather than invoke the idea of human dignity based on man's creation "in the image of God," pro-life advocates appeal to the terminology of "legal rights of fertilized ova outside the mother's body." The problem here is not simply that such scientific and constitutional language falsifies the beliefs of the speaker, nor simply that it places an unfair translation burden on the speaker. For Habermas, the deeper problem is that the full range of moral meaning is lost when religious language is rendered in secular terms: "This *creatural nature* of the image expresses an intuition which in the present context may even speak to those who are tone-deaf to religious connotations. . . . God remains a 'God of free men' only as long as we do not level out the absolute difference that exists between the creator and the creature," in Habermas, "Faith and Knowledge," 114–115, emphasis in the original.

55. Habermas, *Dialectics of Secularization*, 42. Habermas insists that this awareness of the limits of secular reason should lead to an openness to learn from

religious traditions: "Secular citizens or those of other religious persuasions can under certain circumstances learn something from religious contributions; this is, for example, the case if they recognize in the normative truth content of a religious utterance hidden intuitions of their own," in "Religion in the Public Sphere," 10.

56. Habermas, *Dialectics of Secularization*, 45.

57. Jürgen Habermas, "A Conversation about God and the World: Interview with Eduardo Mendieta," in *Religion and Rationality: Essays on Reason, God and Modernity* (Cambridge, UK: Polity, 2002), 162.

58. Habermas, "Pre-political Foundations," 45.

59. Habermas, "A Conversation about God and the World," 162.

60. Jürgen Habermas, "Transcendence from Within, Transcendence in this World," *Religion and Rationality* (Cambridge, UK: Polity, 2002), 74–75.

61. Joseph Ratzinger, in *Dialectics of Secularization*, 65–66, emphasis in the original.

62. Martin Zetterbaum finds Tocqueville to be building on the tradition "originating with Machiavelli and continuing in the natural-rights teaching of Hobbes," in *Tocqueville and the Problem of Democracy* (Stanford, CA: Stanford University Press, 1987), 105. Similarly, John Koritansky believes that "Tocqueville is a thinker in the modern tradition inaugurated by Rousseau," both in his critique of bourgeoisie democracy and in his appeal to the Rousseauian idea of "humanity," in *Alexis de Tocqueville and the New Science of Politics* (Durham, NC: Carolina Academic Press, 2010), 13. As I emphasizes throughout this section, these interpretations tend to minimize the anti-Enlightenment goals of Tocqueville's "new political science."

63. Thomas West regards Tocqueville's omission of natural rights and the Declaration of Independence as a serious "flaw" of *Democracy in America* and a reflection of the sociological bent informing that work, in "Misunderstanding the American Founding," *Interpreting Tocqueville's Democracy in America*, edited by Ken Musagi (Savage, MD: Rowman & Littlefield, 1991). For a similar criticism, see George Anastapolo, who claims that Tocqueville was a "political sociologist" rather than a great political thinker or a political philosopher, in ibid., 459. Harvey Mansfield's response to these criticisms can be found in his *Tocqueville: A Very Short Introduction* (Oxford, UK: Oxford University Press, 2010): Tocqueville "deals with ['the old liberalism' of Locke and the Declaration] by ignoring it" (4, cf. 31). This is the strategy of his "new liberalism in which freedom is the friend of religion and infused with pride as well as impelled by self-interest," 4.

64. Garry Wills, "Did Tocqueville 'Get' America?" in *New York Review of Books*, April 29, 2004, 54. Although he does not mention Tocqueville's views on religion, Rogers Smith makes a similar case in his famous essay "Beyond Tocqueville, Myrdal, and Hartz: The Multiple Traditions in America," *American Political Science Review* 87, no. 3 (1993): 549–566. Smith contends that "the Tocquevillian story is deceptive because it is too narrow," and one of its chief blind spots is that Tocque-

ville fails to give due consideration "to the inegalitarian ideologies and conditions that have shaped the participants and the substance of American politics just as deeply."

65. Victorien Sardou quoted in Phillipe Roger, *L'ennemi américain* (Paris: Seuil, 2002), 88.

66. A number of scholars interpret Tocqueville as a "religious functionalist": Jack Lively, *The Social and Political Thought of Alexis de Tocqueville* (Oxford, UK: Clarendon Press, 1962), 40–41; Sanford Kessler, *Tocqueville's Civil Religion* (Albany: State University of New York Press, 1994), 52–54; and Zetterbaum, *Tocqueville and the Problem of Democracy*, 1–16, 19–21. Lively and Zetterbaum fault Tocqueville for undermining authentic religion by being indifferent to the truth or falsity of religion and by promoting socially useful "myths" in their stead. While this chapter does not reject the view that there is a utilitarian side to Tocqueville's understanding of religion, it aims to demonstrate that it is a misunderstanding of Tocqueville to claim that he reduces religion to its bare utility or that he promotes indifference to religious truth.

67. Sheldon Wolin, *Tocqueville between Two Worlds* (Princeton, NJ: Princeton University Press, 2001).

68. Lively, *The Social and Political Thought of Alexis de Tocqueville*; Koritansky, *Alexis de Tocqueville and the New Science of Politics*; and Zetterbaum, *Tocqueville and the Problem of Democracy*.

69. For an illuminating discussion of the influence of Pascal on Tocqueville's religious teaching, see Peter Augustine Lawler, "Tocqueville's Aristocratic Christianity," *Catholic Social Science Review* 17 (2012): 21–32, and Lawler, *The Restless Mind: Alexis de Tocqueville on the Origin and Perpetuation of Human Liberty* (New York: Rowman & Littlefield, 1993).

70. Wolin, *Tocqueville between Two Worlds*, 324.

71. Ibid., 162, 298, 328. At one point, Wolin goes so far as to suggest that for Tocqueville, "the topic of religion" "reveals how culture is being shaped into a construct which contains, as it were, *directives to the ruling groups* instructing them in the type of powers available for shaping and containing democracy," 328, emphasis added. Wolin does not ask how Tocqueville could have thought religion would fulfill its social purpose if it were understood chiefly as a "construct" rather than as a sincerely held belief.

72. Ibid., 324.

73. Alexis de Tocqueville, *Democracy in America*, ed. Harvey C. Mansfield and Delba Winthrop (Chicago: University of Chicago Press, 2000), 43.

74. It can be tempting to read Tocqueville as prefiguring contemporary interpretations of the American founding, such as the one offered by Gordon Wood in his classic *Creation of the American Republic 1776–1787* (New York: W. W. Norton, 1972), which emphasizes neglected strands of civic and "classical republicanism," and highlights the continuities between America's origins and premodern cove-

nant theology (118). As this chapter has been trying to demonstrate, this misses the theological-political tensions in Tocqueville's account of American democracy.

75. Lawler, "Tocqueville's Aristocratic Christianity," 26.

76. Douglas Kries and Sanford Kessler both suggest that Tocqueville uncovers the germinating seeds of separation of church and state in this tension-ridden "division of labor" that the Puritans embodied: Kries, "Alexis de Tocqueville on 'Civil Religion' and the Catholic Faith," in *Civil Religion in Political Thought*, ed. John von Heyking and Ronald Weed (Washington, DC: Catholic University Press, 2010), 176, and Kessler, "Tocqueville's Puritans: Christianity and the American Founding," *Journal of Politics* 54, no. 3 (1992): 776–792.

77. In this connection, Tocqueville mentions their legal provisions for citizen militia and jury duty, which would seem to indicate that what he wants to highlight in the Puritan experience is how their religious devotion helped them imbue democratic liberty with civic responsibilities and moral restrains, Tocqueville, *Democracy*, 40.

78. Wolin deplores that Tocqueville's account of the function of religion aims to "restrain rather than educate the demos" (Wolin, *Tocqueville between Two Worlds*, 162), when in fact what Tocqueville aims to show is that religion educates the democratic majority precisely by reminding it of the transcendent principles that should circumscribe its uses of power. See especially Tocqueville's account in Chapter 2 of *Democracy* of Winthrop's speech on two versions of freedom—negative freedom, which man shares with beasts, and the noble freedom "to do what is right."

79. Barbara Allen, *Tocqueville, Covenant, and the Democratic Revolution: Harmonizing Earth with Heaven* (Lanham, MD: Lexington Books, 2005). In her thorough study of Tocqueville's political science and the influence of covenant tradition in America, Allen sides with those who stress "continuity": "It would take another century or so for private reason to become the powerful force that Tocqueville saw, *but the foundation for harmonizing heaven with earth on human terms was laid in the Protestant paradox*," 22, emphasis added.

80. Harvey C. Mansfield, "Providence and Democracy," *Claremont Review of Books* 11, no. 1–2 (2011): 74–75.

81. This statement is preceded by Tocqueville's most explicit criticism of classical political philosophy: "The most profound geniuses of Rome and Greece, with the greatest scope, were never able to reach this idea—so general, but at the same time so simple—of the similarity of men and of the equal right to liberty that each one of them bears from birth; and they did their utmost to prove that slavery was natural and that it would always exist," 413.

82. This is especially evident in a quotation that Tocqueville provides from a 1663 sermon denouncing New Englanders for forgetting the original, religious origins of their colony and for devoting themselves to "increasing cent per cent" and to "worldly gain," 688.

83. C.f. Mansfield, "Providence and Democracy," 75: "The puritan point of departure needed to be departed from, and replaced by the principle, or dogma, of 'the sovereignty of the people.' Not wishing to offend religion or praise its enemies, Tocqueville doesn't mention its disestablishment."

84. In a famous interview with the *Commonweal* magazine, John Rawls appealed to these pages from *Democracy in America* to defend his theory of political liberalism against charges that it was hostile to religious commitment. Rawls claimed that political liberalism agrees with Tocqueville's thesis that religion can flourish under separation of church and state.

85. Alan Wolfe, *One Nation, After All* (New York: Viking, 1998), 298–299.

86. Robert D. Putnam and David E. Campbell, *American Grace: How Religion Divides and Unites Us* (New York: Simon & Schuster, 2010), 534–547.

87. This tension between Volume I and II is so jarring that Catherine Zuckert, along with several other scholars, has concluded that by the time he wrote the second half of *Democracy in America*, Tocqueville abandoned his initial hope that religion could provide an effective restraint on democracy, thus changing his mind entirely between the publication of the two volumes. Zuckert, "Not by Preaching: Tocqueville on the Role of Religion in American Democracy," *Review of Politics* 43, no. 2 (1981): 232; Kessler, *Tocqueville's Civil Religion*, 115; Zetterbaum, *Tocqueville and the Problem of Democracy*, 123. As I will show below, while Tocqueville shows that a democratically transformed religion is less capable of restraining public opinion, he maintains the hope that a more traditional religion that responds to man's natural spiritual longings could continue to provide civic restraints that democracy requires.

88. As Ronald Beiner points out, "Catholicism must be Protestantized to cater to a democratic people's natural preference for Protestant simplicity, and yet we are told at the same time that Catholicism holds special cultural advantages over the Protestant sects in precisely those respects in which Catholic Christianity is non-Protestant," in *Civil Religion: A Dialogue in the History of Political Philosophy* (Cambridge, UK: Cambridge University Press, 2010), 255.

89. John Koritansky suggests that Tocqueville's discussion is an implicit attack on the Catholic Church for its continuing demand for doctrinal obedience, in "Two Forms of the Love of Equality in Tocqueville's Practical Teaching for Democracy," *Polity* 6, no. 4 (1974): 488–499, 497n. Lively seems to agree with this view, since he shows that Tocqueville does in effect criticize certain aspects of the French church's practice at the time, in *Social and Political Thought of Alexis de Tocqueville*, 188–194. Both appear to make short shrift of Tocqueville's prediction that Catholicism would find new appeal in democratic centuries, and that it would do so precisely because of the authoritarian, transrational, and dogmatic dimensions of the traditional Catholic teaching, which would fill a spiritual void in the democratic soul.

90. "The religion Tocqueville would preserve is indeed not simply Christian,

although its historical origins are," in Zuckert, "Not by Preaching Alone," 274–275. Others have criticized Tocqueville's approach to American Catholicism as a symptom of a broader failure of his religious teaching, which many critics have found to be far too utilitarian in its treatment of religion (Zetterbaum, *Tocqueville and the Problem of Democracy*; and Lively, *Social and Political Thought of Alexis de Tocqueville*).

91. Letter to Louis de Kergorlay, June 29, 1831, in Tocqueville, *Selected Letters on Politics and Society*, ed. Roger Boesche (Berkeley: University of California Press, 1985). Helpful discussions of this letter can be found in William A. Galston, "Tocqueville on Liberalism and Religion," in *Tocqueville's Political Science: Classic Essays*, ed. Peter Augustine Lawler (New York: Garland, 1992), and Sanford Kessler, "The Secularization Debate: A Tocquevillian Perspective," in *Tocqueville's Defense of Human Liberty: Current Essays*, ed. Peter Augustine Lawler and Joseph Alulis (New York: Garland, 1993).

92. Alexis de Tocqueville, Letter to Kergorlay, October 18, 1847, in *Selected Letters*, 53.

93. In contrast, Koritansky and Kessler both interpret Tocqueville's "civil religion" in Rousseauian terms.

94. Tocqueville, Letter to Kergorlay.

95. Thomas Jefferson, *The Writings of Thomas Jefferson*, 20 vols., ed. Albert Ellery Bergh and Andrew A. Lipscomb (Washington, DC: Thomas Jefferson Memorial Association, 1904), 15:385.

96. Paolo Flores d'Arcais, "Eleven Theses against Habermas," trans. Giacomo Donis, http://www.the-utopian.org/d'Arcais_1.

97. Tocqueville to Gobineau, October 2, 1843, in Tocqueville, *The European Revolution and Correspondence with Gobineau*, ed. and trans. John Lukacs (Garden City, NY: Doubleday, 1959), 205–206.

CONCLUSION: TOLERATION, DEMOCRATIC RELIGION, AND AMERICA'S CIVIC LIFE

1. Alexis de Tocqueville, *Democracy in America*, trans. Harvey C. Mansfield and Delba Winthrop (Chicago: University of Chicago Press, 2000), II.1.5.

2. Robert D. Putnam and David E. Campbell, *American Grace: How Religion Divides and Unites Us* (New York: Simon & Schuster, 2010).

3. For helpful reactions to Putnam and Campbell's *American Grace*, see the Review Symposium in *Perspectives on Politics* 10, no. 1 (2012). My comments on Putnam and Campbell's findings are informed in part by the reviews of their work by Jon A. Shields and Jean Bethke Elshtain that appear in that symposium.

4. The authors emphasize that this edge in civic involvement among the religious is not restricted to service rendered to religious organizations, but extends to secular causes as well: "religion boosts total volunteering so substantially that in addition to their higher rate of religious volunteering, regular churchgoers are

also much more likely to volunteer for secular causes," and "among secular types of volunteering this religious edge is especially marked for service to poor, elderly, and young people, . . . and . . . church attendance is a significant predictor for all types of volunteering except for arts and cultural organizations," Putnam and Campbell, *American Grace*, 447.

5. When charitable giving is measured as a fraction of annual income, "the average person in the most religious fifth of Americans is more than four times as generous as his or her counterpart in the least religious fifth."

6. Robert Putnam, *Bowling Alone: The Collapse and Revival of the American Community* (New York: Touchstone Books by Simon & Schuster, 2001).

7. The authors seem to miss this paradox. Consider, for example, their celebration of the role of religion in mobilizing abolitionism and the civil rights movement, among other "progressive movements" that had "powerful religious roots," Putnam and Campbell, *American Grace*, 114–115, 231–233, 254.

BIBLIOGRAPHY

Abramowitz, Alan, and Kyle Saunders. "Is Polarization a Myth?" *Journal of Politics* 70, no. 2 (2008): 542–555.

Alhstrom, Sydney. *A Religious History of the American People*. New Haven, CT: Yale University Press, 2004.

Allen, Barbara. *Tocqueville, Covenant, and the Democratic Revolution: Harmonizing Earth with Heaven*. Lanham, MD: Lexington Books, 2005.

Anastaplo, George. "On the Central Doctrine of Democracy in America." In *Interpreting Tocqueville's Democracy in America*, edited by Ken Masugi, 425–461. Savage, MD: Rowman & Littlefield, 1991.

Aquinas, Thomas. *Summa Theologiae*. Edited by R. W. Dyson. Cambridge, UK: Cambridge University Press, 2002.

Ashcraft, Richard. *Revolutionary Politics and John Locke's Two Treatises on Government*. Princeton NJ: Princeton University Press, 1986.

———. *Locke's Two Treatises of Government*. New York: Routledge, 1987.

———. "Faith and Knowledge in Locke's Philosophy." In *John Locke: Problems and Perspectives*, edited by John Yolton, 194–223. Cambridge, UK: Cambridge University Press, 1999.

Audi, Robert. *Religious Commitment and Secular Reason*. Cambridge, UK: Cambridge University Press, 2000.

Augustine of Hippo. *City of God*. Translated by Henry Betterson. New York: Penguin Classics, 2004.

Ayers, Michael. *Locke: Volume I: Epistemology*. London: Routledge, 1991.

Baldwin, Lewis V. *The Voice of Conscience: The Church in the Mind of Martin Luther King, Jr.* Oxford, UK: Oxford University Press, 2010.

Barone, Michael. "Throw Out the Maps in 2008." Realclearpolitics.com, 2008. http://www.realclearpolitics.com/articles/2008/03/throw_out_the_maps _in_2008.

Baxter, Hugh. *Habermas: The Discourse Theory of Law and Democracy*. Stanford, CA: Stanford University Press: 2011.

Beiner, Ronald. *Civil Religion: A Dialogue in the History of Political Philosophy*. Cambridge, UK: Cambridge University Press, 2010.

Bellah, Robert N. "Civil Religion in America." *Dædalus* 96, no. 1 (1967): 1–21.

———. *Habits of the Heart: Individualism and Commitment in American Life*. New York: Harper and Row, 1986.

———. *The Broken Covenant: American Civil Religion in Time of Trial*. Chicago: University of Chicago Press, 1992.

Belz, Herman. "Abraham Lincoln and the Natural Law Tradition." *The Witherspoon Institute.* http://www.nlnrac.org/american/lincoln. 2013.

Berger, Peter. "What Happens When a Leftist Philosopher Discovers God?" September 21, 2011. http://www.the-american-interest.com/berger/2011/09/21/what-happens-when-a-leftist-philosopher-discovers-god/.

Black, Sam. "Locke and the Skeptical Argument for Toleration." *History of Philosophy Quarterly* 24, no. 4 (2007): 355–375.

Boettcher, James W. "Habermas, Religion and the Ethics of Citizenship." *Philosophy and Social Criticism* 35, nos. 1–2 (2009): 215–238.

Bolce, Louis, and Gerald Demaio. "Our Secularist Democratic Party." *Public Interest,* Fall (2002): 3–21.

Bou-Habi, Paul. "Locke, Sincerity and the Rationality of Persecution." *Political Studies* 51, no. 4 (2003): 611–626.

Burlingame, Michael. *Abraham Lincoln: A Life.* Vol. 2. Baltimore, MD: Johns Hopkins University Press, 2008.

Burt, John. *Lincoln's Tragic Pragmatism: Lincoln, Douglas, and Moral Conflict.* Cambridge, MA: Harvard University Press, 2013.

Calhoun, Samuel W., and Lucas E. Morel. "Abraham Lincoln's Religion: The Case for His Ultimate Belief in a Personal, Sovereign God." *Journal of the Abraham Lincoln Association* 33, no. 1 (2012): 38–74.

Carson, Clayborne. "Martin Luther King, Jr., and the African-American Social Gospel." In *African-American Christianity,* edited by Paul E. Johnson, 159–177. Berkeley, CA: University of California Press, 1994.

Carter, Stephen L. *Culture of Disbelief: How American Law and Politics Trivialize Religious Devotion.* New York: Anchor Books, 1993.

Catholic Bishops of the United States. *Economic Justice for All: Pastoral Letter on Catholic Social Teaching and the US Economy,* 1986.

———. *Torture Is a Moral Issue: A Catholic Study Guide,* 2008.

Chambers, Simone. "How Religion Speaks to the Agnostic: Habermas on the Persistent Value of Religion." *Constellations* 14, no. 2 (2007): 210–223.

———. "Secularism Minus Exclusion: Developing a Religious-Friendly Idea of Public Reason." *Good Society* 19, no. 2 (2010): 16–21.

Cooke, Maeve. "Salvaging and Secularizing the Semantic Contents of Religion: The Limitations of Habermas's Postmetaphysical Proposal." *International Journal for Philosophy of Religion* 60 (2006): 187–207.

Copeland, Charlton C. "God-Talk in the Age of Obama: Theology and Religious Political Engagement." *Denver University Law Review* 86 (2009): 663–691.

Corbett, Ross. "Locke's Biblical Critique." *Review of Politics* 74, no. 1 (2012): 27–51.

Cousins, Norman. *In God We Trust: The Religious Beliefs and Ideas of the American Founding Fathers.* New York: Harper and Brothers, 1958.

Cowardine, Richard. *Lincoln: A Life of Purpose and Power.* New York: Penguin Random House, 2007.

d'Arcais, Paolo Flores. "Eleven Theses against Habermas." Translated by Giacomo Donis. http://www.the-utopian.org/d'Arcais_1.

Dawkins, Richard. *The God Delusion*. London: Bantam Press, 2008.

Deneen, Patrick J. *Democratic Faith*. Princeton, NJ: Princeton University Press, 2005.

Deutsch, Kenneth L., and Joseph R. Fornieri, eds. *Lincoln's American Dream*. Washington, DC: Potomac Books, 2005.

Dionne Jr., E. J. "Obama's Eloquent Faith." *Washington Post*, April 2006. http://www.washingtonpost.com/wp-dyn/content/article/2006/06/29/AR200606290 1778.html.

———. "Full Faith—Despite Jeremiah Wright, Obama Gets Religion." *New Republic* 238, no. 6 (2008): 23–24.

DiSalvo, Daniel, and Jerome E. Copulsky. "Faith in the Primaries." *Perspectives on Political Science* 38, no. 2 (2009): 99–106.

Donald, David Hebert. *Lincoln*. New York: Simon & Schuster, 1996.

Dorrien, Gary J. *Cross Currents*. http://www.crosscurrents.org/dorrien200506.htm.

———. *The Making of American Liberal Theology: Crisis, Irony, and Postmodernity, 1950–2005*. Louisville, KY: Westminster John Knox Press, 2006.

Douthat, Ross. *Bad Religion: How We Became a Nation of Heretics*. New York: Free Press, 2013.

Dunn, John. *The Political Thought of John Locke: An Historical Account of the Two Treatises of Government*. Cambridge, UK: Cambridge University Press, 1983, 171–193.

———. "What Is Living and What Is Dead in John Locke?" In *Interpreting Political Responsibility*, 9–25. Princeton, NJ: Princeton University Press, 1990.

———. "The Claim to Freedom of Conscience: Freedom of Speech, Freedom of Thought, Freedom of Worship?" In *From Persecution to Toleration*, edited by O. Grell, J. Israel, and N. Tyacke. Oxford, UK: Oxford University Press, 1991.

Dworkin, Ronald. *A Matter of Principle*. Cambridge, MA: Harvard University Press, 1985.

Dyer, Justin, and Kevin Stuart. "Rawlsian Public Reason and the Theological Framework of Martin Luther King's 'Letter from Birmingham Jail.'" *Politics and Religion* 6, no. 1 (2013): 145–163.

Eberle, Christopher. *Religious Conviction in Liberal Politics*. Cambridge, UK: Cambridge University Press, 2002.

Espinosa, Gastón. *Religion, Race, and Barack Obama's New Democratic Pluralism*. London: Routledge, 2012.

Fish, Stanley. "Does Reason Know What It Is Missing?" April 12, 2010. http://opinionator.blogs.nytimes.com/2010/04/12/does-reason-know-what-it-is-missing/?_php=true&_type=blogs&_r=0.

Flanders, Chad. "The Mutability of Public Reason." *Ratio Juris* 25, no. 2 (2012): 180–205.

Fontana, David. "Obama and the American Civil Religion from the Political Left." *George Washington International Law Review* 41 (2010): 909–912.

Forde, Steven. "Natural Law, Theology, and Morality in Locke." *American Journal of Political Science,* 45, no. 2 (2001): 396–409.

———. "What Does Locke Expect Us to Know?" *Review of Politics* 68, no. 2 (2006): 232–258.

Forner, Eric. *The Fiery Trial: Abraham Lincoln and American Slavery.* New York: W. W. Norton, 2010.

Fornier, Joseph R. *Abraham Lincoln's Political Faith.* DeKalb: Northern Illinois University Press, 2005.

Friedland, Michael B. *Lift Up Your Voice Like a Trumpet: White Clergy and the Civil Rights and Antiwar Movements, 1954–1973.* Chapel Hill: University of North Carolina Press, 1998.

Frost, Rainer. *Toleration in Conflict: Past and Present.* Cambridge, UK: Cambridge University Press, 2013.

Galston, William A. "Tocqueville on Liberalism and Religion." In *Tocqueville's Political Science: Classic Essays,* edited by Peter Augustine Lawler, 215–231. New York: Garland, 1992.

Gates, Henry Louis Jr., ed. *Lincoln on Race and Slavery.* Princeton, NJ: Princeton University Press, 2009.

Gaus, Gerald F., and Kevin Vallier. "The Roles of Religious Conviction in a Publicly Justified Polity: The Implications of Convergence, Asymmetry and Political Institutions." *Philosophy & Social Criticism* 35, no. 1–2 (2009): 51–76.

Gedicks, Frederick. "American Civil Religion: An Idea Whose Time Is Past." *George Washington International Law Review* 41 (2010): 891–908.

George, Robert P. *In Defense of Natural Law.* Oxford: Oxford University Press, 2001.

Goldie, Mark, "The Theory of Religious Intolerance in Restoration England." In *From Persecution to Toleration,* edited by Ole Peter Grell, Jonathan I. Israel, and Nicholas Tayacke, 331–368. Oxford, UK: Clarendon Press, 1991.

Gorski, Philip S. "Civil Religion Today" (ARDA Guiding Paper Series). State College, PA: The Association of Religion Data Archives at Pennsylvania State University, 2010. http://www.thearda.com/rrh/papers/guidingpapers/gorski.asp.

———. "Barack Obama and Civil Religion." *Political Power and Social Theory* 22 (2011): 177–211.

Greenawalt, Kent. *Religious Convictions and Political Choice.* Oxford, UK: Oxford University Press, 1988.

Guelzo, Allen. *Abraham Lincoln: Redeemer President.* Grand Rapids, MI: Wm. B. Eerdmans Publishing, 1999.

Gutmann, Amy, and Dennis Thompson. *Democracy and Disagreement: Why Moral Conflict Cannot Be Avoided in Politics, and What Should Be Done about It.* Cambridge, MA: Harvard University Press, 1996.

———. "Religious Freedom and Civic Responsibility." *Washington and Lee Law Review* 56 (1999): 907–922.

Habermas, Jürgen. "On Social Identity." *Telos,* no. 19 (1974): 91–103.

————. *The Theory of Communicative Action*. Translated by Thomas McCarthy. Boston: Beacon Press, 1984.

————. *Postmetaphysical Thinking*. Translated by W. M. Hohengarten. Cambridge, MA: MIT Press, 1992.

————. "A Conversation about God and the World: Interview with Eduardo Mendieta." In *Religion and Rationality: Essays on Reason, God and Modernity*, 147–167. Cambridge, UK: Polity, 2002.

————. "To Seek to Salvage an Unconditional Meaning without God Is a Futile Undertaking." In *Religion and Rationality*. Cambridge, UK: Polity, 2002, 95–109.

————. "Transcendence from Within, Transcendence in This World." In *Religion and Rationality*. Cambridge, UK: Polity, 2002, 67–94.

————. "Faith and Knowledge." In *The Future of Human Nature*. Cambridge, UK: Polity, 2003, 101–115.

————. *The Dialectics of Secularization: On Reason and Religion*. Edited with a foreword by Florian Schuller and translated by Brian McNeil. San Francisco: Ignatius, 2006.

————. "Pre-political Foundations of the Democratic Constitutional State?" In *The Dialectics of Secularization: On Reason and Religion*, edited with a foreword by Florian Schuller and translated by Brian McNeil, 19–52. San Francisco: Ignatius, 2006.

————. "Religion in the Public Sphere." *European Journal of Philosophy* 14, no. 17 (2006): 1–25.

————. *Between Naturalism and Religion*. Cambridge, UK: Polity, 2008.

————. "Notes on a post-secular society." 2008. Available at http://www.signand sight.com/features/1714.html.

————. *Europe: A Faltering Project*. Cambridge, UK: Polity, 2009.

————. "Religion and the Public Sphere: A Response to Paolo Flores d'Arcais." Translated by Yascha Mounk. Available at *The Utopian*, http://www.the-utopian .org/Habermas, last accessed on April 6, 2016.

Harris, Sam. *The End of Faith: Religion, Terror, and the Future of Reason*. New York: Norton, 2005.

Havers, Grant. *Lincoln and the Politics of Christian Love*. Columbia: University of Missouri Press, 2009.

Heclo, Hugo. *Christianity and American Democracy*. Cambridge, MA: Harvard University Press, 2009.

Hendel, Ronald. *The Book of Genesis: A Biography*. Princeton, NJ: Princeton University Press, 2012.

Herndon, William H., and Jesse W. Weik. *Herndon's Life of Lincoln: The History and Personal Reflections of Abraham Lincoln*. New York: Da Capo Press, 1983.

Herold, Aaron. "The Chief Characteristic Mark of the True Church: John Locke's Theology of Toleration and His Case for Civil Religion." *Review of Politics* 76 (2014): 195–221.

Hitchens, Christopher. *God Is Not Great: How Religion Poisons Everything.* Crows Nest, UK: Allen & Unwin, 2007.

Hobbes, Thomas. *Leviathan.* Edited by Edwin Curley. Indianapolis: Hackett Publishing, 1994.

———. *Leviathan.* Edited by Richard Tuck. Cambridge, UK: Cambridge University Press, 1991

Holbreich, Matthew. "In the Valley of Dry Bones: Lincoln's Biblical Rhetoric and the Coming of the Civil War." *History of Political Thought* 35, no. 1 (2013): 121–146.

Holder, R. Ward, and Peter B. Josephson. *The Irony of Barack Obama: Barack Obama, Reinhold Niebuhr and the Problem of Christian Statecraft.* Burlington, VT: Ashgate Publishing, 2011.

Hoover, Judith D. "Reconstruction of the Rhetorical Situation in 'Letter from Birmingham Jail.'" In *Martin Luther King, Jr., and the Sermonic Power of Public Discourse,* edited by Carolyn Calloway-Thomas and John Louis Lucaites. Birmingham: University of Alabama Press, 1993, 50–65.

Horton, John, and Susan Mendus. *John Locke: A Letter Concerning Toleration in Focus.* London: Routledge, 1991.

Horwitz, Paul. "Religion and American Politics: Three Views of the Cathedral." *University of Memphis Law Review* 39 (2009): 973–1035.

Jacoby, Susan. *Freethinkers: A History of American Secularism.* New York: Metropolitan Books, 2005.

Jaffa, Harry. *Crisis of a House Divided.* Chicago: University of Chicago Press, 1959.

Jefferson, Thomas. *The Writings of Thomas Jefferson.* 20 vols. Edited by Albert Ellery Bergh and Andrew A. Lipscomb. Washington, DC: Thomas Jefferson Memorial Association, 1904.

———. *Notes on the State of Virginia.* New York: Harper and Row, 1964.

Jiménez Lobeira, Pablo Cristóbal. "Liberal Democracy: Culture Free? The Habermas-Ratzinger Debate and Its Implications for Europe." *Australian & New Zealand Journal of European Studies* (2011).

Jolley, Nicholas. *Locke: His Philosophical Thought.* Oxford, UK: Oxford University Press, 1999.

———. "Locke on Faith and Reason." In *The Cambridge Companion to Locke's "Essay Concerning Human Understanding,"* edited by Lex Newman, 436–455. New York: Cambridge University Press, 2007.

Kessler, Sanford. "Locke's Influence on Jefferson's 'Bill for Establishing Religious Freedom.'" *Journal of Church and State* 25 (1983): 231–252.

———. "Locke's Legacy of Religious Freedom." *Polity* 17, no. 3 (1985), 484–503.

———. "Tocqueville's Puritans: Christianity and the American Founding." *Journal of Politics* 54, no. 3 (1992): 776–792.

———. "The Secularization Debate: A Tocquevillian Perspective." In *Tocqueville's*

Defense of Human Liberty: Current Essays, edited by Peter Augustine Lawler and Joseph Alulis, 265–282. New York: Garland, 1993.

———. *Tocqueville's Civil Religion*. Albany: State University of New York Press, 1994.

King, Martin Luther, Jr. "The Ethical Demands of Integration." In *A Testament of Hope: The Essential Writings and Speeches of King*, edited by James W. Washington, 117–125. New York: Harper Collins, 1991.

———. "I Have a Dream" (1963). In *A Testament of Hope: The Essential Writings and Speeches of King*, edited by James W. Washington, 217–220. New York: Harper Collins, 1991.

———. "A Letter from Birmingham Jail." (1963). In *A Testament of Hope: The Essential Writings and Speeches of King*, edited by James W. Washington, 289–302. New York: Harper Collins, 1991.

———. "Pilgrimage to Nonviolence" (1960). In *A Testament of Hope: The Essential Writings and Speeches of King*, edited by James W. Washington, 35–40. New York: Harper Collins, 1991.

———. *A Testament of Hope: The Essential Writings and Speeches of King*, edited by James W. Washington. New York: Harper Collins, 1991.

———. "Advice for Living" (1957). In *The Papers of Martin Luther King, Jr.*, vol. 4, edited by Clayborne Carson, 279–281. Berkeley: University of California Press, 2007.

———. "Science and Religion" (September 1948–May 1951, Chester, PA. In *The Papers of Martin Luther King, Jr.*, vol. 6, edited by Clayborne Carson, 108–109. Berkeley: University of California Press, 2007.

———. "The Weakness of Liberal Theology" (1948), Chester, PA. In *The Papers of Martin Luther King, Jr.*, vol. 6, edited by Clayborne Carson, 78–80. Berkeley: University of California Press, 2007.

———. *Stride toward Freedom: The Montgomery Story*. Edited by Clayborne Carson. Boston: Beacon Press, 2010.

Kloppenberg, James T. *Reading Obama: Dreams, Hope, and American Political Tradition*. Princeton, NJ: Princeton University Press, 2010.

Koritansky, John C. "Two Forms of the Love of Equality in Tocqueville's Practical Teaching for Democracy." *Polity* 6, no. 4 (1974): 488–499.

———. *Alexis de Tocqueville and the New Science of Politics*. Durham, NC: Carolina Academic Press, 2010.

Krannawitter, Thomas L. *Vindicating Lincoln: Defending the Politics of Our Greatest President*. New York: Rowman & Littlefield, 2008.

Kraynak, Robert, "John Locke: From Absolutism to Separation." *American Political Science Review* 74, no. 1 (1980): 53–69.

———. *Christian Faith and Modern Democracy: God and Politics in a Fallen World*. Notre Dame, IN: University of Notre Dame Press, 2001.

Kries, Douglas. "Alexis de Tocqueville on 'Civil Religion' and the Catholic Faith." In *Civil Religion in Political Thought*, edited by John von Heyking and Ronald Weed, 167–204. Washington, DC: Catholic University Press, 2010.

Lafont, Christina. "Religion in the Public Sphere: Remarks on Habermas's Conception of Public Deliberation in Postsecular Societies." *Constellations* 14, no. 2 (2007): 239–259.

Lakoff, George. *Don't Think of an Elephant: Know Your Values and Frame the Debate*. White River Junction, VT: Chelsea Green Publishing, 2004.

Larmore, Charles. "Public Reason." In *The Cambridge Companion to Rawls*, edited by Samuel L. Freeman, 368–393. New York: Cambridge University Press.

Lawler, Peter Augustine. *The Restless Mind: Alexis de Tocqueville on the Origin and Perpetuation of Human Liberty*. New York: Rowman & Littlefield, 1993.

———. "Tocqueville's Aristocratic Christianity." *Catholic Social Science Review* 17 (2012): 21–32.

Layman, Geoffrey. *The Great Divide: Religious and Cultural Conflict in American Party Politics*. New York: Columbia University Press, 2001.

Lecler, Joseph. *Toleration and the Reformation*. Translated by T. L. Westow. 2 vols. New York: Association Press, 1960.

Lehning, Percy B. *John Rawls: An Introduction*. Cambridge, UK: Cambridge University Press, 2006.

Lincoln, Abraham. *Collected Works of Abraham Lincoln*. Edited by Roy P. Basler. New Brunswick, NJ: Rutgers University Press, 1953.

———. *The Writings of Abraham Lincoln*. Edited by Steve B. Smith. New Haven, CT: Yale University Press, 2012.

Lively, Jack. *The Social and Political Thought of Alexis de Tocqueville*. Oxford, UK: Clarendon Press, 1962.

Loberia, Pablo C. Jimenez. "Liberal Democracy: Culture Free? The Habermas-Ratzinger Debate and Its Implications for Europe." *Australian and New Zealand Journal of European Studies* 2, no. 2 (2011): 44–57.

Locke, John. *Essay Concerning Human Understanding*. In *The Works of John Locke, in Nine Volumes: The Twelfth Edition*, vols. 1 and 2. London, 1824.

———. *Fourth Letter Concerning Toleration*. In *The Works of John Locke*, vol. 5. London, 1824.

———. *Of the Conduct of the Understanding*. In *The Works of John Locke*, vol. 2. London. 1824.

———. *Reasonableness of Christianity*. In *The Works of John Locke*, vol. 6. London, 1824.

———. *Second Letter Concerning Toleration*. In *The Works of John Locke*, vol. 5. London, 1824.

———. *Third Letter Concerning Toleration*. In *The Works of John Locke*, vol. 5. London, 1824.

———. *An Essay Concerning Human Understanding*. Edited by Peter H. Nidditch. Oxford, UK: Clarendon Press, 1975.

———. *A Letter Concerning Toleration*. Edited by James H. Tully. Indianapolis: Hackett Publishing, 1983.

———. *Two Treatises of Government*. Edited by Peter Laslett. Cambridge, UK: Cambridge University Press, 1988.

———. *Locke: Political Writings*. Edited with an introduction by David Wootton. New York: Penguin Books, 1993.

———. *A Letter Concerning Toleration and Other Writings*. Edited by Mark Goldie. Indianapolis: Liberty Fund, 2010.

Lowenthal, David. *The Mind and Art of Abraham Lincoln: Philosopher Statesman*. Lanham, MD: Lexington Books, 2012.

Macedo, Stephen. "In Defense of Liberal Public Reason: Are Slavery and Abortion Hard Cases?" *American Journal of Jurisprudence* 42, no. 1 (1997): 1–29.

———. "Transformative Constitutionalism and the Case of Religion: Defending the Moderate Hegemony of Liberalism." *Political Theory* 26, no. 1 (1998): 56–80.

———. *Diversity and Distrust: Civic Education in a Multicultural Democracy*. Cambridge, MA: Harvard University Press, 2000.

Macedo, Stephen, ed. *Deliberative Politics: Essays on Democracy and Disagreement*. Oxford, UK: Oxford University Press, 1999.

Machen, John Gresham. *Christianity and Liberalism*. Grand Rapids, MI: Eerdmans Publishing, 2009.

MacIntyre, Alasdair. *After Virtue: A Study in Moral Theory*. Notre Dame, IN: Notre Dame University Press, 1981.

Maddex, Jack P. "Postslavery Millennialism: Social Eschatology in Antebellum Southern Calvinism." *American Quarterly* 31, no. 1 (1979): 46–68.

Manent, Pierre. *Tocqueville and the Nature of Democracy*. Blue Ridge Summit, PA: Rowman & Littlefield, 1996.

Mansfield, Harvey C. *Tocqueville: A Very Short Introduction*. Oxford, UK: Oxford University Press, 2010.

———. "Providence and Democracy." *Claremont Review of Books* 11, no. 1–2 (2011): 74–78.

Mansfield, Harvey C., and Delba Winthrop. "Tocqueville's New Political Science." In *The Cambridge Companion to Tocqueville*. Cambridge, UK: Cambridge University Press, 2006, 81–106.

Mansfield, Stephen. *The Faith of Barack Obama*. Nashville, TN: Thomas Nelson Publishing, 2011.

March, Andrew F. "Rethinking Religious Reasons in Public Justification." *American Political Science Review* 107, no. 3 (2013): 523–539.

Marshall, John. *John Locke: Resistance, Religion and Responsibility*. Cambridge, UK: Cambridge University Press, 1994.

————. *John Locke, Toleration and Early Enlightenment Culture.* Cambridge, UK: Cambridge University Press, 2006.

McConnell, Michael. "Five Reasons to Reject the Claim That Religious Arguments Should Be Excluded from Democratic Deliberation." *Utah Law Review* (1999): 639–657.

————. "Secular Reason and the Misguided Attempt to Exclude Religious Argument from Democratic Deliberation." *Journal of Law, Philosophy and Culture* 2 (2007): 159–174.

Meckler, Laura. "Obama Walks Religious Tightrope Spanning Faithful, Nonbelievers." *Wall Street Journal*, March 24, 2009.

Mitchell, Joshua. "John Locke and the Theological Foundation of Liberal Toleration: A Christian Dialectic of History." *Review of Politics* 52, no. 1 (1990).

Morel, Lucas E. *Lincoln's Sacred Effort.* Lanham, MD: Lexington Books, 2000.

Morgenthau, Hans J. *The Mind of Abraham Lincoln*, edited by Kenneth W. Thompson. Lanham, MD: University Press of America, 1983.

Murphy, John M. "Barack Obama, the Exodus Tradition, and the Joshua Generation." *Quarterly Journal of Speech* 97, no. 4 (2011): 387–410.

Myers, Peter C. *Our Only Star and Compass: Locke and the Struggle for Rationality.* New York: Rowman & Littlefield, 1998.

Nagel, Thomas. "John Rawls and Affirmative Action." *Journal of Blacks in Higher Education* 39 (2003): 82–84.

Neal, Patrick. "Habermas, Religion, and Citizenship." *Politics and Religion* 7, no. 2 (2014): 318–338.

Neely, Mark. "Lincoln's Lyceum Speech and the Origins of a Modern Myth." *Lincoln Lore* 1776, no. 3 (1987): 1–3.

Nichols, Peter. "Locke's Later Letters on Toleration." In *John Locke, A Letter Concerning Toleration, In Focus*, edited by John Horton and Susan Mendus, 163–187. New York: Routledge, 1991.

Niebuhr, Reinhold. *The Nature and Destiny of Man: A Christian Interpretation*, vol. 1. Louisville, KY: Westminster John Knox Press, 1996 (1941).

Noll, Mark. "Lincoln's God." *Journal of Presbyterian History* 82, no. 2 (2004): 77–88.

————. *The Civil War as a Theological Crisis.* Chapel Hill: University of North Carolina Press, 2006.

Obama, Barack. Interview by Kathleen Falsani. *Chicago Sun Times*, March 27, 2004. http://www.patheos.com/blogs/thedudeabides/obama-on-faith-the-exclusive-interview/.

————. Keynote Address at the Democratic National Convention. Boston, MA, July 2004. http://www.washingtonpost.com/wp-dyn/articles/A19751-2004Jul27.html.

————. *The Audacity of Hope.* New York: Crown Publishers, 2006.

————. "Keynote Address." Call to Renewal's Building a Covenant for a New America conference in Washington, DC, 2006. http://www.nytimes.com/2006/06 /28/us/politics/2006obamaspeech.html.

———. "Testing the Waters." Interview with David Remnick. *The New Yorker*, November 6, 2006. http://www.newyorker.com/magazine/2006/11/06/testing -the-waters.

———. Interview by David Brody. Christian Broadcasting Network, July 30, 2007. http://www.cbn.com/cbnnews/204016.aspx.

———. "First Inaugural Address." Washington, DC, January 20, 2009. http:// www.whitehouse.gov/blog/inaugural-address.

———. "Remarks by the President in Commencement Address at the University of Notre Dame." Notre Dame, IN, May 17, 2009. http://www.whitehouse.gov /the-press-office/remarks-president-notre-dame-commencement.

Owen, Judd. "Locke's Case for Religious Toleration: Its Neglected Foundations in the *Essay Concerning Human Understanding*." *Journal of Politics* 69, no. 1 (2007): 156–168.

———. "The Struggle between 'Religion and Nonreligion': Jefferson, Backus, and the Dissonance of America's Founding Principles." *American Political Science Review* 101, no 3 (2007): 493–503.

Owen, Judd J. *Religion and the Demise of Liberal Rationalism*. Chicago: University of Chicago Press, 2002.

Pangle, Thomas L. *The Spirit of Modern Republicanism: The Moral Vision of the American Founders and the Philosophy of Locke*. Chicago: University of Chicago Press, 1988.

Perry, John. *The Pretenses of Loyalty: Locke, Liberal Theory, and American Political Theology*. Oxford, UK: Oxford University Press, 2011.

Perry, Michael. "Religious Arguments in Public Political Debate." *Loyola of Los Angeles Law Review* 29 (1996): 1421–1458.

———. "Why Political Reliance on Religious Grounded Morality Is Not Illegitimate in a Liberal Democracy." *Wake Forest Law Review* 36, no. 2 (2001): 217– 249.

Portier, Philippe. "Religion and Democracy in the Thought of Jürgen Habermas." *Culture and Society* 48 (2011): 426–432.

Proast, Jonas. "Letters on Toleration." *Philosophy of John Locke*, edited by Peter A. Schouls. New York: Garland Publishing, 1984.

Putnam, Robert. *Bowling Alone: The Collapse and Revival of the American Community*. New York: Touchstone Books by Simon & Schuster, 2001.

Putnam, Robert D., and David E. Campbell. *American Grace: How Religion Divides and Unites Us*. New York: Simon & Schuster, 2010.

Rabieh, Michael S. "The Reasonableness of Locke, or the Questionableness of Christianity." *Journal of Politics* 53, no. 4 (1991): 933–957.

Rawls, John. "Social Utility and Primary Goods." In *Utilitarianism and Beyond*, edited by Amartya Sen and Bernard Williams, 159–186. Cambridge, UK: Cambridge University Press, 1982.

———. "Justice as Fairness: Political Not Metaphysical." *Philosophy & Public Affairs* 14, no. 3 (1985): 223–251.

———. "The Idea of Public Reason Revisited." *University of Chicago Law Review* 64, no. 3 (1997): 765–807.

———. *Political Liberalism: Expanded Edition.* New York: Columbia University Press, 2005.

Reichley, James. *Religion in American Public Life.* Washington, DC: Brookings Institution, 1985.

———. *Faith in Politics.* Washington, DC: Brookings Institution, 2002.

Richards, David A. J. "Ethical Religion and the Case for Human Rights: The Case of Martin Luther King, Jr." *Fordham Law Review* 72 (2003): 2105–2152.

Roger, Philippe. *L'ennemi americain.* Paris: Seuil, 2002.

Rorty, Richard. *Contingency, Irony, Solidarity.* Cambridge, UK: Cambridge University Press, 1989.

———. *Objectivity, Relativism, and Truth: Philosophical Papers.* Vol. 1. Cambridge, UK: Cambridge University Press, 1990.

———. "Religion as a Conversation Stopper." In *Philosophy and Social Hope,* 168–174. New York: Penguin Books, 1999.

Ross, Frederick Augustus. *Slavery Ordained of God.* Philadelphia: J. B. Lippincott, 1857.

Russell, Richard B. Speech to the "Georgia General Assembly 8 February 1960." In *Voice of Georgia: Speeches of Richard B. Russell, 1928–1969,* edited by Calvin McLeod Logue and Dwight L. Freshley, 352. Macon, GA: Mercer University Press, 1997.

Sandel, Michael. *Democracy's Discontent: America in Search of a Public Philosophy.* Cambridge, MA: Harvard University Press, 1996.

———. *Liberalism and the Limits of Justice.* Cambridge, UK: Cambridge University Press, 1998.

———. "The Procedural Republic and the Unencumbered Self." In *Public Philosophy: Essays on Morality in Politics,* 156–173. Cambridge, MA: Harvard University Press, 2005.

———. *Justice: What's the Right Thing to Do?* New York: Farrar, Strauss and Giroux, 2009.

Schwartz, Earl. "A Poor Hand to Quote the Scripture: Lincoln on Genesis 3:19." *Journal of the Abraham Lincoln Association* 23, no. 2 (2002): 37–49.

Schwartzman, Micah. "The Relevance of Locke's Religious Arguments for Toleration." *Political Theory* 33, no. 5 (2005): 678–705.

Shields, Jon A. *Democratic Virtues of the Christian Right.* Princeton, NJ: Princeton University Press, 2009.

Siker, Jeffrey S. "President Obama, the Bible, and Political Rhetoric." *Political Theology* 13, no. 5 (2012): 586–609.

Smidt, Corwin, Kevin den Dulk, Bryan Froehle, James Penning, Stephen Monsma, and Douglas Koopman. *The Disappearing God Gap? Religion in the 2008 Presidential Election*. Oxford, UK: Oxford University Press, 2010.

Smith, Rogers. "Beyond Tocqueville, Myrdal, and Hartz: The Multiple Traditions in America." *American Political Science Review* 87, no. 3 (1993): 549–566.

Smith, Rogers M. "The Constitutional Philosophy of Barack Obama." *Social Science Quarterly* 93, no. 5 (2012): 1251–1271.

Smith, Steven B. "How to Read Lincoln's Second Inaugural." In *The Writings of Abraham Lincoln*, edited by Steven B. Smith, 476–492. New Haven, CT: Yale University Press, 2012.

———. *Political Philosophy*. New Haven, CT: Yale University Press, 2012.

Solum, Lawrence B. "Novel Public Reasons." *Loyola of Los Angeles Law Review* 29 (1996): 1459–1486.

Spinoza, Baruch. *The Essential Spinoza: Ethics and Related Writings*. Edited by Michael L. Morgan, translated by Samuel Shirley. Indianapolis: Hackett Publishing, 2006.

Stout, Jeffrey. *Democracy and Tradition*. Princeton, NJ: Princeton University Press, 2004.

Strauss, Leo. *Natural Right and History*. Chicago: University of Chicago Press, 1953.

Sullivan, Amy. "The Origins of the God Gap." *Time*, July 12, 2007.

Sunstein, Cass R. "Beyond the Republican Revival." *Yale Law Journal* 97 (1987–1988): 1539–90.

Tate, John William. "Dividing Locke from God: The Limits of Theology in Locke's Political Philosophy." *Philosophy and Social Criticism* 39, no. 2 (2013): 133–164.

Thiemann, Ronald F. *Religion in Public Life*. Washington, DC: Georgetown University Press, 1996.

Thurow, Glen E. *Abraham Lincoln and American Political Religion*. Albany: State University of New York Press, 1976.

Tocqueville, Alexis de. *The European Revolution and Correspondence with Gobineau*. Edited and translated by John Lukacs. Garden City, NY: Doubleday, 1959.

———. *Selected Letters on Politics and Society*. Edited by Roger Boesche. Berkeley: University of California Press, 1985.

———. *Democracy in America*. Edited and translated by Harvey C. Mansfield and Delba Winthrop. Chicago: University of Chicago Press, 2000.

Tuckness, Alex. "Rethinking Intolerant Locke." *American Journal of Political Science* 46, no. 2 (2002): 288–298.

Tulis, Jeffrey K. "Plausible Futures." In *The Presidency in the Twenty-First Century*, edited by Charles W. Dunn, 169–186. Lexington: University Press of Kentucky, 2011.

Vallier, Kevin. "Against Public Reason Liberalism's Accessibility Requirement." *Journal of Moral Philosophy* 8, no. 3 (2011): 366–389.

Vernon, Richard. *The Career of Toleration: John Locke, Jonas Proast, and After*. Montreal: McGill-Queen's University Press, 1997.

———. "Lockean Toleration: Dialogical Not Theological?" *Political Studies* 61 (2013): 215–230.

Waldron, Jeremy. "Locke: Toleration and the Rationality of Persecution." In *Justifying Toleration: Conceptual and Historical Perspectives*, edited by Susan Mendus, 61–86. Cambridge, UK: Cambridge University Press, 1988.

———. "Religious Contributions in Public Deliberation." *San Diego Law Review* 30 (1993): 817–848.

———. *God, Locke and Equality: The Christian Foundations in Locke's Political Thought*. Cambridge, UK: Cambridge University Press, 2002.

———. "Public Reason and 'Justification' in the Courtroom." *Journal of Law, Philosophy and Culture* 1, no. 1 (2007): 107–134.

———. "Two-Way Translation: The Ethics of Engaging with Religious Contributions in Public Deliberation." *Mercer Law Review* 63, no. 3 (2012): 845–868.

Wallis, Jim. *God's Politics: Why the Right Gets It Wrong and the Left Doesn't Get It*. San Francisco, CA: Harper San Francisco, 2006.

Walmsley, Peter. *Locke's Essay and the Rhetoric of Science*. Lewisburg, PA: Bucknell University Press, 2003.

Weithmann, P. J. *Religion and Contemporary Liberalism*. Notre Dame, IN: University of Notre Dame Press, 1997.

———. *Religion and the Obligations of Citizenship*. Cambridge, UK: Cambridge University Press, 2002.

Weller, Dylan. "Godless Patriots: Toward a New American Civil Religion." *Polity* 45, no. 3 (2013): 372–392.

West, Thomas G. "Misunderstanding the American Founding." In *Interpreting Tocqueville's Democracy in America*, edited by Ken Musagi, 155–177. Savage, MD: Rowman & Littlefield, 1991.

White, Ronald C. *Lincoln's Greatest Speech: The Second Inaugural*. New York: Simon & Schuster, 2002.

———. "Lincoln and the Rhetoric of Freedom." In *Lincoln and Freedom: Slavery, Emancipation, and the Thirteenth Amendment*, edited by Harold Holzer and Sara Vaughn Gabbard, 130–142. Carbondale: Southern Illinois University Press, 2007.

William, James. *The Varieties of Religious Experience: A Study in Human Nature*. Boston, MA: Bedford/St. Martin's Press, 2012.

Williams, Gwyneth I. "Democrats Embrace God: An Unqualified Blessing?" *Fo-*

rum on Public Policy: A Journal of the Oxford Round Table (2007). http://forumon
publicpolicy.com/papersumo7.html.

Wills, Garry. Review of "Did Tocqueville Get America?" *New York Review of Books*,
April 29, 2004.

Winger, Stewart. *Lincoln, Religion, and Romantic Cultural Politics*. DeKalb: Northern Illinois University Press, 2002.

Wolf, Christopher. *Natural Law Liberalism*. Cambridge, UK: Cambridge University
Press, 2006.

Wolfe, Alan. *One Nation, After All*. New York: Viking, 1998.

———. *The Transformation of American Religion: How We Actually Live Our Faith*.
Chicago: University of Chicago Press, 2003.

Wolfson, Adam. "Toleration and Relativism: The Locke-Proast Exchange." *Review
of Politics* 59, no. 2 (1997): 213–231.

———. *Persecution or Toleration: An Explication of the Locke-Proast Quarrel, 1689–
1704*. Lanham, MD: Lexington Books, 2010.

Wolin, Sheldon. *Tocqueville between Two Worlds*. Princeton, NJ: Princeton University Press, 2001.

Wolterstorff, Nicholas. *John Locke and the Ethics of Belief*. Cambridge, UK: Cambridge University Press, 1996.

———. "The Role of Religion in Decision and Discussion of Political Issues."
Religion in the Public Square: The Place of Religious Convictions in Political Debate
(1997): 67–120.

———. "Why We Should Reject What Liberalism Tells Us about Speaking and
Acting in Public for Religious Reasons." In *Religion and Contemporary Liberalism*, edited by Paul Weithmann, 162–181. Notre Dame, IN: Notre Dame University Press, 1997.

Wood, Gordon. *Creation of the American Republic, 1776–1787*. New York: W. W.
Norton, 1972.

Yates, Melissa. "Rawls and Habermas on Religion in the Public Sphere." *Philosophy & Social Criticism* 33 (2007): 880–891.

Zetterbaum, Martin. *Tocqueville and the Problem of Democracy*. Stanford, CA: Stanford University Press, 1967.

Zuckert, Catherine. "Not by Preaching: Tocqueville on the Role of Religion in
American Democracy." *Review of Politics* 43, no. 2 (1981): 259–280.

Zuckert, Michael. *Launching Liberalism: On Lockean Political Philosophy*. Lawrence:
University Press of Kansas, 2002.

———. "Lincoln and the Problem of Civil Religion." In *Lincoln's American Dream*,
edited by Kenneth L. Deutsch and Joseph R. Fornieri, 350–366. Washington,
DC: Potomac Books, 2005.

———. "Locke: Religion: Equality." *Review of Politics* 67, no. 3 (2005).

INDEX